W9-BUC-033

The American Negro Revolution
FROM NONVIOLENCE TO BLACK POWER

1963–1967

BENJAMIN MUSE

The
American Negro Revolution
From Nonviolence to Black Power

1963-1967

Indiana *University Press*

Bloomington, London

FIFTH PRINTING 1973

253-10180-8

Published in Canada by Fitzhenry & Whiteside, Limited,
Scarborough, Ontario
Library of Congress catalog card number: 68-27350
Manufactured in the United States of America

For Beatriz

Contents

Foreword

Many of us, like our forebears, live through epochal events without any sense of being in the presence of history. Such lack of awareness was more understandable in ages past than it is in this day of widespread literacy and mass communication. Unlike, say, a foot soldier in the Trojan war or a shopkeeper in Elizabethan England, the typical American today is inundated by "news." His sense of contemporary history is stunted not because he gets too little information but because he gets too much. Even if he has the skill, he is unlikely to have the time and patience to search out the enduring significance in the transient happenings of the day.

This is what Benjamin Muse has done for us. He has given order and meaning to that bewildering rush of events in recent years that collectively comprise the "Negro revolution"—surely one of the major social forces of our century.

Like all truly good books, this one can be read in several ways. It can be seen as a preview of history as it will be written and read by later generations, for these pages will unquestionably be a major source for future historians. It can be read simply as a stirring chronicle, the story of a long oppressed people's climactic struggle for dignity and opportunity. Above all, it can be read for thoughtful guidance by those who seek a better understanding of how we have thus far failed, and how we may yet succeed, in breathing life into our national promise of equality for all.

Again like all good books, this one tells its story with a deceptive air of ease and simplicity. The reader is untroubled by consciousness of the painstaking research, the first-hand investigation, the conscientious judgments that went into the making of the book.

This virtue is attributable partly to the fact that Mr. Muse is an experienced and consummately skillful reporter. But more important are the personal qualities of the man himself—compassion, humaneness, intellectual honesty, and the immovable conviction that dignity is the natural heritage of every human being. These are the traits that Benjamin Muse has exhibited not only as observer and writer, but also as an able participant in the field of race relations.

The Potomac Institute is pleased that it can claim a share of the credit, however modest, for having made this book possible.

Harold C. Fleming

President, The Potomac Institute
Washington, D.C.

Preface

The purpose of this book is to present a history of the American Negro Revolution from its nonviolent manifestations of 1963 through the crescendo of violence in 1967.

It is difficult to say when the revolution began, but I have regarded its pre-1963 stage as a prelude. The ten years that followed the Supreme Court's 1954 decision outlawing public school segregation were dealt with in my *Ten Years of Prelude* (Viking Press). This book is a sequel, with some overlapping, to that volume.

The end of the Negro revolution is not yet in sight. Yet the civil-rights movement of sit-ins, parades, and nonviolent exhortation that spread across the nation in 1963—and accomplished a significant change in the status of the Negro in the United States —has run its course. The violence which climaxed in the upheavals of Newark and Detroit marked the end of that phase of the revolution and the beginning of another. In carrying the story to the end of 1967, I have attempted merely to raise the curtain on the new phase, whose magnitude and duration no one can predict.

I have not attempted to analyze exhaustively any of the complex problems of Negro-white relations. They have been the subject of innumerable books. But I have sought to bring problems, trends, and events together in an account of what has happened during the past five years and of how we arrived at where we are. It may be said that the time is not yet ripe for this kind of history, and I am fully aware of the limitations and the risks involved. I offer this volume nevertheless in the belief that there is a need for even an unripened account now, and in the hope that it may be of help to historians who will place these events in the perspective that future years will afford.

I am deeply grateful to the Potomac Institute, of Washington, D.C., for its sponsorship of my undertaking, for the use of its files, and above all for the counsel of its officers during my three years of work on this book. Harold C. Fleming, president of the Institute, Arthur J. Levin, staff director, James O. Gibson, and Mrs. Margaret Price were most helpful.

Dr. Leslie W. Dunbar, executive director of the Field Foundation, examined the entire manuscript and gave me invaluable assistance. Others read portions of the manuscript and gave me helpful comment and corrections. Among these were the Reverend Aubrey N. Brown, president, Virginia Council on Human Relations; Lloyd J. Elliott, staff economist, Southern Regional Council; Vernon E. Jordan, Jr., director, Voter Education Project, Southern Regional Council; Dr. Floyd J. Riddick, parliamentarian, United States Senate; Pat Watters, director of information, Southern Regional Council; and Whitney M. Young, Jr., executive director, National Urban League. To all of these and to many others who gave of their time in personal conversation my debt is warmly acknowledged.

Benjamin Muse

Reston, Virginia
December 1967

The American Negro Revolution

FROM NONVIOLENCE TO BLACK POWER

1963–1967

ONE

The March on Washington 1963

On August 28, 1963, one hundred years and 240 days after the signing of the Emancipation Proclamation, 200,000 citizens marched in Washington in protest against oppression of the Negro in the United States. There were 170,000 Negroes, and 30,000 whites marched with them (at minimum estimates). Heads high and chests forward they marched, neatly dressed, respectable and self-respecting.

It was called the "March on Washington." But these marchers carried no arms, engaged in no violence, shook no fists. Russell Baker reported in the *New York Times:* "No one could remember an invading army as gentle as the 200,000 civil-rights marchers who occupied Washington today."

Negroes had begun to gather around the Washington Monument soon after midnight. In the morning sunshine more than 50,000 dotted that familiar rendezvous of American patriotism, the Washington Monument grounds and the Ellipse—all the half mile to the high wrought-iron fence around the garden of the White House, whose occupant they regarded as their great and good friend. President Kennedy, apprehensive in the early stages of the project, had later expressed approval and extended a welcome. He would receive ten of the leaders in the afternoon for a cordial, hour-long chat. (Former President Eisenhower had expressed approval of the March project; Senator Barry Goldwater had expressed approval; former President Truman disapproved, while expressing support for pending civil-rights legislation.)

On all roads leading to Washington the multitude poured in. In addition to those brought by private automobiles and regular trains, buses, and airplanes, 1,514 special buses and 21 special trains had been pressed into service. Bus loads had come all the way from Los Angeles and San Francisco, spending three nights on the road.

At midday the mass of humanity began to move down Constitution and Independence Avenues, nearly a mile, to the Lincoln Memorial for a ceremony and speeches. Marchers carried banners and signs with various slogans, many calling for FREEDOM NOW, DECENT HOUSING NOW, and JOBS AND FREEDOM NOW. Placards urging NO MORE DOUGH FOR JIM CROW were aimed at government support of segregated activities.

They were singing most of the time—hymns and spirituals, patriotic airs, improvised chants of protest. Fervent voices joined repeatedly in the Battle Hymn of the Republic—"Mine eyes have seen the glory of the coming of the Lord. . . ." Rising at all times from some section of the throng were the slow cadences of an old hymn now familiar to millions as the anthem of a nonviolent revolution. "We Shall Overcome" had none of the fire of the "Marseillaise," nor the jaunty swing of "Giovinezza." Though thousands had sung it in the face of angry police and in patrol wagons on the way to jail, it was not a song with which to charge an enemy in battle. The "someday" schedule for triumph was hardly consistent with the "NOW" of the placards that marchers carried. The song had a plaintive note:

> We shall overcome.
> We shall overcome.
> We shall overcome someday.
> Oh deep in my heart
> I do believe
> We shall overcome someday.

It was not a hymn of hatred of the white man. Another verse ran:

> Black and white together,
> We'll walk hand in hand.

A facetious cortege carried a coffin hopefully containing Jim Crow's dead body. There were many good-natured quips and frequent laughter. An atmosphere of festivity pervaded the happy but purposeful throng. Yet the decorum observed has rarely been equaled in a public demonstration of such magnitude anywhere.

Editor Harold E. Fey of the *Christian Century* was a prescient observer. Writing in that magazine's issue of September 11, 1963, Fey said: "The march was disciplined; throughout a long and wearisome day I saw not a single act of discourtesy, nor did I hear one expression of irritation. . . ." But he added: "If the present enlightened and principled leadership of the civil-rights movement fails, if the democratic program of this revolution without hatred is defeated, another 200,000—or it might be 500,000—could march on Washington led by leaders of a different sort who know how to manipulate hatred and violence for their own ends. . . ."*

The world looked on through an unprecedented concentration of news media. Special police passes had been issued to 1,655 visiting press, radio, and television employees, in addition to the 1,200 persons already holding police press cards. Among newsmen from a dozen European and Asian countries, Soviet Russia was represented by a correspondent for *Izvestia*, one for *Pravda*, and three for Tass. In addition to television broadcasts of United States networks flashed to Europe by Telstar, Britain, Canada, Japan, France, and West Germany had television crews on hand. In London, the BBC gave live coverage throughout the day, followed by a special broadcast on its late night show. The Voice of America broadcast the story in thirty-six languages.

From its trans-Atlantic perspective, the London *Daily Herald* said of the March: "America has never seen anything like it. Today, without question, the clock jumped and history changed." Not in that one day, but in the four months since the brutal repression of a series of Negro demonstrations in Birmingham, Alabama—the clock had indeed made a mighty leap.

A few Negro intellectuals had preached rebellion since the turn of the century. Some date the beginning of the revolution from the broadening of racial horizons in World War II, some from the great Supreme Court decision of 1954, some from the Negro resistance to bus segregation in Montgomery, Alabama, in 1956. Who

* Copyright 1963, Christian Century Foundation. Reprinted by permission.

can say when a revolution begins? After Birmingham, it became dynamic, nationwide, and visible to all.

The Supreme Court's *Brown* decision of May 17, 1954, declaring public school segregation unconstitutional, had been the greatest milestone in the Negro's advance since Emancipation. With its subsequent elaboration, that pronouncement removed the last legal foundation for segregation, not only of public schools, but of libraries, auditoriums, parks, and all manner of facilities supported by public funds. However, the dismantling of this mechanism of caste in the South had proved a painful process, often attended by turmoil and violence, and in 1963 it still had a long way to go.

In 1956 the Negroes of Montgomery launched an effective boycott of the buses of that city. The South was startled. At the time and place it seemed to most whites an act of incredible Negro effrontery. The boycott was in protest against the then common practice of segregating Negroes in the back of the bus and giving seating preference to whites; Montgomery Negroes wanted to be treated like other passengers. They persevered for many months, walking to work or crowding into the cars of overworked Negro motorists. And their demands were ultimately upheld by the Supreme Court. Even more important perhaps than this Negro initiative itself was the emergence from it of a leader and a philosophy which were destined to have a profound impact upon the revolution. The leader was Dr. Martin Luther King, the scholarly young pastor of a Negro Baptist church and an admirer of Mahatma Gandhi. King quickly became a national figure and began to call Negroes everywhere to a nonviolent crusade.

The sit-ins of 1960 were another milestone in the rising of the Negro, and they launched a famous technique of the revolution. The sit-in, with its later variations—the pray-in, the wade-in, et cetera—was a technique for breaking through barriers of prejudice and custom to enter restaurants, churches, beaches, and other places formerly reserved for whites. It had been employed earlier in isolated instances, but the sit-in movement was born on February 1, 1960. On that day four Negro college students walked into a variety store in Greensboro, North Carolina, took seats at a lunch counter traditionally reserved for whites, and ordered coffee. They were not served, but they stayed until closing time and came back to complete the performance the next day, and the next and the next—until they were joined by scores of other Negro students, while hundreds more picketed outside. Meanwhile the movement spread rapidly. Soon Negroes were sitting-in and picketing at lunch counters in a dozen Southern cities. And in a few months the race barriers at lunch counters began to fall.

Out of the Montgomery agitation Martin Luther King had launched a new organization, which he named the "Southern Christian Leadership Conference" (colloquially shortened to SCLC). In 1960 he presided over the birth of another organization. In the excitement of the first wave of sit-ins 200 youths, representing most of the Negro colleges, met in Raleigh, North Carolina, and, exhorted by Dr. King, set up the "Student Nonviolent Coordinating Committee" (SNCC, often called "Snick"). The National Association for the Advancement of Colored People (NAACP), which since its establishment in 1909 had borne the brunt of the Negro struggle, the National Urban League, which for almost as long had aided city Negroes in many ways, and the Congress of Racial Equality (CORE) were thus joined by two other burgeoning organizations. Together they were to become the Big Five of the civil-rights movement.

Meanwhile CORE, after functioning inconspicuously in the North since 1942, sprang into aggressive action. In 1961, in the most daring Negro militance yet seen, it launched "Freedom Rides" across the South to break down remaining segregation on interstate buses and in bus and railway terminals. The Freedom Riders, defying the old seating rules, were little molested until their buses reached Alabama, but they were attacked by ferocious white mobs in that state and they were jailed by police in Mississippi.

In April and early May, 1963, Martin Luther King led an attack, in a series of massive demonstrations, upon the whole power structure of the city of Birmingham. King decided on this move, against the advice of cautious liberals, because, he said, "Birmingham is the symbol of racial segregation." The Alabama metropolis was indeed the most segregated of all the large cities in the United States; its schools, theaters, restaurants, drinking fountains, and other facilities were totally segregated. It was a hotbed of explosive intolerance: in six years it had seen 50 Ku-Klux-Klan-style crossburnings and 18 anti-Negro bombings, for which no one had been punished. Now wave after wave of Negroes poured into the Birmingham streets, and were repressed by police with spectacular brutality. Many were injured; over 3,000 were arrested. The name of "Bull" Connor, the raucous city commissioner who directed the Birmingham police, became a byword throughout the nation. During the same period Negro agitation was savagely dealt with also in Jackson, Mississippi, a smaller city, where Negro subservience was even more harshly enforced.

All of this turbulence was luridly publicized throughout the country. Photos of men, women, and children being beaten, attacked by police dogs, and knocked down with streams of water from fire hoses filled press and television. And the centuries-old patience of Negroes in America came at last to an end. In the words of the Negro writer Louis Lomax, "the collective snap of the Negro spirit boomed like thunder across the nation." With Birmingham as a symbol, but acutely conscious of discrimination suffered in every American community, a quarter of a million Negroes took to the streets in demonstrations in forty cities.

With this fire raging it was not surprising that the President should propose civil-rights legislation of such boldness and sweep as a few months earlier would have seemed impossible. President Kennedy had made some recommendations in this field in February. He had requested Congress to require that evidence of a sixth-grade education should be substituted for the literacy tests which in many sections of the South were manipulated to prevent Negroes from registering to vote, to authorize federal referees to register Negro voters in certain circumstances, to authorize federal assistance to school districts faced with the desegregation problem, and to extend the life of the Civil Rights Commission for four more years. The President had evidently sensed that this was as much as Congress and the nation were ready for at that stage. The time was ripe now for something vastly more far-reaching.

The President prepared the way in a television speech June 11, at a moment when a crisis over desegregation of the University of Alabama at Tuscaloosa had riveted the nation's attention on the racial turmoil. Alabama's fiery Governor George Wallace, defying a federal court order, had stood at the front door of the university's administration building and personally barred two Negro students from entering. The impasse was broken only when the commanding general of a federalized National Guard unit appeared with orders from the President. Two hours later President Kennedy addressed the nation. He referred only briefly to the melodrama at the University of Alabama, then pointed to the "fires of frustration and discord . . . burning in every city, North and South . . . a moral crisis," he said, which "cannot be met by repressive police action. . . . It is time to act in the Congress, in your state and local legislative body and, above all, in all of our daily lives."

Later the same night, in the early hours of June 12, the Negro revolt was furnished with an authentic martyr: Medgar Evers, field secretary of the NAACP in Mississippi, was assassinated. The Negro leader was shot from ambush as he returned to his home from a civil-rights rally in Jackson.

On June 19 President Kennedy submitted his program to Congress. It called for: (1) a ban on the exclusion of any person on account of his race from hotels, restaurants, stores, places of amusement, or other facilities; (2) authority for the Attorney General to file suits to speed desegregation of public schools and colleges when those affected could not afford to do so or feared reprisals; (3) a statutory basis for the President's Committee on Equal Employment Opportunity; (4) a ban on discrimination in all federally-assisted programs and activities, with authority to withhold federal funds in cases of violation; and (5) the establishment of a Community Relations Service to help communities through disputes and difficulties in the elimination of racial discrimination. The President also urged prompt action on the proposals he had submitted earlier. "Enactment of the Civil Rights Act of 1963 at this session of Congress," he said, "—however long it may take and however troublesome it may be—is imperative." The package overshadowed all other business of the Congress during most of the ensuing year. It was modified and amended many times, and strengthened, before emerging as the Civil Rights Act of 1964.

While these proposals were being digested and debated by press and public and by committees of Congress (eight months would elapse before they reached the floor of the House of Representatives), the Negro demonstrations continued and spread to more cities. They were scrupulously nonviolent as a rule, but disorder in the streets became a familiar sight. The prospect of a crowning demonstration in the nation's capital was viewed with no little apprehension. It was feared that, in the existing atmosphere, a large gathering of Negroes in Washington could hardly be restrained from violent rampage. Some Southern segregationists, indeed, seemed actually to hope for a convulsion that would embarrass the Negro movement. Women government workers in Washington awaited the event nervously. The Washington *Daily News* sensed a feeling that the Vandals were coming to sack Rome! The anxiety was felt on the New York Stock Exchange. In this atmosphere Negro leaders and their white allies united in a mighty resolve to make the March on Washington not only a spectacular demonstration of protest, but a model of order and dignity.

What manner of men were these who sought the full rights of citizens? Much discussion of the matter has started from a casual premise that the Negroes were a people which had suffered oppression in this country for "350 years" or "three centuries." That is not precisely the case. The first Negroes, twenty individuals, arrived at Jamestown in 1619; only 30,000 are estimated to have reached the colonies by 1715. Some 300,000 arrived in the eighteenth century, and various authorities estimate that of all the Negro slaves coming to this country about half were imported, or smuggled in, during the first half of the nineteenth century.* The Negro ancestors of most American Negroes had reached these shores less than 200 years ago.

Moreover, many of the ancestors of modern "Negroes" were *not Negroes*. According to the best available evidence and expert opinion, from 70 to 80 per cent of Negro Americans are descended in part from whites. Many have slaveholders among their forebears. Among those of predominantly white ancestry, the more light-skinned would be accepted in other countries as Caucasians. But in the United States every person with a known trace of Negro blood in his veins is generally classified as a Negro. Those in this category recognized a common bond, and those classified otherwise were acutely conscious of their separateness from them. Negro Americans were—unhappily from many points of view—a people unto themselves.

There were 18,871,831 of them by the 1960 census. In 1963 the

---

* See Gunnar Myrdal, *An American Dilemma*, Twentieth Century Anniversary edition, pp. 118–19.

number was estimated at 19.3 million. This was less than 11 per cent of the population of the United States. But it was more than the total population of Canada, or of Yugoslavia or East Germany —more than the entire population of the United States in 1840. It was about the number of the peasants of France at the time of the French Revolution.

What kind of people were they? Few white Americans really knew. The persistence of the old image of Negroes as servants and field hands, often as comical characters, prevented many from recognizing the Negro American of the 1960's. It was in the South, where Negroes were most numerous, that the concept of the new Negro was actually most distorted. The average white Southerner was scarcely aware of the existence of Negroes of culture and refinement, even though some lived among them; cultivated Negroes were more isolated than their humbler brethren. In some New England and northwestern states, on the other hand, Negroes were rarely seen. The 1960 census counted only 519 Negroes in the entire state of Vermont, 1,903 in New Hampshire, 777 in North Dakota, 1,467 in Montana. In ten states Negroes were less than one per cent of the total population.

The March on Washington was to millions a revelation. Many white Americans, sitting before television sets, saw Negroes walking with dignity and heard the words of polished Negro spokesmen for the first time. The March presented an illuminating cross-section of the Negro minority and a dramatis personae of the great movement agitating it. It will profit us, therefore, to visit that demonstration again and examine it more closely.

The commander-in-chief of the March was tall, courtly Asa Philip Randolph, president of the Brotherhood of Sleeping Car Porters and a vice-president of the AFL-CIO. Randolph, at seventy-four, was the Grand Old Man of the Negro movement. Long a consultant of American Presidents, he had been chiefly instrumental in securing two of the Negro's most significant gains: Franklin Roosevelt's World War II executive order banning discrimination in government-contract employment and Truman's desegregation of the Armed Forces. Randolph had headed a March-on-Washington Committee in 1941—for a march that was called off when President Roosevelt moved against job discrimination. He began

urging another march in the winter of 1963, contemplating originally merely a march of jobless Negroes. After the Birmingham
upheaval Martin Luther King took up the idea and helped persuade
Randolph to broaden the project to embrace the whole civil-rights
cause. CORE and SNCC followed. The NAACP and the Urban
League joined, with insistence that the march should be orderly
and that whites should be included.

Randolph's chief of staff was Bayard Rustin, a tense, chain-
smoking Negro intellectual of fifty-three. For Rustin this was the
climax of a long career of organizing demonstrations. He had set
up the first Aldermaston Ban-the-Bomb protest in Britain, and he
led marchers who set off across the Sahara in 1960 to stop a French
nuclear explosion. Some of his earlier activities—among them identification with the Young Communist League for several years
around the beginning of World War II—had given him a somewhat embarrassing record. Since 1941 Randolph had been his
protector, mentor, and idol. Rustin's management of the many
complex details of the great March—including remarkable step-
by-step cooperation with the Washington police—proved a marvel
of administrative efficiency, and his voice was to be heard with
new authority from then on as a spokesman for the Negro movement.

Randolph headed an official body of ten—six Negroes and four
whites—called the Organizing Committee. The other Negroes
were leaders of the Big Five civil-rights organizations: Roy Wilkins of the NAACP, Martin Luther King of SCLC, James Farmer
of CORE, Whitney Young of the National Urban League, and
John Lewis of SNCC.

Roy Wilkins at sixty-two was, like Randolph, a veteran of the
Negro struggle. In his manner and speech, and in his appearance,
except for his light brown skin, Wilkins resembled a familiar type
of white political leader; and he displayed qualities that could well
be called statesmanship. Though he came to the March beaming
under a gay NAACP cap and bedecked with slogan buttons, Wilkins' usual approach to problems was one of stubborn dignity and
relentless common sense.

Martin Luther King asserted the power of prayer and love. It
was said of one of the planning sessions that, when all except King
had spoken and the group turned toward him expectantly, the

clergyman dropped to his knees and said: "Gentlemen, please let us pray"! At thirty-four years of age, King's religious fervor, his learning, his eloquence, a degree of mysticism, and no little histrionic talent had won him nationwide primacy among Negro leaders. To the general public he had become a symbol of the revolution. To millions of Negroes he was a Moses come to lead his people out of Egypt—and in one respect the lawgiver: the commandment that he brought down from Mount Sinai to refrain from violence had been embraced by virtually the whole civil-rights movement.

Whitney Young, the forty-two-year-old executive director of the National Urban League, was the least spectacular of the Big Five leaders. His name was unfamiliar to many of the rank and file. But he was well known to Negro leadership, and also to a wide circle of influential whites, many of whom aided or cooperated in his Urban League work. Tactful and soft-spoken, he was at home in executive suites where the economic problems of the Negro were discussed. He was an alert, imaginative, and personable leader, who would become one of the most respected spokesmen for the Negro minority.

All of the organizers of the March on Washington subscribed to the principle of nonviolence, but had this been a revolution of barricades and bullets, it probably would have found its chieftain in tough, masterful James Farmer. An apostle of audacity, more and always audacity, the forty-three-year-old Farmer suggested a more dapper Danton. But Farmer was not there. Characteristically on the day of the Washington demonstration he was languishing in a Plaquemines, Louisiana, jail after leading a night march on the city hall of the fiercely segregated town. CORE was represented by its chairman, Floyd B. McKissick, a Durham, North Carolina, lawyer. It is noteworthy that McKissick was particularly impressed by the strong participation of whites in the March. He said to a *New York Times* reporter that it signaled "the end of the Negro protest and the beginning of the American protest."

Wilkins, King, Young, and Farmer—they were the Big Four. It was the nation's great good fortune that the Negro revolt when it came should have found its leaders in men of their character, stability, and patriotism. When one spoke of the Big Five, referring to individuals rather than organizations, the fifth was likely to be labor leader Randolph rather than any of the youthful officers of SNCC. Some of the latter showed promise—notably its chairman John Lewis, its executive director James Forman, and Robert Moses, a field director—but none had achieved national stature. Lewis, who represented SNCC in the March, was a veteran of the bloody Freedom Rides and many sit-ins; he had been arrested twenty-four times and would be in jail again four weeks later.

The four white members of the Organizing Committee were distinguished representatives of the three major religious faiths and of organized labor: Mathew Ahmann, executive director of the National Catholic Conference for Interracial Justice; Dr. Eugene Carson Blake, Presbyterian leader and chairman of the Commission on Religion and Race of the National Council of Churches (he was elected general secretary of the World Council of Churches in 1966); Rabbi Joachim Prinz, president of the American Jewish Congress; and Walter P. Reuther, president of the United Automobile Workers and vice president of the AFL-CIO. Dr. Blake himself had been arrested for participation in civil-rights demonstrations. Reuther, the second most powerful figure in organized labor, had sharply criticized the action of the AFL-CIO's executive council two weeks earlier when it expressed sympathy with the Negro aims but failed to endorse the March on Washington. Members of his union carried placards proclaiming: "Whenever Men March for Freedom UAW Marches Too."

The number who rallied to the March exceeded all predictions. The leaders had set 100,000 as a hopeful goal and would have regarded it as an achievement if 75,000 had appeared. In the event, the number of participants probably exceeded 200,000; no serious estimates were lower than that figure. Poor Negroes had used hard-earned savings for the trip. In some Southern towns Washington pilgrims had been aided with contributions by their neighbors, and envious Negroes left at home had cheered their departing comrades. (If any Negro economic level was unrepresented, it was an elusive handful of the very rich who, with a few exceptions, displayed little eagerness to change the status quo.)

Jaundiced segregationists in the South had attempted to discredit the March with a warning that it would be infiltrated with Communists and criminals. Some Communists came from New York with the party's secretary Gus Hall; police estimated the total number of Communists in the throng at 130. Few of the marchers were aware of their presence. And not in many years had Washington passed a day so free from crime. The only persons arrested in connection with the March were three anti-Negro whites. One had stoned a bus on the way to the scene; another had torn a placard from a marcher. The third was Karl R. Allen, "Deputy Leader" of a handful of truculent adventurers who called themselves the "American Nazi Party"; Allen was speaking on park grounds without a permit.

The Negro-baiting Ku Klux Klan, which preferred night prowls in the Deep South, was nowhere in evidence. At the other pole of racial hatred, the extremist Black Muslims were ingloriously ignored. Only a tiny handful of listeners heard their chief spokesman Malcolm X hold forth in a Washington hotel, denouncing the demonstrators for "seeking favors" from "the white man's government."

A number of well-known whites who were not directly identified with the Negro movement were noted in the crowd. Norman Thomas, the respected Socialist leader, at seventy-nine, was "glad I lived long enough to see this day." Harold E. Stassen marched as president of the American Baptist Convention. Mayor Robert Wagner led a contingent of New York city officials and employees. (In both New York and Chicago city employees had been given time off to participate in the March.) The Most Reverend Patrick J. O'Boyle, Roman Catholic archbishop of Washington, pronounced the invocation at the afternoon ceremonies; Archbishop Lawrence J. Shehan (now Cardinal) came from Baltimore. Ten Episcopal bishops and fifty rabbis were there. Formal endorsement of the March by many church bodies and the participation of thousands of the clergy and members of church organizations—who made up the bulk of the white contingent—bore witness to the growing effort of religious leaders to arouse the conscience of the nation. A small hostile organization of segregationists and right-wing extremists, called the "American Council of Christian Churches," established "Opposition Headquarters" at the Hotel Washington, but this tiny ripple was lost in the liberal tidal wave of the Negro's Great Day.

Conspicuous in the March also were Negroes famous in fields other than civil-rights leadership—among them: Ralph Bunche, undersecretary of the United Nations and a winner of the Nobel Peace Prize; Jackie Robinson, a former baseball hero recognized as the game's "most valuable player," now a business executive; playwright Ossie Davis; and James Baldwin, some of whose writings on the white man's sin against the Negro were not only best-sellers but literary masterpieces.

A platform had been erected on the Washington Monument grounds, where entertainment and exhortation were provided until the March began. There a galaxy of stars, both white and Negro, gave evidence of the prominence which Negroes had attained on stage and screen; evidence too of the conspicuous sympathy of "big-name" white actors with the Negro Movement. Negroes Harry Belafonte, Sidney Poitier, Dick Gregory, and Sammy Davis mingled with Marlon Brando, Charlton Heston, Paul Newman, and Burt Lancaster in jovial camaraderie. Conspicuous also among those who appeared during the day were such Negro women celebrities as Lena Horne, Mahalia Jackson, Marian Anderson—and Josephine Baker, who at sixty had flown over from her long exile in France.

The advertised purpose of the March had been to press for enactment of the civil-rights bill, which was dragging unpromisingly through committees of Congress. Threats of some kind of sit-in maneuver on Capitol Hill had contributed to the earlier alarm. In the procedure which was adopted, members of the Organizing Committee and three other leaders held half-hour conferences during the morning with Congressional leaders in an atmosphere of courtesy and restraint.

Congress was grappling at the time with a threatened railroad strike. The House passed the arbitration bill that day. Nevertheless, between 75 and 100 senators and representatives reached the demonstration during the afternoon ceremonies. Negroes cheered as they filed in from behind the Lincoln Memorial, and cries of "Roosevelt!," "Humphrey!," "Javits!" arose as favorites were recognized. There were five Negro members of Congress, one of whom was Representative Adam Clayton Powell of New York. A clergyman-politician-playboy, Powell was a problem for civil-rights leaders, with whom he was generally at odds, but his swashbuckling manner and his air of sophisticated arrogance toward whites were a tonic to the Negro's browbeaten ego and he had a host of admirers. When this tall, handsome, olive-complexioned man walked down the Memorial steps, many yelled, "Powell!" in jubilant surprise.

The sea of humanity now spread in a semicircle under the great elms and oaks and stretched almost a mile east from the Lincoln Memorial on both sides of the Reflecting Pool. There the multitude listened for almost three hours to speeches interspersed with songs, amplified from the Memorial steps. Archbishop O'Boyle prayed that Christian love might "replace the coldness that springs from prejudice and bitterness." The revolution's anthem was sung by Joan Baez, who captured as no one else could the strength and poignancy of "We Shall Overcome." Mahalia Jackson's tremendous voice warmed Negro hearts with spirituals.

Speakers called for passage of the civil-rights bill before Congress, but declared that more would be needed. Randolph, Wilkins, and Reuther urged that provision for a Fair Employment Practices Commission (FEPC) should be included in the package (as it later was). Police brutality was denounced: "We are beaten and kicked and maltreated and shot and killed by law enforcement officers," Wilkins said. Dr. Blake sought to arouse the nation's churches. "If all members and all the ministers of the constituency I represent here today," he said, "were ready to stand and march with you for jobs and freedom for the Negro community, together with all the Roman Catholic Church and all of the synagogues in America, then the battle for full civil rights and dignity would be already won. . . . We come late—late, late we come. . . ."

SNCC's John Lewis had come to Washington with a prepared speech more warlike than befitted the occasion. When Archbishop O'Boyle read an advance copy the night before, he threatened to withdraw from the program unless changes were made. Aided by Randolph and Reuther, the prelate got the speech revised. Instead of: "We will march through the South, through the heart of Dixie, the way Sherman did. We shall pursue our own scorched-earth policy and burn Jim Crow to the ground, nonviolently" Lewis was induced to say that his people would march through the streets of cities "with the spirit of love and with the spirit of dignity that we have shown here today." Nevertheless, Lewis' originally intended language was indicative of the temper of the youths of the Student Nonviolent Coordinating Committee, many of whom, learning of the incident later, regretted the change.

Nine speeches had been listened to when Martin Luther King's turn came, yet when the prophet arose a great roar welled up from the crowd. A band played the Battle Hymn of the Republic. He was not a big man and his manner was deliberate and gentle, but his broad, sloping face and heavily-muscled neck and shoulders lent his five-foot-eight frame an aspect of physical power.

"There will be neither rest nor tranquility in America," he said, "until the Negro is granted his citizenship rights. The whirlwinds of revolt will continue to shake the foundations of our nation until the bright day of justice emerges."

But the apostle of nonviolence admonished his people:

> In the process of gaining our rightful place we must not be guilty of wrongful deeds.... Again and again we must rise to the majestic heights of meeting physical force with soul force. The marvelous new militancy which has engulfed the Negro community must not lead us to a distrust of all white people, for many of our white brothers, as evidenced by their presence here today, have come to realize that their destiny is tied up with our destiny.

King continued with mounting fervor. His delivery was moving though restrained; his thoughts flowed as smoothly as his rich baritone voice. In conclusion, he told of a great dream.

> I have a dream that one day this nation will rise up and live out the true meaning of its creed: "We hold these truths to be self-evident, that all men are created equal...."
>
> I have a dream that one day on the red hills of Georgia the sons of former slaves and the sons of former slaveholders will be able to sit down together at the table of brotherhood.
>
> I have a dream that one day even the state of Mississippi, a state sweltering with the people's injustice, sweltering with the heat of oppression, will be transformed into an oasis of freedom and justice.
>
> I have a dream that my four little children will one day live in a nation where they will not be judged by the color of their skin, but by the content of their character.
>
> This is our hope. This is the faith that I go back to the South with. With this faith we will be able to hew out of the mountain of despair a stone of hope.

The Nonviolent Battalions
1963

A fuller picture needs to be given of the principal civil-rights organizations that rallied and propelled the Negro revolution. We met them in the March on Washington and they will be with us to the end of this volume. But first a word on the revolution's terminology.

"Civil rights" had come into universal use in the United States to denote the aim of the Negro movement. The term was applied to all manner of activities related to the movement and to legislation looking toward justice for the Negro. The label "civil-rights organizations" was given to the Big Five—that is to say the National Association for the Advancement of Colored People, the National Urban League, the Congress of Racial Equality, the Southern Christian Leadership Conference, and the Student Nonviolent Coordinating Committee—and to a less extent to other groups allied with them. In recent years there had also been a proliferation of predominantly white organizations combating race discrimination, unofficial councils and committees as well as state and city commissions. These generally took names using not "civil rights" but "human relations" or "community relations" (as, for example, the "Memphis Committee on Community Relations" or the "New York State Commission for Human Relations").

Incidentally, "civil rights" was often translated by European journalists—with substantial accuracy—as "Negro rights." That is indeed what the agitation was mainly about. Discrimination against 900,000 Puerto Ricans in the Northeast, against three million citizens of Mexican origin in the Southwest, against the country's half a million Indians and against Jews received some attention under the head of civil rights; but in common parlance in the United States in the 1960's "civil rights" denoted the claim of the Negro to equal status with the white man.

The Big Five organizations were directed by Negroes, but each had some white participation and received substantial white financial support. They had diverse backgrounds. The NAACP and the Urban League, both established largely on white initiative, had functioned for more than half a century; CORE dated from 1942; SCLC and SNCC were from their inception a part of the Negro upsurge of the late 1950's and the 1960's. They differed also in their approach to the problem. There was rivalry and dissension among them and they lacked over-all planning and coordination. The unity that was achieved (with some difficulty) in the March on Washington would not be seen again. At the same time the variety of organizations made it possible for people of many philosophies and temperaments to find a place in the movement.

The NAACP

Whether judged by its formidable list of accomplishments in the long past or measured by its far-reaching representation of the Negro minority in the 1960's, the greatest of the Big Five was the National Association for the Advancement of Colored People. It had 535,000 dues-paying members in 1963—and no other group had anything approaching its nationwide structure of seven regional offices and over 1,700 state and local units. A large proportion of the Negroes in high government positions and many leaders of other civil-rights organizations had been active at some time in the NAACP.

NAACP members were drawn predominantly from the Negro middle class (a circumstance which would prove a weakness later when attention focused on rioting slum-dwellers at the bottom of the economic pile). Members' dues, at a minimum rate of two dollars a year, supplied the bulk of the Association's funds—in contrast to the other four civil-rights organizations, whose funds came mainly from philanthropic foundations and other outside sources. In recent years the NAACP had operated on an annual budget in excess of one million dollars; its income in 1963 totaled $1,437,675.

In its early years the board of directors of the NAACP had been predominantly white. In 1963 four-fifths of its board members were Negroes. Arthur B. Spingarn, a white attorney in his eighty-fifth year, was serving his twenty-fourth year as the Association's president. Roy Wilkins, on the staff since 1931, and executive secretary since 1955, enjoyed high prestige in civil-rights councils and a popularity among the Negro public exceeded only by that of the charismatic Martin Luther King.

The NAACP had for many years been virtually synonymous with the Negro protest movement. Segregationists in the South had become accustomed to thinking of it as the source of all their racial troubles. Many of these Southerners in 1963, confused by the new organizational spectrum of the Negro revolution, still focused their hatred and their execrations on the NAACP. But the NAACP and the Urban League were the most conservative of the Big Five—the Urban League in the nature of its special functions; the NAACP by reason of its sheer size and institutional nature, the composition of its membership, its age and the age level of its leaders.

The NAACP had relied traditionally on peaceful protest and the slow processes of law. Throughout the long struggle to secure compliance with the Supreme Court's ruling against public school segregation it had placed chief emphasis on court action and law enforcement. Now with Negro demonstrations breaking the tranquillity of a hundred cities, law enforcement had acquired a different connotation, and impatient members of CORE, SCLC, and SNCC chided the NAACP on its moderation. Nevertheless the venerable NAACP was moving to adapt itself to the bolder stance and newer techniques, and there was some justification for its claim: "In every area of civil-rights activity the NAACP and its units have collectively borne the lion's share of the burden. This is the case whether the target has been in housing, in employment, in vote denials or in public accommodations."*

The NAACP Legal Defense and Educational Fund

This organization, an offshoot of the NAACP, and frequently identified with it in the public mind, was in fact a separate entity,

* John A. Morsell in *Annals of the American Academy of Political Science*, January, 1965.

and it merits a place among the most effective instruments in the civil-rights movement in its own right. The Legal Defense and Educational Fund handled an ever growing mass of court action in the defense of Negroes and in furtherance of the Negro cause. (Its educational program was a minor activity.) The Fund was established in 1939 for the purpose of separating the bulk of the costly legal work from the Association's lobbying and propaganda activities, thus making contributions to its financial support deductible from income tax.

In 1963 the Fund's New York office was manned by 16 attorneys, with 102 cooperating lawyers across the country. In that year it defended 10,487 citizens arrested during civil-rights demonstrations, represented Negroes in 30 cases carried to the Supreme Court, and fought 168 separate groups of legal actions in 15 states, involving integration of schools, medical services, public facilities, recreation, employment, and housing. The Fund's annual budget had multiplied five times in ten years; in 1964 it reached $1,460,965.

The Supreme Court's memorable decision of 1954 declaring public school segregation unconstitutional was a shining triumph for lawyers of the Legal Defense Fund, led by Thurgood Marshall (now an associate justice of the Supreme Court). Marshall served as the Fund's director-counsel for twenty-two years, before resigning in 1961 to accept a judgeship on the federal circuit court of appeals. He was succeeded by Jack Greenberg, a dedicated white civil-rights crusader, who had been an associate of Marshall in the 1954 Supreme Court fight.

The National Urban League

Although it helped to organize the March on Washington, the National Urban League was the civil-rights organization least involved in the struggle in the streets. It had nonetheless a dynamic part in the movement. Its role was one of negotiation and advocacy of reform, while aiding urban Negroes, as it had done for half a century, in many practical ways. Its work tended to complement the militant crusade: while other organizations marched, picketed, and boycotted to open doors to Negro employment, the Urban League negotiated with employers and labored to place individual Negroes in jobs.

The League was formed in 1910 for the purpose of assisting unadjusted Negroes migrating to the cities. It had been a sorely needed friend of the urban Negro in an era when his subservient status was scarcely challenged. For many years it strove to get even the smallest economic openings for Negro workers. Its activities touched problems of education, home and neighborhood, recreation, vocational guidance, housing, health, and morals, but the primary task for all its branches was to find jobs for Negroes. A social service organization rather than a voice of protest, it had leaned heavily upon the good will of the white community. Most of its local Leagues were members of city-wide Community Chests. Many white businessmen contributed directly to their financial support or even had a part in their administration.

With the wave of Negro militancy and self-assertion of the 1960's the Urban League had expanded and adopted a more aggressive attitude. While continuing its social service activities, it moved vigorously to take advantage of the new opportunities that civil-rights agitation was opening to Negroes. And at the intellectual level it joined in the fight. Its leaders presented thoughtful and cogent arguments to government, industry, and the public in a campaign "to wipe out the last vestiges and barriers of discrimination." The personal stature of the League's urbane but stubborn executive director helped it to hold a solid place among the Big Five. Whitney Young and Roy Wilkins were listened to with particular respect by committees of Congress and were the Negro leaders most often called to the White House for consultation.

Congress of Racial Equality

The forces of CORE, SNCC, and SCLC were the shock troops of the nonviolent offensive. As national director of CORE, James Farmer commanded a nonviolent army of 13 field secretaries, from 17 to 30 field workers, and hundreds of more or less trained crusaders, who were deployed on one trouble front after another. Thousands of other CORE members and unaffiliated local Negroes joined in CORE demonstrations in various communities. Small and little known before the 1961 Freedom Rides, its growth since then had been phenomenal. Its membership and budget had quadrupled in four years. There were 61,000 members in 1963. Membership dues and larger individual contributions brought its annual income to $900,000 in 1964.

CORE came into being in the spring of 1942, in response to a memorandum circulated by James Farmer. It was actually a pioneer in nonviolent resistance techniques, including the sit-in, but it remained tiny and without a paid staff until the mid-1950's. It was then also that it first entered the South, where, in 1963, 32 of its 70 chapters were located. Its leader, for all his tactical belligerency, was a thoughtful student of the broad implications of the Negro revolution. James Farmer had served previously as race relations secretary for the pacifist Fellowship of Reconciliation, and had studied originally for the Methodist ministry.

Southern Christian Leadership Conference

The Southern Christian Leadership Conference was the least known of the Big Five organizations, but Martin Luther King, its founder and president, was by far the best known of their leaders. King was *Time* Magazine's Man of the Year for 1963. "King has neither the quiet brilliance nor the sharp administrative capabilities of the NAACP's Roy Wilkins," *Time* said. "He has none of the sophistication of the National Urban League's Whitney Young. . . . He has neither the inventiveness of CORE's James Farmer nor the raw militancy of Snick's John Lewis. . . . Yet he has an indescribable capacity for empathy that is the touchstone of leadership . . ." King's call for action without violence was well illustrated by his admonition to a group of angry Negro militants in Alabama which *Time* quoted: "Some of you have knives, and I ask you to put them up. Some of you may have arms, and I ask you to put them up. Get the weapon of nonviolence, the breastplate of righteousness, the armor of truth, and just keep marching."

Though other able leaders were associated with King and some conducted campaigns on their own, SCLC was essentially the organizational embodiment of this preeminent symbol of the Negro movement. King was SCLC's president, the Reverend Ralph Abernathy its vice president and treasurer. Its busy and growing staff, which was headed in 1963 by the Reverend Wyatt T. Walker, engaged in research and issued some publications, but its primary concerns were fund-raising, organizing campaigns, and the manifold arrangements for King's personal appearances. Funds, fluctuating in times of calm and crisis but exceeding $1 million a year, came from collections at rallies which the leader addressed and contributions from many other well-wishers across the nation.

Student Nonviolent Coordinating Committee

SNCC, or "Snick," was the youngest, the angriest, and the most impatient of the five organizations. A majority of SNCC's crusaders were in their early twenties—youths who could hardly remember the day of the Supreme Court's great decision of 1954 and who were little concerned with it anyway. To them segregation and discrimination were simply preposterous wrongs, not to be tolerated. Nonviolent though SNCC men were, they exposed themselves to violence unceasingly.

They believed that their goal of revolutionizing the Deep South could be accomplished only by unrelenting, single-minded struggle on the part of individuals fearless of the consequences to themselves. In their ranks were Northern students of "far-out" brands of liberalism, also bearded men and trousered young women—ideologies as well as fashions that, while common in the North, were rare and suspect in the Deep South. Critics said SNCC workers invited violence. Certainly danger of imprisonment, beatings, and even death did not deter them from moving into areas of fierce hostility. The good will of local whites was of minimum concern to these young idealists, but their often heroic efforts gave courage, hope, and organization to thousands of oppressed Negroes.

SNCC was expressly "not a membership organization, but rather an agency attempting to stimulate and foster the growth of local protest movements." Chairman James Forman and Executive Director John Lewis, directing about 200 field secretaries who lived on close to subsistence salaries, sparked SNCC's activities—in which many unaffiliated local Negroes joined. Financial support came from voluntary contributions, largely from Northern student groups and wealthy individuals. Coming into being with the sit-in movement of 1960, its first target had been segregated lunch counters. Its chief battleground in 1963 was around the franchise, from which most Negroes in the Deep South were still excluded.

The Southern Regional Council

The Southern Regional Council was sometimes labeled a "civil-rights organization." It was limited to one region in its primary concern and it engaged in no direct-action militancy, but it was, and had been for many years, a force of the first importance in the movement toward interracial justice. It was best known for its reports and publications chronicling and interpreting developments—and exposing injustice—in the field of race relations. These, which enjoyed a high reputation for accuracy and objectivity— within its commitment to the cause—were widely quoted and were used with confidence by many public men. The Council also stimulated the forming of biracial state and local human relations councils in the South and aided their work. In 1963 SRC was planning, coordinating, and reporting progress in a massive campaign of the Big Five and other groups to increase voter registration.

The SRC was formed in 1944, growing out of an earlier Commission on Interracial Cooperation, which had labored in the race-relations field since 1919. Its members—about 100 outstanding Southern Negroes and liberal white leaders—formed a board which gave it over-all direction. A staff of specialists carried on the day-to-day work of its Atlanta office, where a succession of distinguished Southerners had served as its executive director. The incumbent in 1963 was Dr. Leslie W. Dunbar, a scholarly and a widely respected student of the problem of race relations in the United States. His predecessor, Harold Fleming, had moved on in 1961 to somewhat similar work as executive vice president of the Potomac Institute in Washington, D.C.

The Black Muslims

The Black Muslims could not be called a civil-rights organization, and the Gandhi-King principle of nonviolence was far removed from their ideology. They forswore violence unless attacked, and incidents in which they had actually been involved in violence were rare, but their preaching vaguely contemplated some widespread violence to come. Above all they preached hatred of the white man—in contrast to the ideal of love, which Martin Luther King set for the civil-rights movement. Yet the Muslims need to be mentioned here, because—while more revolutionary than the revolution—they had an impact upon both Negroes and whites that made them a part of it.

The Black Muslim prophet, or "Messenger of Allah," Elijah Muhammad (once a Georgia Negro named Elijah Poole), prophesied that in a coming Armageddon the white race would be destroyed and the black man would inherit the earth. The Brotherhood's more limited stated goal was a territory of the size of a number of states within the United States to be set apart for Negroes only. There were other features of Muslim doctrine beside these fantasies that repelled intelligent Negroes. The Brotherhood's rejection of the Christian religion was ill calculated to appeal to militants of the Big Five, who often met in Christian churches and included many clergymen among their leaders. Muslims also urged, not an end to segregation, but more complete segregation. Nevertheless millions of Negroes applauded their execrations of the "white devil," and this revelation of the mood of Negroes gave an added jolt to white complacency.

The number of Black Muslims was variously estimated at from 20,000 to over 100,000, depending in part on how close those counted were to the disciplined inner circle of the cult. Muhammad was sixty-six years of age. Flourishing in 1963 as his voluble spokesman and second ranking Muslim leader was thirty-eight-year-old Malcolm X (the Muslim faithful often used "X" in lieu of their white-originating surnames). Malcolm X was a man of considerable ability and personal magnetism. At the end of 1963 he lost favor with the Messenger and launched upon an independent career (which ended with his assassination in early 1965).

On the constructive side the Black Muslims preached scholastic diligence, industry, cleanliness, and sexual morality, and they did much to imbue their followers with self-respect and pride in the Negro race. This emphasis on pride and self-improvement, together with their lurid denunciation of the wrongs done to Negroes by whites, made civil-rights leaders hesitate to repudiate the Muslims and provided a base on which some kind of cooperation might in time be built.

THREE

The Attack
1963

In the March on Washington the Negro revolt reached its highest level of decorum. In a deed perpetrated in Birmingham eighteen days later, anti-Negro fanaticism descended to the nadir of infamy.

Alabama had experienced its first week of public school desegregation in minimum adjustment to the Supreme Court's 1954 decision. A handful of Negro children had been admitted to white schools in the cities of Birmingham, Mobile, Tuskegee, and Huntsville. In spite of the pyrotechnics of Governor Wallace, who had declared that he would personally stand at the schoolhouse door to prevent it, the step actually had met with no physical resistance and little public disorder. For a few days the crisis seemed indeed to have passed. But at 9:22 A.M. the following Sunday morning, September 15, an explosion in a Negro Baptist church in Birmingham sent a wave of horror across the nation and the world.

The church was bombed while it was filled with children attending Sunday School. Four girls from eleven to fourteen years of age were killed; twenty others were injured. After this, holding the city's seething Negro populace in check became the frantic concern of Birmingham police, and a policeman shot and killed a Negro boy. During the day's turmoil another Negro boy was callously murdered by two white youths, bringing the death toll to six. (Half a year later the two white youths were sentenced to seven months each in the county jail, but were released on probation. To this date the perpetrators of the bombing have not been apprehended.)

President Kennedy expressed "a deep sense of outrage and grief." With apparent reference to Governor Wallace's inflammatory behavior, he said: "It is regrettable that public disparagement of law and order has encouraged violence which has fallen on the innocent." Roy Wilkins said the President should cut off "every nickel of federal aid to Alabama." Martin Luther King, flying to Birmingham to restrain angry Negroes, declared: "The Army ought to take over this city and run it because the Negroes are tired now, tireder than ever before." The reaction of Negroes throughout the nation ranged from grief and prayer to demands for Wallace's arrest. Impromptu demonstrations took place in the larger cities. Negroes and Negro-sympathizers marched before the United Nations.

By the end of September the white public had turned its attention to other matters—including the annoyance of Negro demonstrations nearer home. But bitterness over the Birmingham horror sank deep and would dwell long in Negro hearts. The protest movement continued without significant change. Let it be said, however, that its usual manifestations bore little resemblance to the great parade in the nation's capital. Negroes did not rely simply upon submission of grievances and appeals to the conscience of the white majority. The campaign upon which they had embarked was one of pressure and harassment. It was indeed nonviolent, but it used coercion as well as persuasion.

Martin Luther King explained the policy in a letter which he wrote while in a Birmingham jail during the April disturbances in that city. Eight leading white Alabama clergymen, including four bishops and one rabbi, had issued a public statement urging the Negroes "to withdraw support from these demonstrations, and to unite locally in working peacefully for a better Birmingham." King produced an 8,000-word reply. "It would have been much shorter," he said, "had I been writing from a comfortable desk, but what else is there to do when you are alone for days in the dull monotony of a narrow cell other than write long letters, think strange thoughts, and pray long prayers?" The document, a masterpiece of cogent reasoning and lofty sentiment, became a classic of the Negro revolution.

Addressing his white fellow clergymen, King wrote: "You may

well ask, 'Why direct action? Why sit-ins, marches, etc.? Isn't negotiation a better path?' You are exactly right in your call for negotiation. Indeed, this is the purpose of direct action. Nonviolent direct action seeks to create such a crisis and establish such creative tension that a community that has constantly refused to negotiate is forced to confront the issue. It seeks so to dramatize the issue that it can no longer be ignored. . . . We know through painful experience that freedom is never voluntarily given by the oppressor; it must be demanded by the oppressed. . . ."

"For years now," King said, "I have heard the word 'Wait!' It rings in the ear of every Negro with a piercing familiarity. . . . The nations of Asia and Africa are moving with jet-like speed toward the goal of political independence, and we creep at horse-and-buggy pace toward the gaining of a cup of coffee at a lunch counter. I guess it is easy for those who have never felt the stinging darts of segregation to say, 'Wait.' But when you have seen vicious mobs lynch your mothers and fathers at will and drown your sisters and brothers at whim; when you have seen hate-filled policemen curse, kick, brutalize and even kill your black brothers and sisters with impunity; . . . when you take a cross country drive and find it necessary to sleep night after night in the uncomfortable corners of your automobile because no motel will accept you; when you are humiliated day in and day out by nagging signs reading 'white' and 'colored'; when you are harried by day and haunted by night by the fact that you are a Negro . . . then you will understand why we find it difficult to wait. . . ."

On the delicate subject of civil disobedience he wrote: "You express a great deal of anxiety over our willingness to break laws. This is certainly a legitimate concern. . . . One may well ask, 'How can you advocate breaking some laws and obeying others?' The answer is found in the fact that there are two types of laws: There are *just* and there are *unjust* laws. I would agree with Saint Augustine that 'An unjust law is no law at all.' "

However, King did not "advocate evading or defying the law as the rabid segregationist would do. This," he said, "would lead to anarchy. One who breaks an unjust law must do it *openly, lovingly*, . . . and with a willingness to accept the penalty. I submit that an individual who breaks a law that conscience tells him is unjust, and willingly accepts the penalty by staying in jail to arouse the conscience of the community over its injustice, is in reality expressing the very highest respect for law."

He paid tribute to "some of our white brothers" who, "like Ralph McGill, Lillian Smith, Harry Golden and James Dabbs, have written about our struggle in eloquent, prophetic and understanding terms. Others," he said, "have marched with us down nameless streets of the South. They have languished in filthy, roach-infested jails, suffering the abuse and brutality of angry policemen who see them as 'dirty nigger-lovers'. . . ."

But he was "greatly disappointed with the white church and its leadership."

There was a time when the church was very powerful. It was during that period when the early Christians rejoiced when they were deemed worthy to suffer for what they believed. In those days the church was not merely a thermometer that recorded the ideas and principles of popular opinion; it was a thermostat that transformed the mores of society. Wherever the early Christians entered a town, the power structure got disturbed and immediately sought to convict them for being "disturbers of the peace" and "outside agitators." But they went on with the conviction that they were "a colony of heaven," and had to obey God rather than man. They were small in number but big in commitment. They were too God-intoxicated to be "astronomically intimidated." They brought an end to such ancient evils as infanticide and gladiatorial contests.

Things are different now. The contemporary church is often a weak, ineffectual voice with an uncertain sound. It is so often the arch supporter of the status quo. Far from being disturbed by the presence of the church, the power structure of the average community is consoled by the church's silent and often vocal sanction of things as they are.

In closing, King said to the white ministers:

I hope this letter finds you strong in the faith. I also hope that circumstances will soon make it possible for me to meet each of you, not as an integrationist or a civil-rights leader, but as a fellow clergyman and a Christian brother. Let us hope that the dark clouds of racial prejudice will soon pass away and the deep fog of misunderstanding will be lifted from our fear-drenched communities and in some not too distant tomorrow the radiant stars of love and brotherhood will shine over our great nation with all their scintillating beauty.

Many factors contributed to this climax in the upsurge of the Negro; but if we ask why, after centuries of submission, the Negro was not only aroused but ready to mount a sustained, nationwide revolt at this moment in history, we shall find much of the answer in two discoveries which he had made. First, he had discovered that with the techniques of nonviolent action it was possible to picket and boycott and sit-in, with consequences which, though they might involve manhandling or imprisonment for some, were far short of bloody conflict. Second, he had found that such tactics bore fruit. Both of these discoveries had flashed out from the 1960 attack upon segregated lunch counters in the South. The white public was amazed then at the audacity of Negro youth, but hostility was actually mingled with some admiration, reprisals were minimal, and after a few months of Negro demonstrations, the walls of Jericho began to fall. Within a year lunch counters previously restricted to whites were serving Negroes in a hundred cities and towns. Similar boldness began to bring other Negro gains.

It is not to be inferred that wide inroads had been made so soon upon the pervasive structure of race discrimination. The great majority of Southern hotels, motels, and eating places were still segregated; they would yield slowly, many only under the ultimate compulsion of federal law, to the new order. But steady improvement was visible in response to Negro pressure even in the South—Negro policemen employed here and there; WHITE and COLORED signs removed from public conveniences; theaters, parks, or swimming pools desegregated; a few more jobs opened to Negroes. Negotiation played a part, but it was the sit-in and the street demonstration, or the threat of them, that made negotiations productive. Businessmen and public authorities not yet under attack were often moved to make concessions by the agitation and disorder which they observed in other cities. In short, harassment was succeeding where supplication had failed. Offending the white man was proving more effective than pleasing him.

The mass of Negro Americans was not suddenly transformed from mice into men. Many took no part in the militant movement. Thousands were still inhibited by fear or habit and a deeply ingrained humility. Some leaders thought civil-rights organizations were relying too much on direct action, too little on persuasion. A considerable element still cherished the belief, inherited from Booker T. Washington (now widely discredited among Negroes), that the Negro's best hope lay not in noisy protest but in diligent self-improvement. Such sentiment found its largest expression in the National Baptist Convention, U.S.A., Inc.—which, incidentally, was the biggest single Negro organization of any kind. The five million members of this body were by no means of one mind on the issue—sharp dissension often characterized its annual meetings; but the Convention's dominant leadership frowned upon militant protest. Its assembly, in session in Cleveland on September 5, 1963, re-elected the Reverend Dr. J. H. Jackson, of Chicago, to his eleventh one-year term as president. Dr. Jackson urged prayer and industry rather than demonstrations, "pressure by production" rather than "pressure by protest."

Another well-known opponent of civil-rights militancy was S. B. Fuller, of Chicago, one of the rare Negro millionaires. Starting life in poverty, he had amassed a fortune in the cosmetics industry, specializing in bleaching and hair-straightening products for the Negro market. The Fuller Products Company was grossing over ten million dollars a year. About 20 per cent of its several thousand employees and salesmen were white. Fuller held that the way to Negro advancement lay through thrift and business enterprise.

Fuller also addressed the Assembly at Cleveland. "If we could save money as well as save souls," he told the Negro Baptists, "many of our troubles would be solved." In an interview with *United States News and World Report* of August 19, Fuller said of Martin Luther King and his associates that they spoke "only for certain small groups of people." "Those who are demonstrating and 'sitting-in'," he said, "are a very small minority of the Negroes. . . . There are more moderates than we hear of, but some are afraid to give their opinion. They are being muzzled. . . ."

Fuller vastly underestimated the sweep of the Negro revolt, though he was right in saying that many "moderates" and "gradualists" among Negro leaders were silenced by the odium that now descended upon such spokesmen. Dr. Jackson himself, though his position largely protected him from public attack, was anathema in many Negro circles. He had been booed from the speakers' stand

—along with the mayor of the city—at a boisterous NAACP rally in Chicago on July 4.

Even James H. Meredith, the sensitive young Negro for whose admission to the University of Mississippi federal marshals and troops had fought white rioters in 1962, and whose quiet courage in the hostile atmosphere of his year's attendance at that institution had aroused general admiration, found himself under attack for his nonbelligerent attitude. In a speech to the youth group at the July convention of the NAACP in Chicago Meredith said: "Anyone of you burr heads out there could be the owner or manager of a large department store, president of a corporation, or even mayor of the city of Chicago. Only believe; all things are possible if you only believe."

The man so recently hailed as a hero was not booed, but he got a cool reception and only a few polite handclaps. After he left the room, James Davis, an NAACP student leader, arose to attack him, and Davis' vehement speech was received with shouts and cheers. The expression "burr heads," though not so intended, was needlessly offensive, but the NAACP youths had been disappointed also in Meredith's failure to issue a call to battle. "I am extremely sorry," Davis said, "anyone would come before you and tell you 'Only believe'!"

An extensive survey conducted by *Newsweek* Magazine in July led to the conclusion that the "revolution" had "won the allegiance of vast majorities of Negroes wherever they live and whatever their age or economic lot." Millions of Negroes who had taken no part in demonstrations, many only vaguely conscious of the revolution, nevertheless rejoiced in it. And militancy was the fashion. A Louis Harris poll, which formed the basis of the *Newsweek* survey, reported after lengthy interviews with over 1,250 Negroes that "as of now, 40 per cent of Negroes say they have taken part in a sit-in, marched in a mass protest or picketed a store." The Negro press, Negro intellectuals, Negroes who were vocal were overwhelmingly on the side of aggressive action: pressure and more pressure.

Let us take a closer look at the kind of pressure that was being exerted—and making daily newspaper headlines—in the summer and fall of 1963. On the day when the mayor of New York signed a proclamation designating August 28 as "Jobs and Freedom Day" and urging all citizens to "lend their heartfelt support to the peaceful purposes" of the March on Washington, pickets were singing, littering, and hurling abuse outside his office. Pickets had squatted there for forty-four days, protesting discrimination against Negroes and Puerto Ricans in the building-trade unions. The next day an attempt by Negroes to chain themselves to a pillar resulted in a melee with police until Mayor Wagner ordered their removal. A few days earlier members of CORE had driven a truckload of rubbish to City Hall Plaza and were dumping broken furniture, torn mattresses, and the like until they were stopped by police. These were protesting conditions in the New York tenements in which Negroes lived.

In Philadelphia, CORE members attempted to dump a truckload of junk on the lawn of an owner of Negro-occupied tenements and, when stopped by police, dumped it in the street. In Chicago, during the week before the March on Washington, pickets charged through barricades to prostrate themselves in thick mud in the path of construction machinery. This protest was against the construction of mobile schools in a Negro neighborhood instead of sending the Negro pupils to predominantly white schools in an adjoining residential district. In Detroit pickets protesting the failure of a bank to employ Negroes had to be carried away by police on stretchers; they had stood in line until reaching the teller's cage, then sat on the floor, blocking the access of others. A clapping, singing group of seventy demonstrators sat on the floor of a leading hotel in Syracuse, New York, to protest against its discriminatory hiring policy.

The campaign against the exclusion of Negroes from building-trade unions developed some of the most grotesque tactics. In Elizabeth, New Jersey, Negro youths sat down in the street, arm in arm, blocking the roadway used by cement-mixing trucks until twenty-nine of them were taken away by police. Ten demonstrators chained themselves together and defied police to move them; the latter, armed with bolt-cutters, severed the chains and removed them at last.

Such displays of mischievous ingenuity were rarely promoted by responsible Negro leaders. Most of the demonstrations took conventional forms of parades and picketing. But even these were inconveniencing the public, disrupting traffic, making businessmen and city officials uneasy, and placing a heavy burden upon police everywhere.

Meanwhile a new Negro complaint was beginning to assume epidemic proportions. This was called *"de facto"* public school segregation—since it was not pursuant to laws, not *de jure*, but *de facto*. Outside of the officially segregated areas of the South, in cities where segregation had long been unlawful or contrary to official policy, many public schools were in fact attended only, or almost entirely, by pupils of one race. This situation had received little attention in past years. Now it became a burning issue. Negro leaders demanded a redistribution of pupils, with expanded transportation arrangements, to achieve a better "racial balance" in the various public schools. This complex problem will be examined in detail in later chapters; we note here that in the fall of 1963 it had become a major source of Negro unrest.

The revolt in the South differed in many respects from that in the rest of the nation. The Negro was more intimidated and repressed in the South. Concern for public order in this region was qualified and confused in the minds of many officials by the ancient imperative of "keeping the Negro in his place." In some Southern states, Negro demonstrations of protest, however orderly, were regarded as a kind of outrage; police handled the demonstrators as if they were criminals. At the same time white anti-Negro terrorists enjoyed a large measure of public favor and did their criminal work with almost complete impunity.

The Southern Negro also had a longer road to travel to reach the goal of equal citizenship. In spite of visible advance, he still lagged far behind his brethren in other sections. His push therefore was generally directed toward more elementary objectives. Much of his effort was focused on hurdles in areas of public accommodations, officially segregated public education, and the franchise—which remained to be cleared only in the South. In the rest of the nation, and now in most of the South, Negroes were voting freely and without molestation. But in Mississippi and in many counties of Alabama, Louisiana, and Georgia most of the blood, tears, and sweat of civil-rights crusaders were being expended in a struggle to enable Negroes to register for voting.

Racial disturbances were not more numerous in the South at this stage than in some other sections, but they were uglier and resulted in far more Negroes being herded into jails. The Southern Regional Council, which kept a running tally in this region, issued this Year-End Summary:

> During 1963 an estimated 930 individual public protest demonstrations took place in at least 115 cities in 11 Southern states.
>
> More than 20,083 of the persons, Negro and white, who have so demonstrated have been arrested.
>
> Ten persons have died under circumstances directly related to racial protests.
>
> And 35 known bombings have occurred.

Birmingham and Jackson were centers of perpetual tension, ruthless police action, and Negro frustration. Half a dozen other Southern cities had for months been running sores of interracial strife: Albany and Americus, Georgia; Danville, Virginia; Jacksonville and St. Augustine, Florida; and Williamston, North Carolina. Cambridge, Maryland, a border state town with Southern characteristics, was similarly afflicted. In these unhappy communities a peculiarly vexing situation had developed, and the pattern was similar in each.

The fever began with relatively mild protests on the part of Negro citizens against their traditional exclusion from eating places, libraries, swimming pools, churches, etc.—and from job opportunities. Initial Negro demonstrations met with harassment by white fanatics and with police repression. These in turn stimulated larger and more desperate Negro demonstrations, which received a progressively more ruthless white response. As collision succeeded collision, bitterness and tension mounted; exaggerated rumors multiplied. Fear of obloquy and reprisal from extremist elements prevented even those whites who were so disposed from urging consideration of the Negroes' grievances. At the same time Negroes hardened in their determination not to desist until visible gains were achieved. They were adhering to a basic tenet of the revolution: never to abandon a campaign merely because of the virulence of white opposition. The inevitability of the Negro advance had to be demonstrated. That would be demonstrated ultimately, but in the meantime Negroes in these cities tirelessly sat-in and picketed and marched and went singing and praying to jail in unrelenting struggle against intransigent whites.

The unrest in the summer and fall of 1963—and continuing for many months thereafter—was unlike anything the nation had witnessed before, in two significant respects. First of all, it saw the flowering of the doctrine of nonviolent action, which promised to give the American Negro revolution a signal place in the history of social reform. Seldom, if ever, have we seen in any country such widespread, sustained, and purposeful turmoil with so little bloodshed as in the United States at this time. American race riots of the past had come at long intervals and were generally confined to one metropolitan area at a time. But the death toll in them was high. More persons were killed in three days of rioting in either East St. Louis, Illinois, in July, 1917, or in Detroit in June, 1943, than lost their lives in 2,000 civil-rights demonstrations in 300 cities in 1963.

Undisciplined Negroes sometimes overstepped the bounds of nonviolence in minor incidents, and the threat of eventual resort to violence was heard in many quarters; but in the broad picture of nationwide agitation, the deviations thus far had been rare. Happily also, the reactions of the white public reflected a clear advance in interracial tolerance in the United States. Organized white countermilitancy, for instance, was practically unknown outside of the South. The Negro campaign against *de facto* public school segregation in the North was leading to a white counter-movement in defense of the neighborhood school, but the promoters of this were careful to disavow anti-Negro bias and professed sympathy with other Negro objectives. Although there were occasional announcements of the formation of an "Association for the Advancement of White People," a "Society for the Prevention of Negroes Getting Everything" or something else of that sort, these, like the buffoonery of the American Nazi Party, were little more than publicity gestures.

In many sections of the South the old spirit of passionate mass intolerance still prevailed. In the half dozen cities that we described as running sores, white attackers of Negroes often reached mob proportions. Police dispersed crowds of from 500 to several thousand angry whites in Concord and High Point, North Carolina, in September. The Southern anti-Negro organizations—of which the Citizens' Councils were the best known and the most respectable—were not as ubiquitous as in the late 1950's, but they had become more ruthless, and their criminal elements were coming more to the fore as their strength declined. In Mississippi, the center of the Citizens' Council movement, many were leaving that group for the more violent company of the Ku Klux Klansmen or for a new "Americans for the Preservation of the White Race." The fanatical bullies of the Klan received fresh stimulus from the 1963 turmoil. Klan leaders' estimates of Klan membership ran to hundreds of thousands. The Anti-Defamation League of B'nai B'rith, the most reliable watchdog on the Klan, estimated its "probable hard-core membership" at 10,000, but reported that "an additional 25,000 to 35,000 like-minded racists . . . stand ready to do its work of terror."

Outside of the South, however, the rarity of interracial collision was remarkable. Police were heavily involved, but the only other whites who disturbed Negro demonstrations were a few rock-throwing young hoodlums. Among the general public, Negro audacities that half a century earlier might have set off frenzied mobs thirsting for Negro blood were watched by whites now with relative detachment. It remained, precariously but still in fact, a peaceful revolution.

Nevertheless, the initiative which had been taken by the Negro minority was a phenomenon that never ceased to bewilder or frighten the white public. The race riots of old had been mainly white attacks upon Negroes. Though they had often been precipitated by some obscure or fancied Negro offense, Negro participation in the ensuing battle was generally in self-defense or in desperate retaliation. Whites still rioted and engaged in terrorism in some sections of the South, but the turbulence that spread across the land in 1963 sprang from Negro impulse.

One type of disorder, it is true, was created entirely by whites. From time to time violence resulted from the exercise by a Negro family of a simple legal and moral right in the choice of a home. This evil was much older than the revolution of the 1960's, but ugly incidents still occurred. In Chicago in late July, when two Negro families moved to the edge of a white residential district ten blocks south of the stockyards, bricks, bottles, and firecrackers were hurled at the Negro homes by sullen whites milling in the streets. On the day of the March on Washington, the attempt of a Negro couple to move into an all-white suburb of Philadelphia produced a night of turbulence. The Negroes' chosen home was damaged and a fire was started by a homemade bomb thrown into a back bedroom; the heater was upset, the plumbing was ripped out, and windows were broken. Rioting prevented the couple from entering until two days later, when they did so only under heavy police escort and amid a barrage of taunts and stones.

Yet these shameful white contributions to the general commotion, and even the barbarities of Negrophobes in the Deep South, were overshadowed by the nationwide display of aggressiveness on the part of the once meek and long-suffering colored man. An unprecedented sense of manhood and self-assertion had seized millions of Negro Americans. Sympathetic observers saw in the phenomenon a healthy release of the human spirit, with incalculable possibilities of future Negro achievement. Critics wondered if it would carry the Negro offensive beyond the point of righting wrongs.

FOUR

The White Revolution
1963

The Negro revolt had become the nation's greatest domestic concern. In fact, except during transient international crises, it took precedence over foreign policy in the public mind. The *United States News and World Report* of July 29, 1963 observed: "War dangers no longer dominate thinking. . . . Race issues, instead, have moved out in front in people's thoughts."

Whether viewed with approval, or with hostility or alarm, the agitation could not be ignored. And few whites were immune from some liberalization of attitude toward the Negro. Many who regarded him as a nuisance, or a menace, began to recognize him for the first time as a fellow citizen. Many others took up cudgels on his behalf. Consciousness of wrongs done to the Negro was reflected in an outpouring of newspaper and magazine articles, books, television programs, sermons, and politicians' pronouncements. An increasing number of white enthusiasts were crusading for interracial justice with ardor equal to that of their Negro brethren. A great white movement had arisen to support and complement the Negro revolt.

A statistically-minded librarian estimated that nonfiction books on the Negro and the race problem, including paperback reprints, were issuing from American publishing houses at the average rate of nine a week. A few books came forth, mainly from Southern writers, to preach racism and segregation—or state rights, having in mind a right to discriminate against Negroes—but these were submerged in the flood of volumes discussing the problem from a liberal point of view. On radio and TV, while defenders of segregation had opportunities to express their views, most of the programs offered the public dealt sympathetically with the Negro upsurge.

Many Southern newspapers still defended the old order, but a trend toward acceptance of the new was clearly visible, even in the Southern press; half a dozen of the largest Southern newspapers were working diligently to combat prejudice. Among important newspapers in the rest of the country, or among magazines of national circulation, any attitude other than disapproval of racial discrimination was rare. It is true that tactics and specific demands of civil-rights demonstrators were often criticized, but nearly all published comment started from a routine assumption that racial prejudice was unworthy of men of intelligence and good will. It entered the catalog of unquestioned evils—like water pollution or reckless driving—to be combated as a matter of course by the communications media. An immense and heterogeneous journalistic family seemed united in a desire to expound the nature and causes of Negro discontent. Ultrasophisticated publications like the *Wall Street Journal*, the *New Yorker*, and *Esquire* shared in the endeavor with magazines of mass circulation like *Time*, *Newsweek*, *Life*, *Look*, and the *Saturday Evening Post*, and a long list of other major publications of literary, political, and religious commentary. Public opinion lagged behind its molders in this matter, to be sure, but the mobilization of liberal influences was extraordinary.

The revolution entered the campuses of white universities and colleges. It agitated students, and engaged the attention of departments of sociology, psychology, anthropology, law, and political science in a manner generally favorable to Negro aspirations. Leaders of organized labor were seeking with varying zeal to liberalize their locals and their rank-and-file membership. In Congress most members, even if not committed to support of the civil-rights bill, expressed sympathy with the Negro's yearning for equal status; only a few Southern members were indifferent or hostile. The Supreme Court was a mighty bulwark of the revolution; the national administration a towering ally. President Kennedy had declared in his June 11 broadcast; "A great change is at hand—our task, our obligation, is to make that revolution that change, peaceful and constructive for all."

The Supreme Court had traveled a long way from the Dred Scott decision of 1857 to the Brown decision of 1954. Now the most liberal Supreme Court in history, it had taken a position of leadership in the social revolution. By declaring unceasingly that the Constitution does not condone racial discrimination or segregation, it profoundly influenced Congress, the executive branch of government, and the public. The Court's new concern for the rights of Negroes, beginning in the early 1930's, reached a climax in its 1954 decision which declared that "separate educational facilities are inherently unequal," depriving the plaintiffs "of the equal protection of the laws guaranteed by the Fourteenth Amendment." In subsequent cases the Supreme Court and lower courts, taking the cue, had applied that principle to the whole field of public facilities—libraries, parks, golf courses, swimming pools, and the rest. In a long series of decisions since the Scottsboro cases of 1932 the Court had affirmed with increasing emphasis the right of Negro defendants to a fair trial in court. In the numerous cases that came to it out of the turmoil of the 1960's, the Supreme Court had insisted upon the right of Negroes to engage in peaceful demonstrations of protest, turning back most of the state prosecutions arising out of such demonstrations and based on trespass, disturbance of the peace, and segregation laws.

The Administration's drive for civil rights was centered in the Department of Justice. The caliber of the men at the head of that Department under President Kennedy was remarkable. In the fall of 1963 the President's brother, Robert F. Kennedy (now Senator) was Attorney General, and Nicholas de Belleville Katzenbach (now Under Secretary of State) was serving as Deputy Attorney General. Katzenbach's predecessor in the latter office, Byron R. White, had been elevated to the Supreme Court in 1962. Katzenbach later succeeded Kennedy as Attorney General. In charge of the Department's crucial Civil Rights Division was Assistant Attorney General Burke Marshall, an official of quiet tact and effectiveness, who enjoyed to a rare degree the respect of all parties to civil-rights disputes.

These men and their assistants had drafted the President's omnibus civil-rights bill, and were working intensively to secure its enactment. They were carrying on a volume of litigation related to school desegregation and voting rights that strained the capacity of the Civil Rights Division's forty overworked lawyers. The Department kept an eye on all developments in the Negro revolution, tabulating demonstrations and desegregation moves. At the end of each year it issued a comprehensive "Review of the Activities of the Department of Justice in Civil Rights"—which was in part also a report on the progress of the revolution. Its 1963 report gave a further idea of the range of the Department's activities in this field:

> Beyond the Justice Department's statutory responsibilities in the civil-rights field, Department officials here worked to assist elected officials and civic leaders of troubled communities in anticipating, preventing or responding to racial problems.
>
> For example, at the direction of President Kennedy, Burke Marshall, Assistant Attorney General for Civil Rights, went to Birmingham when several disorders occurred in May. He served as a mediator and succeeded in re-establishing communication between the white and Negro communities.
>
> His first assistant, John Doar, prevented a riot in Jackson, Mississippi, by walking into the middle of a crowd of demonstrators and urging them to leave. Other Department officials went to Danville, Virginia; Cambridge, Maryland; Gadsden, Alabama; Greenwood, Mississippi, and elsewhere to help resolve racial conflicts peacefully.

The Department was criticized in some quarters for not doing more—particularly for its reluctance to proceed against the molesting of civil-rights workers by Southern racists. It was felt that FBI agents should make arrests when they witnessed flagrant assault or other violations of civil rights. Complaint was also made that the Department's mediatory efforts in racial disputes were aimed more at restoring public tranquillity than at advancing Negro rights.

Among White House activities the Justice Department's report noted:

> Between last May 22 and July 12, the Administration called 21 meetings of public officials, businessmen, attorneys and leaders of religious, women's, labor and education organizations, from North and South. A total of 1,700 persons participated.
>
> The purpose of the meetings was to appraise what these people and their organizations could do on their own to help erase racial discrimination from all aspects of our National life....

By June 21, a month after the first meetings, desegregation of some public facilities, like hotels and restaurants, had taken place in 161 cities, and biracial committees were established in another 18 cities for a total of 179 cities, 36 per cent of the 566 cities. By February 11, 1964, the date of the last reports to the Department from businessmen, the total had increased to 391 cities or 69 per cent.

Listing some of "the work of other groups who participated in the Washington meetings," the Department reported that religious leaders "established interfaith biracial committees in 30 communities"; "the National Council of Churches sent teams of workers to a number of Southern communities to assist in the resolution of racial problems"; "more than 200 attorneys from all over the country volunteered for service" on a "Lawyers' Committee on Civil Rights Under Law"; the president of the AFL-CIO had "begun a program, working through 800 central labor organizations, to act against racial discrimination, particularly in employment and housing"; and 13 major national women's organizations had "joined in a National Women's Committee for Civil Rights."

In areas where the executive had power without new legislation, the Administration was attacking the problem of job discrimination with unprecedented vigor. On March 6, 1961, President Kennedy had set up an impressive committee to see to the elimination of racial discrimination among the two and a half million federal employees, and to use the lever of federal contract awards to reform the employment practices of a large segment of industry. The thirty-one members of the Committee on Equal Employment Opportunity included three members of the cabinet, the Secretaries of the Army, Navy, and Air Force, and the chairman of the Civil Service Commission. The committee was headed by Vice President Lyndon Baines Johnson—who had become an outspoken foe of racial discrimination. Federal agencies had stepped up the recruiting and upgrading of Negroes. The rule of equal opportunity at all levels was being publicized throughout the federal establishment. The Civil Service Commission was embarked on a program, including visits to Negro colleges, to encourage qualified Negroes to apply for federal jobs. The military departments, which administer the greatest dollar volume of federal contracts, were employing specialists to assist their contract management officials in enforcing the requirement that companies should eliminate employment discrimination.

The United States Commission on Civil Rights was a useful watch-tower and a clear liberal voice in the field of race relations. Established by Congress in 1957, this commission was composed of six distinguished white and Negro citizens, appointed by the President from both parties. Dr. John A. Hannah, president of Michigan State University, was its chairman. It possessed no enforcement authority, but, aided by a professional staff and an advisory committee in each of the fifty states, it gathered a mass of enlightening information which, by throwing a spotlight on mistreatment of Negroes, had a deterrent influence. But the Civil Rights Commission was a kind of undernourished official orphan. It was anathema to a powerful minority in the Congress which created it—and which still granted it only two years of life at a time. At the same time its boldly independent activities were not easily coordinated with policy of the executive branch.

In the fall of 1963 the uncertainty of tenure had told on the morale of members of the commission, and positions on its staff no longer offered attractive careers to race-relations specialists. Several staff members, including their capable director, Berl I. Bernhard, had resigned. The commission's latest lease on life was due to expire at the end of November, and the gloom was increased by pessimism over the prospects of early passage of the pending civil-rights bill, to which its next renewal was tied. In the first week of October Congress turned from controversy and maneuver over that measure, and passed a separate bill extending the commission's life for one more year.

Attention was drawn in the fall of 1963 to the racial situation in the military. The armed forces—in which from time immemorial Negro soldiers had been separated from whites—were desegregated following an executive order of President Truman in 1948. President Kennedy appointed a special committee in 1962 to look into the treatment being accorded servicemen of minority groups both within the military establishment and in civilian communities near bases at which they were stationed. The Civil Rights Commission, making a simultaneous study with a more intensive investigation of specific community situations, collaborated with the President's Committee and embodied its own similar findings in its biennial report. The Committee on Equal Opportunity in the Armed Forces submitted its first and main report on June 22, 1963. The Defense Department issued a comprehensive directive July 26 and took successive steps during the following year to deal with inequalities cited by the committee. A Deputy Assistant Secretary of Defense was appointed to supervise a remedial program.

The committee had reported a marked backwardness on the part of the Navy and the Marine Corps in recruiting and promoting Negro personnel. In the Army, 12.2 per cent of the personnel were Negroes; in the Air Force, 9.1 per cent; but of Navymen and Marines, only 5.22 per cent and 7.59 per cent respectively were Negroes. Of the 2,674,000 men in uniform, only 8.2 per cent were Negroes, although they represented approximately 11 per cent of the country's total population. Negroes were underrepresented in the officer corps of all services. Only 3.2 per cent of the officers in the Army were Negroes, 1.24 per cent of those in the Air Force, 0.24 per cent of those in the Navy, and 0.21 per cent of those in the Marine Corps.

The only significant controversy arose from the committee's recommendation, and the Defense Department's directive, calling for positive activity on the part of post commanders, looking toward the elimination of discrimination against Negro servicemen in neighboring civilian communities. Although commanders were expected to "limit their concern to problems affecting the morale and efficiency of members of their command," the move was criticized in some quarters as an attempt to use the military to impose social reform. Much of the need for such efforts on the part of military commanders would be removed by the Civil Rights Act of 1964.

The experience of the military furnished valuable lessons beyond the matter of the shortcomings of racial integration, on which the President's Committee was assigned to report. The writer—who was a member of that committee—was more impressed with the unmistakable success of integration in the armed forces. Race prejudice existed and discrimination was still practiced, sometimes unconsciously, but the exhibit of some 220,000 Negro servicemen intermingled and working harmoniously with 2,454,000 whites was a hopeful harbinger of an ultimate solution of the problem in the nation. Difficulties of a racial origin among servicemen were rare. I was told that white recruits, even from sections of the South where racial prejudice was most deeply rooted, adjusted themselves in but a few months to the experience of having Negro comrades, even Negro superiors. Commanders found Negro officers and sergeants notably efficient, and no significant problem of discipline arose from the fact that they commanded white soldiers. It was the stripes on the sergeant's sleeve that mattered, not the color of his skin. In the Army, there were more Negro sergeants than white in proportion to the total personnel of each race: 16.3 per cent of the sergeants in grade E_5 were Negroes. Negroes were conspicuous in sports, filling more than their proportionate share of positions on football and baseball teams. White fans cheered the battalion team no less when it was predominantly Negro.

The experience of the Armed Forces tended to refute a saying that laws cannot change the hearts of men. It proved that race discrimination, and, in some measure, prejudice itself, yield quietly to military discipline. Whites, compelled to mingle with Negroes in the Armed Forces, generally found that it made no difference, or even that they liked it. The command changed first the behavior, then the attitudes of soldiers.

The Negro revolt and the companion movement of enlightenment, persuasion, and remedial action—the one, of course, predominantly Negro and the other predominantly white—overlapped at many points. White students, clergymen, and others were picketing, sitting-in, and going to jail along with Negroes in the revolt; talented Negro writers made a resounding contribution to the literature of enlightenment and persuasion. The movement had become an outlet for American idealism not unlike that offered by the Peace Corps. White volunteers came from all social levels, and they entered all phases of the crusade. David Rusk, the twenty-three-year-old son of the Secretary of State and a Phi Beta Kappa scholar, joined the staff of the Washington Urban League. Mrs. Malcolm Peabody, the mother of the governor of Massachusetts, was among a group of white ladies who, in scenes of turmoil in St. Augustine, Florida a few months later, joined Negro demonstrators and went to jail along with them for two days.

White crusaders were most likely to be found in local bodies of the "human relations council" type, which were active now in many cities. Here the idealist was joined by citizens of a more practical mind for whom "public-spirited" is a better description —seeking adjustment to the Negro advance as a means of avoiding tension and turmoil in their communities. Active in these groups also were many Negroes, some of whom were members at the same time of civil-rights organizations. Opposed to segregation, these organizations were naturally biracial, but in their inspiration, leadership, and membership they were essentially a part of the white effort.

Early prototypes were the Councils on Human Relations set up by the Southern Regional Council in the eleven former Confederate states, plus Kentucky. These were generally small local groups of from a dozen to several hundred white and Negro citizens, meeting once a month, united in state Councils on Human Relations. Pioneer councils had been obliged to operate furtively and they had had some stormy experiences during an earlier period of segregationist hostility; in parts of the Deep South councils were still persecuted. But in most of the South in 1963 they had become accepted, and even respected, institutions. Public authorities felt a need for their services of conciliation. The aggregate membership of these groups, associated with the Southern Regional Council, rose from a few hundred in the mid-1950's to 6,338 in 1962. It had jumped to 8,257 in 1963.

In the meantime hundreds of other human relations bodies had been set up across the nation, some of them with religious affiliation or with the authority of governmental agencies. Catholic Interracial Councils had labored for years in half a dozen large cities, the first having been established in New York in 1934. By the end of 1963, 65 such Roman Catholic organizations had been formed in 30 states, and the number would more than double within the next two years. Mayors of cities appointed human relations committees either to meet temporary emergencies or as permanent agencies. Some were advisory only; others were invested with a degree of authority to end discriminatory practices. One hundred and three official city committees were established in 1963. Twenty-seven states had commissions to combat racial discrimination, 22 of them with enforcement powers. Approximately 1,000 agencies and organizations working for race-relations reform were represented in a National Association of Intergroup Relations Officials.

In lifting the curse of racial prejudice, not only in areas with which legislation could deal, but in a boundless field of human intercourse beyond the reach of laws, conscience had to be the driving force. And conscience is assuredly the business of churches. The American clergy had inherited a historic stain from its acquiescence in the sin of slavery. Since Emancipation—always with noble exceptions—the clergy had connived at segregation and degradation of the Negro. Now when the psychological moment to invoke the commandment to "love thy neighbor" had come, how were the nation's religious leaders meeting the challenge?

Feebly, courageously, ignominiously, nobly, too aggressively, or not at all. The answer depended on where one stood—both physically and ideologically. In the South many laymen charged liberal ministers with forsaking their role as spiritual leaders to engage in "sociological" and "political" activity. On the other hand, liberals throughout the land were pointing a finger of scorn at the "silent clergymen." The answer depended also on the base of comparison: indubitably far more ministers were preaching against racial prejudice in 1963 than in 1962, and more each month than the last.

One who mingled with the 650 Protestant, Catholic, and Jewish leaders in the National Conference on Religion and Race of January, 1963, could easily have received an impression of the churches marching in the cause of interracial brotherhood. That impression might have been gained also by one of the 1,100 delegates to a great Methodist Conference on Human Relations which met on August 30; this meeting urged legislation to open all public facilities "to all persons without regard to race" and expressed pride "that Methodist youths have participated in nonviolent demonstrations all over the land." Yet the total number of clergymen who attended gatherings like these was only a fraction of the several hundred thousand in the United States. Millions of church-goers, had they relied only on their pastors, would have been unaware in 1963 that a social revolution of the utmost relevance to the Christian ethic was in progress.

Yet it would be unjust to fail to salute the army of inspired clergymen who were in the battle line, and misleading to underrate their impact upon the nation. Some millions of white church-goers did hear from their pastors that racial discrimination was immoral. Some saw their pastors carry the banner of brotherhood in public demonstrations. Clergymen were the mainstay of human-relations councils throughout the land; hardly a biracial committee, council, or commission was without one or more white men of the cloth. Most important of all in its immediate effect, church leaders were mustering needed support for the pending civil-rights bill.

At the highest levels, the religious community was emphatically on the side of the Negro movement. The National Council of Churches (under its former name) had declared in 1946: "The Federal Council of Churches in America hereby renounces the pattern of segregation in race relations as unnecessary and undesirable and a violation of the Gospel of love and human brotherhood." In June, 1963, the Council's general board called upon the Church "to confess her sin of omission and delay, and to move forward to witness to her essential belief that every child of God is a brother to every other." The Roman Catholic bishops of the United States had condemned racial segregation and discrimination in a solemn statement of November, 1958. A week before the March on Washington the bishops issued a pastoral letter to be read in all Catholic churches declaring that "the conscience of the nation is on trial" and calling for action "to see that voting, jobs, housing, education and public facilities are freely available to every American. . . ."

Anti-Negro prejudice was sometimes found among Jews (like anti-Semitism among Negroes), but the five and a half million members of the nation's Jewish congregations were more nearly united than any other white religious group in opposition to racial discrimination. Many Jews were active in the fight; Jewish laymen gave it powerful support in the Anti-Defamation League of B'nai B'rith; rabbis and laymen worked together in the American Jewish Committee and the American Jewish Congress.

In the multitudinous Christian family the Roman Catholic Church, with 44 million communicants, was able in the nature of its administration to move with more system and uniformity than the loosely organized National Council of Churches. Catholic attitudes were irregular, nevertheless. "Prudence," or apathy, silenced some bishops and many of the 60,000 Catholic priests, in spite of the brave language of the episcopal body. Some bishops restrained eager priests on the ground that action should be cautious and gradual. One prince of the Church was sharply out of line: James Cardinal McIntyre, Archbishop of Los Angeles, in his seventy-eighth year in 1963, thought Negroes had little cause for complaint, and ruled civil-rights agitation out of order. Controversy and stifled rebellion among priests resulted. Vestiges of segregation remained in Catholic hospitals and parochial schools, but Catholic churches everywhere were open to Negroes and whites alike. The National Catholic Conference for Interracial Justice, which had opened its office in Chicago at the beginning of 1961, stimulated the spread of Catholic Interracial Councils and coordinated the Catholic civil-rights drive throughout the country.

The heads of the thirty-one Protestant and Eastern Orthodox denominations (with some 40 million members) in the National Council of Churches had virtually all taken strong stands in support of the Negro movement. Bishop Arthur Lichtenberger of the Protestant Episcopal Church declared that "men, women and children are risking their livelihood and their lives in protesting for their rights," and called on the 3,300,000 Episcopalians to "support and strengthen their protest in every way possible. . . ." The young men of the Episcopal Society for Cultural and Racial Unity marched with their executive director, the Reverend John B. Morris, in some of the most daring civil-rights demonstrations (to the horror, it must be said, of some of the Church's more conservative clergy). The president of the Lutheran Church in America, Dr. Franklin Clark Fry (who was also president of the Lutheran World Federation), urged the nation's 8,549,906 Lutherans to "act and lead others by precept and example" to bring racial discrimination to an end. The United Presbyterian Church in the U.S.A., with 3,265,234 members, was in the forefront of the movement; we met its stated clerk, Dr. Eugene Carson Blake, in the March on Washington. Crusaders were also to be found among the *Southern* Presbyterians, organized separately as the Presbyterian Church in the United States, with 928,055 members, and in the Methodist Church, one-third of whose 10 million members were in the South.

Among smaller denominations, the Quakers, historic champions of the Negro, had redoubled their efforts in the modern context.

The American Friends Service Committee contributed to the flow of educational pamphlets and labored with notable effectiveness through its various regional offices to further the process of adjustment to the new order.

Groups representing approximately one-third of American Protestants were not members of the National Council of Churches. The largest of those not identified with it was the Southern Baptist Convention, which with 10,191,303 members was also the largest non-Catholic religious body in the United States. In June, 1954, following the Supreme Court decision outlawing public school segregation, the Southern Baptist Convention said in a mild statement: "We recognize the fact that this Supreme Court decision is in harmony with the constitutional guarantee of equal freedom to all citizens, and Christian principles of equal justice and love for all men." But in 1963 *Time* magazine observed: "In the rearguard of the civil-rights battle comes the Southern Baptist Convention, many of whose members believe that segregation derives from the law of God." There were liberal ministers in this body—dozens of them had lost their pulpits for attempting integration moves—but all efforts to induce the Convention to take a forceful stand against racial discrimination had failed. A Negro was rarely to be seen in any of its 33,000 churches. The smaller American Baptist Convention, on the other hand, was active in the civil-rights movement. Its 1,559,103 members, scattered widely across the nation, included 50,000 Negroes, and more than half of its churches had Negro members.

The National Council of Churches was denounced by extreme segregationists as a "Communistic" body. Some of its constituent churches in the Deep South ceased contributing to it. In the summer of 1963 the Council sent teams of clergymen and laymen to help alleviate racial tensions in Alabama, Georgia, Mississippi, North Carolina, and Virginia. The team which visited Selma, Alabama, in October was not only rebuffed by city officials, but its clergyman member, the Reverend Arthur Thomas—a white Methodist minister—was turned away from Selma's Methodist church at the Sunday morning service. An usher told him: "We don't want trouble-makers in our congregation."

One group of churches was openly hostile to the National Council and to the civil-rights movement. An uncertain number of embittered churchmen had joined the aggressively segregationist entity called the "American Council of Christian Churches." This organization, founded by the Reverend Carl McIntire, a famous preacher and broadcaster of the far Right, combined racism with a bundle of doctrines of the John Birch Society, to which it was ideologically related. Up to 10 million members were claimed by the group's promoters. The listeners to McIntire's extremist broadcasts were indeed to be counted in the millions, but the aggregate membership of the churches identified with the American Council —generally from obscure fundamentalist sects—was hardly more than 100,000.

An interesting by-product of the church campaign against racial discrimination was the impetus given in the United States to the ecumenical movement. Protestant, Catholic, and Jewish leaders united in the National Conference on Religion and Race of January, 1963. Rabbi Balfour Brickner, of the Social Action Commission of Reform Judaism, and the Reverend Dr. Robert W. Spike, of the National Council of Churches, both addressed the meeting of the National Catholic Conference for Interracial Justice held in Chicago in July. Catholic and Jewish divines also addressed meetings of the National Council of Churches. The annual convention of the Catholic Conference and that of the Episcopal Society for Cultural and Racial Unity were held simultaneously in November at the same hotel in Washington, the two groups fraternizing and meeting jointly in some sessions. Speakers were exchanged at many other church gatherings, and representatives of the three faiths took counsel together on innumerable occasions. At the community level it was not unusual to see a priest or a rabbi and a Protestant minister going together to call on local officials or to canvass businessmen, urging desegregation of facilities and employment of Negroes. The movement brought Catholics and Protestants together in a comradeship the like of which had not been seen since the Reformation.

The powerful influences at work in the nation and the example of so many respected leaders might suggest a greater abatement of prejudice against the Negro in the United States than was actually taking place. The gap between the attitude of informed leadership and that of the masses is nowhere wider than in the clouded and complex problem of race. The cruelty and injustice of racial discrimination are not readily comprehended from a distance—from the distance at which most white people stood. The average white man—the average individual in 160 million white people—rarely talked with Negroes except in giving orders to servants. He read sensational accounts of Negro demonstrations, but he never opened a book on the race problem.

A very large number of whites still clung to a belief, or a feeling —one which was not often expressed, but which resisted all argument—that Negroes were creatures of an inferior order. Among those who accepted the broad principle that discrimination on account of race was wrong, many showed no inclination to apply it to their own personal situations. In religious terms, if Christianity bade that Negroes be treated as brothers, they regarded the injunction as a remote ideal—like the command to "love your enemies"—which none but saints were expected to take seriously.

Two public opinion surveys, one by Stewart Alsop and Oliver Quayle, reported in the *Saturday Evening Post* of September 7 and one by Louis Harris for *Newsweek* of October 24, found majorities in favor of equality for Negroes in voting, in access to restaurants, etc., and in employment opportunity. But widespread prejudice appeared when racial questions were brought nearer home. Alsop and Quayle reported that only 23 per cent of whites thought a Negro should have the right to buy a residence anywhere he chose; Louis Harris' findings indicated that 56 per cent would oppose federal legislation prohibiting discrimination in housing. In a June Gallup Poll only 22 per cent of the whites questioned said they would remain in their neighborhood if large numbers of Negroes moved into it. All surveys reported disapproval by a majority of whites of picketing, sit-ins, and the like. The *United States News and World Report* observed "a widespread feeling that Negroes are pushing too hard, demanding too much too soon."

The Objectives
1963

The Negro's grievances were the subject of a massive literature. Recently, thoughtful writers had been putting forth a stream of theories—some ill-conceived, some quixotic, many sound, all difficult to carry out—as to what needed to be done to set things right. It was of course not merely a matter of certain specific wrongs and categorical remedies, but these five major objectives formed rallying points in the Negro revolt:

Equal voting rights in every section.

Equal access to places of public accommodation.

Equal opportunity in employment.

Equal and unsegregated education.

Equal opportunity to make a home anywhere within one's means.

Equal Voting Rights

In the late 1950's, a kind of Negrophobia raged in all the Southern states. The area of its infection had contracted by 1963, but in a smaller region near the Gulf of Mexico it was more virulent than ever. "Persecution" better described the treatment of Negroes there than discrimination, and it was practiced not only by the white populace, but by the public authorities themselves. Outrages perpetrated against Negroes in the Deep South furnished constant fuel for the fires of the Negro unrest throughout the land. But what was to be done? What *could* be done by the national government in our federal system? The use of federal military force was urged by some. Presidents had resorted to this temporarily—

Eisenhower in Little Rock in 1957 and Kennedy at the University of Mississippi in 1962—when the issue was enforcement of definitive orders of federal courts. But precise situations which would make military occupation helpful, or constitutionally possible, were not there. Some foresaw, or actually hoped for, a desperate Negro uprising in Mississippi or Alabama which would throw the inhibitions of nonviolence to the winds, precipitating a bloody cataclysm and the unavoidable dispatch of federal troops.

One elementary and completely legal remedy commended itself —it would be nonviolent too, as far as Negro action was concerned: the exercise of the franchise. More often than not the areas in which Negroes were most oppressed were those in which Negroes were most flagrantly prevented from voting. There were also communities in which Negroes were numerous, sometimes a majority of the population. Once the Negro became a factor in the election of public officials, the climate would undoubtedly change. Wresting from hostile whites the right to participate meaningfully in elections promised to be a long and hazardous undertaking, but it might be the Negro's ultimate salvation. It became a major objective of the civil-rights movement.

Echoes of the struggle of the Negro for the vote and of this last stand of white resistance in the South mingled with reports of racial disturbances nearer home to most Americans. This was but one phase of the ferment throughout the country and it did not arouse the general public in 1963. But it was destined in the next two years to cause much tragedy and bloodshed, and crises which would shake the nation. The episode was to close at last a chapter of American history which began in 1870 with the adoption of the Fifteenth Amendment of the Constitution, providing: "The rights of citizens of the United States to vote shall not be denied or abridged by the United States or by any State on account of race, color or previous condition of servitude." Efforts to circumvent or frustrate that prohibition were long a preoccupation of white citizens throughout the former Southern Confederacy. For half a century after Emancipation many of the most respectable whites felt justified in going to great lengths to free their communities from the danger of political control by illiterate Negroes. But that unhappy era had passed. In the greater part of the South in the 1960's the Negro's right to vote was recognized and respected.

Yet in some sections (generally communities which in more ways than one were dismal relics of the Reconstruction period) this right was stubbornly, ingeniously, and fiercely denied.

The poll tax, or a tax of one or several dollars levied as a prerequisite to voting, had been used effectively at an earlier period to eliminate Negroes from Southern voter lists. But as the amount of the tax became somewhat easier to come by it became a less reliable deterrent, and it tended to discourage potential white voters. The poll tax in fact was going out; in 1963 it was retained as a prerequisite for voting only by Alabama, Arkansas, Mississippi, Texas, and Virginia. Many other devices were used to keep Negroes from the polls.

The 1961 report of the Civil Rights Commission, *Voting*, observed that "the problem of denials of the right to vote because of race appears to occur in only eight Southern states—Alabama, Florida, Georgia, Louisiana, Mississippi, North Carolina, South Carolina and Tennessee." The Commission added that "in Florida, North Carolina and Tennessee it is limited to only a few isolated counties." That left only five states where the right to vote was regularly denied, and only a few sections of some of these. The Commission's investigations had pointed to about 100 counties "in which there is reason to believe that substantial discriminatory disfranchisement of Negroes still exists."

In those counties, intimidation prevented many Negroes from attempting to register for voting—intimidation which had adopted some modern techniques, but which, as in the old days, did not stop at murder. Where Negroes were brave enough to apply for registration, the stratagems used to frustrate their attempts were almost incredible. Some of these, had they not been in grim earnest, would have suggested tricks of mischievous children.

"Literacy tests" were the favorite weapon. Negro literacy was "tested" with grotesquely difficult questions; whites were given easy questions, or none at all. In eleven Alabama counties, where most of the whites had scant education, the number of white names on the voting lists was actually greater than the number of white residents of voting age. In the same eleven counties only a tiny fraction of the Negroes were registered. In two of them, where Negroes made up approximately 80 per cent of the population, not a single Negro was registered to vote.

The application form itself provided excuses for the rejection of Negroes on account of alleged imperfections in its execution. A Department of Justice report noted that "one registrar rejected an applicant because he wrote 'Negro' in answer to the question as to his color. Another registrar, insisting that 'Negro' was the proper answer, rejected an applicant because he wrote 'brown'." An excerpt from the Civil Rights Commission's 1961 report on its intensive investigation in Louisiana throws further light on the shenanigans which were common in the recalcitrant counties:

> Witnesses from Plaquemines and East Carroll Parishes testified that they had difficulty getting in touch with the registrars. Only after Negroes filed suit in a federal court was a permanent office for registration located in Plaquemines Parish. One of the witnesses stated that before suit was filed, finding the registrar "was something like a game of hide and seek. We would go to the Court house and go over to the clerk of the court's office. They said they did not know where the registrar was or that he could not be contacted." A witness, told by the registrar to go to the next door, returned to find that the door to the registrar's office had been locked.

The situation would be described succinctly by President Johnson—when the nation was at last aroused—in an address to Congress of March 15, 1965:

> Every device of which human ingenuity is capable has been used to deny this right. The Negro citizen may go to register only to be told that the day is wrong, the hour is late, or the official in charge is absent.
>
> If he persists, and manages to present himself to the registrar, he may be disqualified because he did not spell out his middle name or because he abbreviated a word on the application.
>
> If he manages to fill out an application he is given a test. The registrar is the sole judge of whether he passes this test. He may be asked to recite the entire Constitution or explain the most complex provision of state law. Even a college degree cannot be used to prove that he can read or write.
>
> For the fact is that the only way to pass these barriers is to show a white skin.

While a few brave Negroes struggled against these iniquities in 100 counties, elsewhere in the South a problem existed among Negroes themselves. Most Negroes had not yet acquired the voting habit. Even where no white machinations stood in the way, a lingering fear of displeasing white men, or sheer apathy, still kept many away from the polls. Of more than five million Negroes of voting age in the eleven former Confederate states in early 1962, only 1,386,654 were registered. More than two-thirds of the whites of voting age were registered.

To thoughtful leaders and friends of the Negro—including officials high in the national Administration—it seemed in 1961 that his rising militancy could find no more appropriate outlet than in a massive campaign for Negro voter registration in the South. Out of this came the biggest and best organized single undertaking of the civil-rights movement. After some months of planning and organization, it went into operation on April 1, 1962—as the Voter Education Project (VEP). Each of the Big Five organizations participated, along with smaller allied groups. The Southern Regional Council took the responsibility of the Project's central administration. Philanthropic foundations came forward with generous grants; by the end of 1963 the financial support totaled nearly $600,000. The formal purpose was to study the causes of low voter registration and methods used to increase it, while developing educational programs calculated to provide potential voters with the necessary knowledge and will to register. In the existing situation, the latter activity amounted in practice to an intensive drive to get Negroes registered.

Whites in many of the recalcitrant counties responded with unrestrained hostility. A VEP report of March 31, 1963, listed twenty-eight acts of violence and intimidation—beatings, shootings, burning of Negro properties, etc.—during the first year of the project in Mississippi alone. (Harassment of voter registration workers took an even more ferocious and sanguinary form during the second and third years.) In most of the last-stand communities, the accomplishment also was statistically disappointing. In Mississippi, by the end of 1963, only about 3,500 Negroes had been added to the 25,000 previously on the voter rolls. However, in the many Southern communities where Negroes were unhampered in the voting procedure, impressive progress was made. In the entire South, 327,588 Negro voters had been registered, bringing the total to 1,752,000.

The Department of Justice had been given a responsibility by the Civil Rights Act of 1957 and 1960 to take legal action in cases where the vote was flagrantly denied. It tried to secure voluntary action by local authorities, and failing this, filed suits in federal courts—25 of them in 1963. The Department's review of its civil-rights activities noted that at the beginning of that year there were 19 counties in which no Negroes at all had been permitted to register. It added: "As a result of Department activity, or court action, during the year, there was for the first time in decades or even in history, actual registration of Negro voters in nine of these counties, and court cases are pending in two others."

Equal Access to Places of Public Accommodation

Ending segregation in places of public accommodation was one of the hardest problems in the persuasion stage; but in the doing, it was the easiest and least complicated of the five on the civil-rights objectives list. The ban on this kind of racial discrimination aroused more controversy than any other proposition in the package before Congress; many felt that it would have to be eliminated if the bill were ever to pass. Actually, however, opening previously segregated restaurants and hotels to all—when proprietors for whatever reason felt impelled to take this step—was neither a dangerous nor a very difficult thing to do. In the North and West, 18 states had prohibited discrimination in places of public accommodation since the turn of the century. In 1963, 31 states and five cities had laws forbidding it.

To be turned away from a hotel or a restaurant because of his color was not only one of the cruelest humiliations that the sensitive Negro suffered, but the practice imposed serious physical hardships. Unthinking whites often asked: "Why don't they go to their own restaurants?" But where the Negro population was widely dispersed, "their own restaurants" were nonexistent, and Negroes represented less than 5 per cent of the population in 260 Southern counties. Even where Negroes were numerous, their restaurants, operated with scant capital for a largely impoverished clientele, were necessarily poor.

It was here that segregation found least rational justification. In addition to strictly racial prejudices, segregationists often confused racial tolerance with equalitarianism. They envisioned, upon the removal of the racial barrier, a rush of uncouth Negroes to inundate even the better white restaurants. White business executives saw themselves rubbing shoulders with their janitors, and white ladies with their kitchen maids. When restaurants were in fact desegregated, it was found that Negroes patronized them discreetly, more or less in accordance with their individual means and cultural level.

A variety of strategies was employed by apprehensive proprietors to soften the initial impact upon white customers; competition often dictated simultaneous action by all similar establishments in a community. But the remedy for Negro exclusion was essentially simple. It could be expressed in one word: Stop. However vociferous the opposition might have been, when restaurants opened their doors to Negroes for the first time, fears generally evaporated, and the fact that Negroes and whites were eating in the same room soon ceased to cause disturbance or even to attract attention.

Equal Opportunity in Employment

In contrast, the ideal of giving the Negro an equal chance to earn his daily bread and to rise in the economic sphere to the extent of his ability presented endless difficulties. There were situations of rank discrimination against Negroes in which it was possible to say categorically: This must cease. But the problem of integrating the Negro equitably in the national economy was one of infinite complexity. It demanded the utmost in wisdom and good will on the part of both statesmen and industrialists. Moreover, despite the long delay in grappling with it and the impatience of the now awakened Negro, it would take a long time. It would also take continuing, unrelenting Negro pressure.

Notwithstanding heavy migration to the cities in recent years, a quarter of a million Negroes still operated farms in the South. About half of these were owners or part-owners of the land, the rest tenants. On the average their acreage was less than one-third that of white farmers, and the living they wrested from the soil was meager. But these made up the largest group of Negroes who could be called self-employed.

A handful of talented Negroes had achieved distinction and affluence in literature and entertainment, and the number of Negro lawyers, doctors, and dentists had shown a sharp increase in recent years, though Negroes were still underrepresented in the professions. However, in the potentially large field of independent business, Negroes were strangely lacking. In many a Southern community the Negro funeral parlor was the only substantial Negro enterprise, and the undertaker was the most prosperous Negro in town. In cities everywhere one saw restaurants, shops, laundries, etc., run by members of Chinese, Greek, Armenian, Puerto Rican, or other ethnic groups, but rarely an establishment run by a Negro. Negroes in the United States had no tradition as merchants. Whatever the disabilities that prejudice had imposed in the past, a program to encourage Negro entrepreneurship was not the least among the undertakings that the situation called for.

By and large the Negro worked for the white man. His chance of getting a job and the kind of jobs open to him depended on the customs and prejudices of white people. He was protected to some extent by fair employment practices (FEP) legislation, which 25 states and 40 municipalities had enacted; but these laws, administered feebly complaint by complaint, had made only a minor dent in the pervasive structure of job discrimination. Most private employment agencies routinely accepted orders to fill jobs with white persons only. In many segments of business and industry the absence of Negro employees had long gone almost unnoticed. The National Urban League investigated 10 leading advertising agencies in New York and found only 11 Negroes among their 23,600 employees. Negroes were most likely to find employment at the lowest levels; they were welcome in menial jobs. Fifty-four per cent of all Negroes in the labor force were relegated to unskilled and service occupations.

In the federal work force Negroes made up 13 per cent, more than the Negro proportion of the total population; but Negroes were scandalously underrepresented in the higher classifications. The main thrust of the new federal effort had been to raise the level of positions held by Negroes. In the year ending in June 1963, the number of Negroes in middle-level white-collar jobs increased almost 15 per cent. A more striking advance was made in upper-level federal jobs, in which Negro employment rose 39 per cent. In the postal field service the number of Negroes in superior positions increased by 56 per cent.

The companies under contract with the federal government comprised an enormous segment of American industry. The 100 largest contractors and subcontractors in the area of national defense alone employed 10 million persons. The accomplishment of the President's Committee on Equal Employment Opportunity in this vast field had been disappointing to many; but the Committee was working sedulously—with authority which bodies with a similar purpose in the past had lacked—and progress was being made. A September report showed that in the last half of 1962 nonwhites received 38 per cent of the 45,728 new jobs in 75 companies subscribing to what the Committee called its "Plans for Progress."

The Department of Labor's "Report on Manpower Requirements, Resources, Utilization and Training," transmitted by the President to the Congress in March, 1964, drew from a mass of statistics a series of over-all conclusions, among which the following references to the Negro sector told much in a few words:

> High rates of unemployment among Negroes are related to their educational handicaps and concentration in low-skilled occupations. However, unemployment rates for Negroes are much higher than for whites in all occupations. . . .
>
> Many Negroes are employed in occupations below their educational level. . . .
>
> Despite important breakthroughs in employment fostered by federal, state and local efforts, the progress toward equal employment opportunity for Negroes has been very limited. . . .

Generally, across the country the unemployment rate was 5.6 per cent, but among Negroes it was 11 per cent. Even if all concerned had so desired, the imbalance could not be redressed forthwith, nor for long years to come. Many jobs required training, experience, or general education that Negroes lacked. Even if a fairy's wand could have wafted the right proportion of Negroes into the labor force, it would have sent many whites into the ranks of the unemployed—and no white man could be discharged to make room for a Negro. Discrimination had to be attacked only in promotions, apprenticeships, and the annual intake of new employees. If Negroes received a fair share—say 11 per cent—of the new jobs, it would still take a long time for them to catch up. Should preference be given to Negro workers to make up for the years of rejection that had left them so far behind? Should quotas be established in the new hiring?

The idea of racial quotas was much tossed about during the summer and fall of 1963, but, though it appealed to many Negroes, responsible leaders hesitated to advance the proposal. The percentage of Negroes in a given labor force was a helpful index: it was constantly used to gauge progress, or the lack of progress, toward equal opportunity of employment. But to fix quotas to be filled by Negroes in preference to white applicants would be discrimination in reverse. The use of race as a determinant, even if it might cause temporary Negro gains, was a thing which the whole civil-rights movement was trying to eliminate from American life.

That some preference should be given to Negroes in employment, at least informally, was urged nonetheless by the National Urban League. Whitney Young called it "indemnification" for past discrimination. Mahlon T. Puryear, the League's associate director, said: "Whatever they did before to avoid hiring Negroes . . . , we are now asking that they reverse. Bend the rules for a while to hire Negroes." Young wrote in his book *To Be Equal:* "Neither the Negro nor the Urban League is asking for three hundred years of preferential treatment such as white citizens have had. We are asking for only a decade of dedicated special effort."

Some companies *were* discriminating in favor of Negroes in their hiring at this stage—out of a feeling that it was due them because of their exclusion in the past or from a desire to make a good appearance. Many made special efforts in their recruiting campaigns to interest Negroes. Large corporations, especially those under contract with the federal government, engaged race relations specialists to assist them in instituting a system of equal job opportunity. Difficulties presented themselves which were beyond the employer's control. Most serious of these was the lack of educational preparation among most Negroes for the better-paying jobs. Another was the powerful hold on employment of organized labor. Employment was often limited to union members, and unions also controlled admissions to apprenticeship programs.

In labor, as in other groups, appeared the familiar pattern of liberal commitment in the higher echelons meeting with indifference, or resistance, as it worked down to the rank and file. An objective of the AFL-CIO, stated in its constitution, was "to encourage all workers without regard to race, creed, color, national origin, or ancestry to share equally in the full benefits of union organization." The AFL-CIO's president, George Meany, was officially—and its other most conspicuous leader, Walter Reuther, was aggressively—opposed to racial discrimination. But the AFL-CIO had no direct control over local unions—a number of craft unions were virtually autonomous. The Brotherhood of Locomotive Firemen and Enginemen removed the ban on nonwhite membership from its constitution only in July, 1963. Negroes were receiving a less than cordial welcome in many unions, and some excluded them. In the Deep South, the race issue caused some rebellion against national union leadership; in Alabama, while the state AFL-CIO remained loyal to national policy, segregationist locals with approximately 30,000 members had defected during the past two years.

Discrimination was most flagrant in the building trade unions, and, as we have seen, some of the most desperate Negro demonstrations were directed against these. An old tradition of father-son unionism was a factor here. In one New York plumbers' local it was found that 80 per cent of those admitted to membership in recent years were sons or nephews of members. Many unions of ironworkers, steam fitters, plumbers, electrical workers, sheet metal workers, asbestos workers, pile drivers, elevator constructors, hoisting engineers, glassworkers, and sign painters had only an insignificant number of Negro workers or none at all.

As more jobs were opened to Negroes, their lack of training and skills became more and more apparent. In some cases there was an actual demand for Negro personnel that could not be met. Employers who were anxious to place Negroes in some of the higher-paying jobs found it difficult or impossible to secure qualified Negroes. At lower levels, new techniques and the rapid advance of automation were steadily reducing the number of jobs which could be filled without specialized skills.

The unpreparedness of Negroes for the better jobs was itself a result of the place in society to which prejudice had long relegated them. For the most part, they had family backgrounds of poverty and ignorance, and the schools which they attended were generally inferior; Negroes were on the average far behind whites in general education. Public schools for Negroes had been largely geared to the expectation—which both administrators and pupils shared—that they were unlikely to rise in life above menial and common-labor roles. A widely prevailing attitude was illustrated by a remark of the director of vocational education in a Southern Negro high school, made to a representative of the Civil Rights Commission—that the curriculum was set up to provide training in "those occupations that Negroes could get employed in in this community." Even at the college level, few careers were contemplated for Negroes except teaching in Negro schools and preaching to Negro congregations. Apart from the instructional offering, the effect of all this upon incentive of course had been deadly. The Negro youth saw little reason to struggle with learning; only the white youth could aim at the stars.

True, this picture at its gloomiest belonged to the past. Things were changing. But this was the educational background of many of the Negro adults who now demanded full integration in the national economy. The new generation would have it better. The schools attended by Negroes were being improved; vocational training programs were being expanded. Some Negro colleges were instituting technical and scientific training courses geared to the needs of industry in the nuclear age, and Negro students were rubbing shoulders with whites in formerly segregated institutions of higher learning. Though all were not yet convinced that Negro merit could be rewarded in a white-dominated world, many Negro youths were raising their sights. Improvements indeed, but they were still inadequate and affected too few. Much greater effort and much more time would be needed before the Negro could compete on equal terms with the white man.

Whitney Young conceived of a "Marshall Plan" for Negroes in the United States. He saw in the plight of the Negro a comparison with the bankruptcy of Europe following World War II and recalled the vast aid by which the United States had put Europe on its feet again. The plan put forward by the National Urban League included job training and apprenticeship programs, scholarships, health programs and hospital construction, capitalization of co-operative business and industrial enterprises, purchase of land and equipment for farms, programs for nursery children and working mothers, book-buying and tutoring programs.

Could a great program of the federal government lift Negroes out of the slough of ignorance and poverty? Conceivably it could. But any such undertaking would have to lift whites also who, for whatever reason, were in the same slough. It was idle to talk of indemnification for the wrongs of the past, yet the slate might be wiped clean and, in a general and even-handed rehabilitation of the backward, the Negro could rise in accordance with his true worth. A "War on Poverty" would later be directed toward this goal.

Equal and Unsegregated Education

Economic, educational, and housing disabilities were closely related. Each contributed to the feeling—and the reality of the experience—that Negroes were not wanted in a white-dominated world, and each had a causal relation to the other two. Poverty and lack of education nourished the prejudice that made Negroes unwelcome in white residential areas. Their concentration in Negro neighborhoods restricted employment in that they could not take jobs wherever jobs could be had with assurance of finding homes at a convenient distance from their work. It also resulted in their schools being largely segregated, even outside of the South; and educational shortcomings, as we have seen, left Negroes ill equipped for many types of employment. Indeed, the virtual imprisonment of thousands of Negroes in degrading big city ghettos reduced their fitness for employment, or for healthy citizenship, in many ways.

Segregation in Southern public schools was a problem unto itself. There school segregation had long been a matter of public policy—and still was, mitigated by only token adjustments to the Supreme Court decision which forbade it. Until the Negro revolt spread across the nation in 1963, efforts to enforce that 1954 ruling in the South, with their accompanying turmoil, had held the center of attention in the civil-rights movement. This situation had now stabilized from the point of view of public tranquillity. The initial hard breakthrough had been accomplished in every state but one: the first Negro children were not admitted to white schools in Mississippi until 1964. The fabric of school segregation was being slowly unpinned, and disorderly resistance to the change in most of the South had virtually ceased. But the process of bringing segregation to an end was still only at the beginning. The hope prevailed that, by admitting half a dozen, or a score, of Negro children to a white school here and a white school there, the general framework of segregation could be retained for a very long time. By December, 1963, only 30,798 of the 2,901,671 Negro pupils in the eleven former Confederate states were attending schools with whites.

The lagging reform in the South was overshadowed now by an attack upon *de facto* public school segregation in the rest of the nation. The Civil Rights Commission noted in the summer of 1962 that "agitation against segregation and discrimination Northern style is actively being pursued in 43 cities in 14 Northern and Western States. Numerically it is doubtful that any single 18-months period has seen as much intensive activity even in the South." By the fall of 1963, the NAACP reported that the battle was being waged in 75 cities in 18 states.

In this fight, Negroes had no categorical Supreme Court decision to fall back upon: the Constitution prohibited only segregation that was governmentally imposed. Federal district courts had forbidden intentional gerrymandering of districts to effect segregation (first in New Rochelle, New York), but had refused to order desegregation where predominantly Negro schools merely reflected the local neighborhood (in Gary, Indiana). Both of these opinions had been, or soon would be, upheld in effect by the Supreme Court.

Negroes also lacked the degree of white sympathy here that supported them in other objectives. The agitation was widely resented. Though the situation had long disturbed Negro intellectuals and probing white sociologists, the general public was surprised to hear that there might be anything racially wrong with public schools outside of the South. Negroes were carrying things too far, many said—making a fetish of integration. The concentration of Negroes in certain schools merely followed the residential pattern; to disperse them among white schools hither and yon would destroy the (suddenly sacred) "principle" of the neighborhood school. Even more intolerable was the idea of sending white children away from their neighborhoods to correct "racial imbalance" in predominantly Negro schools; many white parents in big cities had horrid visions of their children being sent to school in foul-smelling Negro ghettos. Whites began to organize "in defense of the neighborhood school." No less a champion of the Negro cause than the *Washington Post* said: "Integration has a positive social value, and it is to be welcomed where it can be achieved by shifting school boundaries. But where it requires the massive transportation of small children across a large city, then it begins to cost time and money that might more usefully be invested in teaching." In Congress, it was found prudent to stipulate in the pending civil-rights bill that " 'desegregation' shall not mean the assignment of students to public schools in order to overcome racial imbalance."

Nevertheless the Negro offensive continued unabated. Demonstrations and sit-ins plagued school administration offices; schools were boycotted here and there to make the point. In Chicago in October, 225,000 children participated in a mammoth one-day boycott of the public schools, while 8,000 adults circled the city hall, waving signs and singing. School administrators of great cities, with the need to satisfy budgetmakers as well as the press, teachers, reformers, and hundreds of thousands of parents, even under normal circumstances, have no easy job. Many of them in 1963 found the *de facto* segregation problem their most time-consuming and nerve-racking concern.

In a region in which Negroes were only a small minority of the total population, there were 738 public schools in which "minority-group" (overwhelmingly Negro) pupils constituted from 90 per cent to all of the enrollment. More than half of these schools were in six great cities—New York, Chicago, Philadelphia, Detroit, Cleveland, and Los Angeles; the rest in over 100 cities and towns. Of course, this was largely the way Negroes resided—concentrated in big ghettos and scattered enclaves. If schools were segregated, it was because communities were so for the most part, but not entirely.

There were cases in which Negro children residing in a small pocket of Negro homes in a predominantly white residential section were being transported—past white schools—to schools in the larger Negro neighborhood some distance away. That was rare in 1963, but, in the border zones between white and Negro neighborhoods, it was not unusual to find Negroes in virtually segregated schools when there were white schools as near or nearer to their homes. For instance, the vast Negro ghetto of Chicago is a configuration of two long, narrow strips, the main one extending north and south, the other, north of the Loop, extending east and west. From many points in the heart of this ghetto one can walk a few blocks and find himself in a predominantly white residential area. A substantial amount of Chicago's *de facto* segregation could have been conveniently avoided if sites had been selected and districts drawn to bring white and Negro children together across the ghetto boundary. Gerrymandering of school districts to accomplish segregation had come under court scrutiny and was difficult to prove; but there were abundant indications that in doubtful situations a desire to place pupils among companions of their own race had weighed heavily in school board decisions. Traditionally segregation had been *fostered*—sometimes unconsciously, as a matter of routine—in the delineation of school districts and in the selection of building sites. This tendency could be reversed and school segregation could be substantially reduced without significant damage to the principle of the neighborhood school.

The Supreme Court in its 1954 decision declared that segregation of Negro school children "generates a feeling of inferiority as to their status in the community that may affect their hearts and minds in a way unlikely ever to be undone." Segregation also made it easy to follow a common propensity on the part of white administrators to neglect the Negro part of the school population. Predominantly Negro schools were generally inferior to predominantly white schools in physical plant and equipment as well as in the quality of instruction. Inexcusably, too, Negro schools were very often overcrowded while nearby white schools had space to spare—a situation which, from a purely practical point of view, counseled a more even distribution of pupils.

Probably no phase of the civil-rights struggle brought forth more of "the folly of those who want what is and the unreason of those who want what should be." The basic question also was one of degree—the hardest kind to decide with precision and consensus. How wrong was *de facto* school segregation, and how much of it was it possible or just or vitally necessary to undo? Negroes fell out among themselves; whites differed sharply both from Negroes and from one another. Adding to the confusion, many *ad hoc* Negro organizations sprang up to fight *de facto* segregation independently of the Big Five civil-rights organizations.

School authorities everywhere were taking a new look at the racial composition of their schools. Survey after survey was being made. Racial integration was being accepted generally as the proper aim, and was beginning to determine policy in borderline situations. Some Negro children were being transferred to predominantly white schools at a distance, and other steps were being studied or taken experimentally which involved retreat from the neighborhood rule. A celebrated device called the "Princeton Plan" (after Princeton, New Jersey, where it was first adopted), was the "pairing" of schools where one had been attended predominantly by whites and the other by Negroes; white and Negro children in the lower grades would be placed together in one school and those in the higher grades, both white and Negroes, would attend the other.

New York was laboring more constructively with the problem than Chicago. It had more Negroes than any other city (about one million to Chicago's 800,000)—and more *de facto* segregated schools. The great metropolis, along with other cities of New York State, had been prodded for some years by James E. Allen, Jr., the state commissioner of education, who fixed 50 per cent as the maximum desirable proportion of Negroes in any school. The New York City school administration had been moving some children out of overcrowded Negro schools to uncrowded schools in white areas, changing school district boundaries, building new schools in "fringe areas" between white and Negro neighborhoods, and permitting pupils to transfer out of predominantly Negro schools to any other school with space available. Some 75,000 pupils had been shifted in the interest of racial balance. But this had made little change in the total picture, and the outcry against *de facto* segregation continued to rise. Sit-ins besieged the board of education offices; the resignation of Superintendent Calvin E. Gross was demanded. An interim report, issued by the school administration December 9, on the progress of desegregation, proved a disappointment to Negro leaders, and plans began to take shape for a massive boycott of the city's schools. By the end of the year, the date for the great boycott had been fixed—February 3, 1964.

Equal Opportunity in Housing

The problem of open housing, of free dispersal of Negro homes without restrictions on account of race—and escape from the opposite extreme, which was the ghetto—has already received considerable mention in these pages; it figures largely in the story of the next four years and remains in 1968 still far from being resolved. In 1963, both effort and accomplishment were less conspicuous in housing than in other civil-rights fields. Crusaders were able at best only to slow down the trend. Housing across the nation was becoming not less, but more segregated.

It was in the matter of homes that segregation was most strongly tied to "the hearts of men." It was not precisely public opinion that it was tied to, though that was not firmly on the side of open housing. It was that other force, so difficult to gauge and yet so potent in all questions involving the Negro: *private* opinion, or the private feeling of individuals. Many a white man who joined the chorus of indignation over the murder of Negro children in Birmingham, or who favored equal rights for Negroes in the abstract, reacted differently to living next door to a Negro family. Children, social prestige, and property values had to be considered; and the prejudice which he thought he had cast aside came back at the prospect of having colored neighbors. The attitudes of millions of individuals had to be changed. A majority would not be enough. In many matters the will of the majority could be expressed in legislation which would govern the behavior of all; but no law could make a Negro family welcome in a white neighborhood.

Seventeen states and sixty cities had laws affecting discrimination in housing; they ranged from the broad coverage of New York City's open housing ordinance to measures which reached only a tiny part of the housing market. But many wiles could be employed to make a home seem attractive to some and unattractive to others, and who could know what went on in the private conversations of property-owners and brokers with home-seekers? Though not every Negro newcomer in a white residential district met with violence or physical harassment, the occasional well-publicized instances of this deterred many Negroes from taking the risk. Others hesitated to move to a white neighborhood merely because they thought they would be socially uncomfortable there.

In spite of all this, Negroes were gaining a foothold in previously all-white neighborhoods. Legislation could and did help. But what was to prevent the whites from moving away? If all the whites left, a ghetto was born. Where a substantial number of whites held on, a stable biracial community might develop. There were some of these. But across the country, whites were fleeing from the proximity of colored people. Negroes from rural districts of the South were pouring into the big cities. In twenty years the Negro population of New York, Philadelphia, and Boston had more than doubled, that of Chicago and Detroit had approximately trebled; that of Los Angeles had multiplied five times; and that of San Francisco had jumped from 5,000 to 74,000. Factors other than racial prejudice were involved in the comparable exodus of whites, but they were moving to the suburbs, which for the most part, and for a time at least, offered a haven of racial exclusiveness.

The federal government, in spite of its many programs and vast expenditures in the field of public housing, had been slow to concern itself with housing segregation. An estimated 80 per cent of public housing projects were segregated. The fact that whites held back when Negroes poured into a development accounted for much of this segregation; and in some nearly all-white sections, no Negroes applied for houses. But in many cases Negroes were unable to rent or purchase even homes erected in part with public funds.

Until the late 1940's the tendency of federal housing agencies had been frankly to support racial homogeneity in housing. Subsequently federal policy had undergone minor revisions tending to encourage integration. In President Kennedy's Executive Order 11063 of November 20, 1962, it was at last officially recognized that "segregated patterns of housing . . . necessarily produce other forms of discrimination and segregation which deprive many Americans of equal opportunity in the exercise of their inalienable right to life, liberty, and the pursuit of happiness." The order prohibited discrimination in housing to be constructed thenceforth by the federal government or with federal financial assistance. It also created the President's Committee on Equal Opportunity in Housing to review the implementation of the order, recommend policies to effectuate it, and encourage educational programs to eliminate the basic cause of discrimination. Five cabinet members and the heads of housing agencies were ex officio members of this committee. On January 11, 1963, the President announced the appointment of David R. Lawrence, about to retire as governor of Pennsylvania, as its chairman.

The practical effect of Executive Order 11063, however, had been slight. The order did not apply to any existing housing, even public housing. Nearly two million housing units already built or under construction before November 20, 1962, and still receiving federal financial assistance, were excluded. The order directed federal housing agencies to "use their good offices, and to take other appropriate action permitted by law . . . to promote the abandonment of discriminatory practices" in housing "heretofore" built with federal aid; but more than "good offices" was needed and little action of any kind was taken. A nationwide survey completed by the *Wall Street Journal* in July, 1964, found "that the executive order has had little impact on housing patterns in most parts of the country."

Moreover, getting Negroes into a white residential area was only half or less than half of the problem. It was also necessary to prevent whites from leaving it. Economic considerations, largely born of misconceptions and hysteria, were added to racial prejudice in the flight of whites before the advance of Negro residents. That the coming of Negro families reduced property values in white neighborhoods was denied on the basis of research by many students of the subject. But this was believed by most whites—indeed, it had long been taken for granted—and in the early stages of Negro entry it was often proving true in fact. As usual in situations of panic, a rush of whites to sell their homes pushed prices down. Unscrupulous real estate brokers helped to spread alarm among white homeowners in order to acquire their properties at bargain prices. "Block-busting," this practice was called: one house sold to a Negro could lead to the sale of the remaining houses in a white block. "Block-busting" was increasingly frowned upon; five cities had special legislation against engaging in practices designed to induce panic selling of real estate.

A few public-spirited developers were pioneering in housing projects especially designed to attract homeseekers of both races. Morris Milgram and a corporation which he headed, called Modern Developers, Inc., had assisted in the planning and financing of such projects in Chicago and Washington suburbs, Philadelphia, Providence, and Wilmington, Delaware. In one of Milgram's Philadelphia projects, 75 of the homes were occupied by whites and 64 by Negroes; in another, 6 by Negroes and 13 by whites (including Milgram himself). The mayor of Trenton, New Jersey, to aid the open-housing cause, bought his own home in a biracial neighborhood and "For Sale" signs on several nearby white properties promptly came down.

Groups of dedicated people were working in many cities to allay the fears of white residents and promote the development of biracial communities. The American Friends Service Committee was outstanding in this field. A National Committee Against Discrimination in Housing, which had been formed in 1950, numbered thirty-seven leading religious, civil-rights, labor and civic organizations among its members. The National Urban League, the NAACP, and CORE were among these, along with the National Council of Churches, the National Catholic Conference for Interracial Justice, a number of Protestant denominational bodies, and five Jewish organizations. White communities which Negroes were entering for the first time were sometimes canvassed by these workers house by house. Some homeowners were induced to affix placards reading: "This House Not for Sale. We Believe in Democracy." Campaigns were undertaken to collect white signatures to pledges similar to one offered in a pamphlet issued by the National Committee and the Friends Committee which read:

> I believe: that every person has the moral and constitutional right to purchase or rent a home anywhere without limitations based on race, religion or national origin.
>
> I believe: it is imperative that within our metropolitan area all persons of good will unite with others of like conviction to take an active role in helping to achieve equal opportunity in housing.
>
> Therefore, I will welcome into my neighborhood any responsible person of whatever race, religion or national origin, and I will work with him and other neighbors to create a desirable community for all.

Militant civil-rights organizations did not give high priority to open housing in 1963, but their efforts were directed increasingly toward that objective in the next several years. As rioting drew attention to the problem of the ghettos, housing segregation became a matter of the gravest national concern.

How a Great Civil Rights Law Was Passed 1963-1964

The civil-rights bill before the Congress embraced in some fashion all of the objectives discussed in the foregoing chapter, except that of open housing. To many, like *Newsweek* magazine, it seemed to go "virtually as far as the law can reach to end the Negro's lot as a second-class citizen." It did not go that far. The bill as finally passed by Congress went farther than the Administration's proposals, but still left much ground to be covered. It had no provisions, for instance, to protect Negroes and civil-rights workers from racist violence in the South, a matter in which federal legislation was badly needed. Its failure to attack the problem of discrimination in housing left the Negro without one vastly important freedom—the freedom the white man enjoyed to choose the neighborhood in which he wished to live. Nevertheless, against the long background of unwillingness to really face the problem of the Negro's inferior status in the United States, the bill was revolutionary and it went very far indeed.

It prohibited soda fountains, lunch counters, restaurants, hotels, motels, and gasoline stations as well as theaters, concert halls, and sports stadiums from turning away any person because of his race. The impact of this section, when it came into effect, was anticlimactic. It was followed with excited interest for a few weeks (in expectation of public disorders which did not occur); isolated cases of overt resistance caused uneasiness for a few months; and then as a matter of active national concern it receded into history. But as a national recognition of the equal citizenship and humanness of Negroes, its significance was profound.

To the bill's original provision authorizing the Attorney General to move against remaining public school segregation Congress added another, enabling him to bring suit to end discrimination in public libraries, museums, playgrounds, hospitals, or other facilities owned or operated by states or political subdivisions. What proved to be a more effective weapon against racial discrimination in all these areas lay in the bill's provisions threatening federally assisted activities practicing discrimination with the loss of federal funds. In the matter of job discrimination, instead of mere statutory authority for the President's limited Committee on Equal Employment Opportunity, the final bill prohibited discrimination by employers and labor unions—beginning in 1965 with those having as many as 100 employees or members, and reaching those with 25 or more by 1968; and it created a new government agency, the Equal Employment Opportunity Commission.

In September, 1963, several bills embodying some or all of the President's program were still dragging through hearings in committees of Congress. The outlook for the legislation was not considered bright. Yet nine months later, not watered down but strengthened, it became the Civil Rights Act of 1964—to stand with the Emancipation Proclamation and the Supreme Court's *Brown* decision among the great milestones in the elevation of the Negro to equal citizenship in the Great Republic.

The enormous difficulty in enacting legislation which a majority in Congress favored from the beginning—the many vicissitudes in the bill's year-long journey to final passage and its narrow escapes from defeat or emasculation—drew much attention to the impediments with which procedural rules, custom, and a fetish of seniority have encumbered the national legislative machinery. "Three months," Walter Lippmann fumed, "is plenty of time to hear all the arguments of all the experts and all the interested people pro and con and to bring the issue before the Congress for decision." Yet it was well, since the bill survived unimpaired, that this law should have been the product of travail, of long and searching examination and exhaustive discussion. In addition to the House and Senate debates, which filled several thousand pages of the *Congressional Record*, the testimony of 269 witnesses before six committees filled eight volumes totaling 5,791 pages. There was, of course, much demagoguery, nonsense, and repetition; but no one could say that significant views had not been heard. The bill was not idle for any long period, other than the seven weeks it slumbered in the House Rules Committee, and that period embraced the season of mourning for President Kennedy. Every provision, every sentence in the bill was tirelessly worked over. And the majorities which approved it were so overwhelming that its final passage represented an unmistakable expression of the national will.

It was a bipartisan accomplishment. It had to be. The Democratic party held a large majority of the seats both in the Senate and in the House of Representatives; but that included the Southern Democrats—and they were the enemy. It was they who had to be outwitted, outmaneuvered, and outvoted with sufficient preponderance. The party division in the Eighty-eighth Congress was: in the House of Representatives, 257 Democrats and 178 Republicans; in the Senate, 67 Democrats, 33 Republicans. From the eleven Southern states of the onetime Confederacy, there were 22 senators and 105 representatives—all Democrats except six representatives and Senator John G. Tower of Texas. In the presidential campaign a year later, the party of Lincoln followed a leader who voted against the civil-rights bill. Yet—with hesitation on the part of some, and with due opposition-party skepticism, but very generally in the end—Republicans in Congress gave the bill their support. No Republicans, outside of the handful from the South, displayed hostility comparable to that of Southern Democrats.

A group of Republican liberals had chided President Kennedy for many months for his failure to present a strong civil-rights bill. They had introduced one of their own in January. Representative Charles A. Halleck, the House minority leader, noted a Republican identification with the program when the Kennedy bill was introduced. "Republicans will move expeditiously and in a spirit of cooperation," he said, "to get hearings started in the House Judiciary Committee on the civil-rights proposals offered by the President today and by many individual Republicans earlier this year." Senate Minority Leader Everett McKinley Dirksen joined in sponsoring a version of the Administration bill that embraced all but the section on public accommodations; he ultimately accepted that feature as well.

An interesting tit-for-tat of interparty badinage developed when Assistant Attorney General Marshall testified before the Senate Commerce Committee on July 20—underlining the tardiness of both parties in coming to grips with the problem of discrimination against the Negro in the United States. Republican Senator Hugh Scott of Pennsylvania asked whether a law like that under discussion had not been just as important in 1961 (President Kennedy's first year in office).

"Yes, Senator," Marshall replied—"and in 1960 and 1959," (years of Republican administration).

"And in 1962" (the second Kennedy year), Scott shot back.

"Yes," said Marshall, "and in 1958" (again a Republican year).

"And in 1948," Scott said. This was a year of Democratic administration under President Truman.

Marshall smiled, saying such legislation had been needed indeed since the 1870's.

Many white Southerners considered the bill to be directed against *them*, and the region most affected was indeed the South. But the common use of the word "Southern," as synonymous with opposition to civil-rights legislation—the "Southern position," the "Southern argument," etc.—was inaccurate. Though it was still politically dangerous to relent on the race issue, the liberal trend was somewhat more pronounced among the public in the South than among its representatives in Congress. Gallup polls showed only 82 per cent of Southern whites in June, 1963—declining to 72 per cent in February, 1964—opposed to federal legislation banning discrimination in hotels, restaurants, theaters, and the like. Mayor Ivan Allen of Atlanta, Georgia was an outspoken supporter of the civil-rights bill, and newspapers in Atlanta, Miami, Norfolk, Charlotte, Winston-Salem, Raleigh, Greensboro, Memphis, Nashville, Chattanooga, Knoxville, and Little Rock gave the bill their support.

Nevertheless, with few exceptions, the Southerners in Congress were prepared to fight the bill by every means at their command.

And the representatives of no other region, or no other group of equal number, were as powerful as they when it came to thwarting the will of the majority in Congress. As representatives of a virtually one-party region, where re-election was almost automatic, their long experience had made them past masters in the arts of obstruction and delay, while their seniority had given them the chairmanships of powerful committees.

Some members of the Southern bloc were statesmen of high caliber. From the opposite camp, the NAACP's Roy Wilkins, testifying before a Senate committee, referred to their leader, Senator Richard Russell, as "the distinguished Senator from Georgia" adding: "—and, except in the field of human rights, he *is* distinguished." On the Senate side, the 18-man "Southern team" included the chairmen of nine of the Senate's 16 standing committees. Russell's own personal position reflected faintly the changing Southern attitude. He recognized that the nation faced a "social revolution," and he conceded—as few Southerners were ready to concede five years earlier—that "the Negro has been imposed upon." "But," he said, "we shouldn't upset the whole scheme of constitutional government and expect people to swallow laws governing their most intimate social relations. The tempo of change is the crux of the whole matter. . . ."

Two of the committees of Congress that handled the bill were headed by the most intransigent of Southerners—the Senate Judiciary Committee, headed by Senator James O. Eastland of Mississippi, and the House Rules Committee, whose chairman was eighty-year-old Representative Howard W. Smith of Virginia. The prospect of a filibuster in the Senate made it necessary to aim at winning more than a mere majority of the members of that body. To end a filibuster required a vote of two-thirds of the senators present, and some objected to cloture on principle; it had been voted only five times in the forty-seven-year history of the cloture rule.

In order to navigate through the mine-fields of obstruction from Southerners, the President's program was presented in several different forms. The full bill was introduced in the Senate by Majority Leader Mike Mansfield, but this document was known to be doomed: it went to the Judiciary Committee, dominated by southerners, and was never reported to the Senate floor. The section banning discrimination in places of public accommodation was excerpted and introduced by Mansfield as a separate bill. As this had to do with interstate commerce, it went to the friendly Commerce Committee; if approved there, it could later be amended from the floor to include the whole civil-rights package. A third bill, containing all but the public accommodations section, was introduced in the Senate jointly by the majority and minority leaders. In the House, the Administration bill was introduced by Representative Emmanuel Celler of New York, chairman of the House Judiciary Committee, which was as hospitable to the proposals as that of the Senate was hostile. It would be in friendly hands in the House until it reached "Judge" Smith's Rules Committee.

It was in these committees that the issue was debated during the first seven months. The bill did not reach the floor of either chamber until February, 1964. But debate there was, and it was echoed throughout the country. The heavily publicized committee hearings were like seminars. The questions put by committee members were often in the nature of argument, and most of the witnesses called had strong opinions on one side or the other. Cabinet members and other government officials appeared, Attorney General Kennedy leading the fight from the Administration end. Southern governors testified, including the two most vociferously opposed to the bill—George Wallace of Alabama and Ross P. Barnett of Mississippi. Negro leaders, clergymen, scholars, and businessmen were heard. The House Judiciary Committee had the longest run: by the end of the summer, it had heard 91 witnesses. The Senate Commerce Committee heard 46. The Senate Judiciary Committee, in 11 days of hearings, heard only one witness, Attorney General Kennedy—in a running debate with Senator Sam Ervin of North Carolina.

The prohibition of discrimination in places of public accommodation and entertainment, in Title II of the bill, was more passionately and extensively debated both in and out of Congress than any other section. It seemed to symbolize the whole civil-rights issue. The fact that the most respectable Negro could be turned away from a restaurant or hotel, solely because of his race, was an exasperating reminder of the Negro's inferior status. (Some Negro veterans of World War II remembered seeing German prisoners of war being served in restaurants from which they were barred because of their color.) At the same time, federal interference with this indignity represented to many the most alarming intrusion of the government in the affairs of individual citizens and enterprises. "Many of our most sacred rights, including the right to own and use private property," Senator Lister Hill of Alabama said of this section, "have been laid on the altar of political expediency."

Roy Wilkins presented to the Senate Commerce Committee an effect of racial discrimination that had not occurred to many white people—the traumatic experiences of Negroes traveling by car in an area where uncertainty existed as to whether they would be admitted to places of public accommodation. "How far do you drive each day?"—the NAACP leader asked. "Where and under what conditions can you and your family eat? Where can they use a rest-room? Can you stop driving after a reasonable day behind the wheel or must you drive until you reach a city where relatives or friends will accommodate you and yours for the night? . . ."

Secretary of State Dean Rusk reminded the committee that "racial discrimination here at home has important effects on our foreign relations." "We cannot expect the friendship and respect of non-white nations," he said, "if we humiliate their representatives by denying them, say, services in a highway restaurant or city cafe. . . . Yet within the last two years, scores of incidents involving foreign diplomats accredited to this country have come to the attention of the Department of State." The diplomats, denied service along a Maryland highway or barred from hotels in Birmingham and Jacksonville, were likely to carry away resentments that outweighed millions in aid granted their countries.

Senator Ervin, a constitutional lawyer, took much of the time of the Senate Judiciary Committee hearings to present the legal argument of the Southern opposition. Title II rested—entirely at first—on the power given to the Congress in the Constitution to regulate interstate commerce. The North Carolina senator contended that the commerce clause could not be stretched to cover establishments that were not adjuncts of interstate commerce, such as restaurants in railway, airline, and bus terminals. Attorney General Kennedy insisted that discrimination in a broader field was a burden on interstate commerce, with which Congress was indeed empowered to deal. Many Republican supporters of the bill preferred invoking the Fourteenth Amendment's command that no person should be denied equal protection of the laws by any state. The validity of the application of this to private establishments was also challenged by Senator Ervin. It was attacked and defended in other quarters. In the end, both constitutional bases were used, the bill being amended to apply to any establishment, "if its operations affect commerce, or if discrimination or segregation by it is supported by state action."

The Senate Commerce Committee, whose bill contained only the provisions on places of public accommodation, approved its bill October 8, but did not report it until the following February —when it was set aside. Majority Leader Mansfield had by then decided that the Senate should wait for the House bill—which could be "met at the door" and made the pending business without getting into the hands of Eastland's Judiciary Committee. In the meantime, a crisis had developed on the House side.

The subcommittee of the House Judiciary Committee on September 25 tentatively approved a civil-rights bill which was far more comprehensive, and provocative, than the Kennedy recommendations. One addition made by the subcommittee was favored by the Administration and became an important part of the act. Expanding the ban on employment discrimination to cover not merely the federal government and companies under federal government contract, but practically all businesses and labor unions with over twenty-five workers, it had provided at last for the establishment of an "FEPC." The commission to be set up would have a different alphabetical designation, but "FEPC" had been used through years of unsuccessful efforts to revive the Fair Employment Practices Committee set up by President Roosevelt during World War II. The President's bill had not included an FEPC, though he had expressed support for FEPC bills already pending in Congress.

But the civil-rights enthusiasts in the subcommittee had sharpened and expanded the bill in many other particulars. (Among these enthusiasts was Representative John Lindsay, who two years later would be elected mayor of New York.) They had extended the public-accommodations section to cover a broad field of enterprises operating under state "authorization, permission or license," and they wanted to give the Department of Justice almost unlimited powers in filing suits over asserted violations of civil rights. The immediate result of this performance was a situation of chaos. It produced a variety of paradoxical reactions. Negro leaders rejoiced. But the revision also delighted some Southern opponents, who sensed that it would result in defeat of the bill. Some white liberals were pleased: the *New York Times* called for "a clear voice from the President in support of legislation that would carry forward his stated principles more effectively than his own." But others, including the Administration, were alarmed. It seemed that the bill was being overloaded to the point where it was likely to capsize.

In a month of conferences and negotiations, the Administration, which was pressing so ardently for a strong civil-rights bill, now strove frantically to stop the advancement of one as strong as this. Attorney General Kennedy told committee members the draft as it stood would give his office vast powers which it neither wanted nor should have. It might even lead to a national police force. Other subcommittee changes were attacked as unwise or likely to provoke unnecessary opposition to the bill. Negroes meanwhile, cried: "A sell-out!" Sensitive to political repercussions, the liberal committee members, both Democrats and Republicans, were loath to take responsibility for dropping any of the provisions that Negro leaders favored. The Attorney General advised the President that only the latter's direct and immediate intervention would prevent the House Judiciary Committee from voting out the drastic version.

In an extraordinary White House meeting—one of the kind generally reserved for grave foreign policy conferences—President Kennedy told House and committee leaders that a civil-rights act was imperative and that he doubted if there would be one if this draft should be insisted upon. The legislators then worked long hours through the week-end. Monday morning a group got together in a hotel room—along with Deputy Attorney General Katzenbach, Assistant Attorney General Marshall, and Republican legal advisers—and hammered out a 56-page revision. Minority Leader Halleck conferred with the President at the White House, and that afternoon (October 29) the Judiciary Committee approved the compromise bill by a vote of 20 to 14. It still went beyond the original in the new fair employment provisions, and in several other respects. Nevertheless Attorney General Kennedy declared it "a better bill than the Administration's," and the President said it had "significantly improved the prospects for enactment of effective civil-rights legislation."

The bill then went, on November 21, to the House Rules Committee. The next day the life of its great proponent ended in a tragedy which shook the nation and the world. President Kennedy was assassinated and Vice President Johnson succeeded to the presidency.

In his thousand days as President, John Fitzgerald Kennedy had established himself in the eyes of the world as a champion of freedom and justice for all men. The British Prime Minister noted in his tribute: "He was a man who hated bigotry and believed all men are created equal." At home his belief "in the dignity and equality of all human beings" was stressed by Chief Justice Earl Warren and many others. Yet Kennedy's work for equal rights for Negroes had cost him some popularity. In some sections of the South, the feeling of whites toward the President had reached a point of incredibly bitter hatred. In the hours of national desolation, a sense of decency silenced most adult criticism, but the extent to which vilification of the President had become a commonplace in many households was revealed in the reaction of Southern children: some of them applauded when the announcement of his death was made at school.

Negroes felt they had lost a true friend; weeping Negroes were conspicuous in the crowds of mourners everywhere. Yet from a practical point of view, Negroes had found much to criticize in Kennedy's performance. He had not gone far enough or fast enough for civil-rights crusaders, though many other people thought he was doing too much too soon. Until the turmoil and pressures of 1963, the President had hoped to avoid new legislation, relying on executive action to advance the cause. Elected by a precariously thin margin, and lacking the toughness and peculiar skill needed to carry Congress along with his policies, he had taken a cautious view of the "art of the possible."

In some of his judicial appointments in the South his sense of political exigencies had led to what seemed a betrayal of the cause. Many federal judges appointed by Kennedy were openly hostile to the civil-rights movement and critical of the Supreme Court's antidiscrimination rulings, which they were in duty bound to enforce. Efforts to secure redress of Negroes' grievances through the courts often met with delay or frustration as a result. With one or two exceptions, Eisenhower appointees were more to be relied upon. Such appointments are a constitutional responsibility of the President, but they are subject to approval by the Senate, and long-established practice has given a senator of the President's party something like a veto over appointments in his state. Under a Republican administration the President had a freer hand in choosing Southern judges. Critics insisted nonetheless that President Kennedy might have risked some senatorial displeasure, made better bargains, or delayed some appointments indefinitely.

There was some compensation in his judicial appointments outside of the South. Presidents Taft, Wilson, Harding, Coolidge, Hoover, Franklin Roosevelt, Truman, and Eisenhower, each appointing, or reappointing, one or two Negro judges, had all together placed the first eight Negroes on the federal court bench. Kennedy alone appointed eight more Negro judges. In federal government departments and agencies he named more Negroes to high positions than had ever been given such responsibilities before. Negroes formerly had entered the White House only on rare occasions; during his administration they were constantly coming and going there. Within his powers as President, he took positive steps to advance the cause of justice for Negroes in the fields of employment, housing, military service, and voting. He helped to make Americans aware of the wrongs done to Negroes and urged reform in his public speeches, in his brilliant press conferences, and in apt remarks on innumerable occasions.

In his address of June 19, 1963, President Kennedy said to the Congress: "I ask you to look into your hearts—not in search of charity, for the Negro neither wants nor needs condescension—but for the one, plain, proud and priceless quality that unites us all as Americans: a sense of justice. In this year of the Emancipation Centennial, justice requires us to insure the blessings of liberty for all Americans and their posterity—not merely for reasons of economic efficiency, world diplomacy and domestic tranquility—but above all, because it is right." His example and his words, which lifted the spirit of America, shed a special glow over the struggle for interracial justice and inspired all who labored in it.

The new President was a rough-hewn, practical man in contrast to the radiant young statesman whose life had been cut short. But in their service to civil rights they complemented each other. The Chicago *Daily News* observed: "It would not, we think, unduly derogate the abilities of Mr. Kennedy to point out that dealing with Congress was not one of his major talents. It may, on the other hand, prove to be the greatest talent his successor possesses." For all his lofty idealism, Kennedy's death left not only the civil-rights bill, but virtually his whole domestic legislative program in a stalemate. Then came Johnson, the doer, the veteran of Senate leadership—"the greatest political craftsman of our time," former Vice President Richard M. Nixon called him. When the new President, a few days after taking office, placed himself resolutely behind the civil-rights bill, the prospects for its passage brightened overnight. The assassination itself had tended to strengthen support for the things the martyred President stood for.

In his first message to Congress as President, on November 27, Johnson placed this matter in the forefront of pressing business. "First," he said, "no memorial or eulogy could more eloquently honor President Kennedy's memory than the earliest possible passage of the civil-rights bill, for which he fought so long."

Negro leaders were much impressed—Martin Luther King called the President's speech "a heroic and courageous affirmation of our democratic ideals"—and Johnson lost no time in getting in touch with them. He received Roy Wilkins at the White House two days later, and in the course of a week he conferred, one by one, with each of the others of the Big Five: Young, King, Farmer, and Randolph.

The immediate hold-up was the House Rules Committee, whose octogenarian chairman had no intention of moving the "nefarious" bill any faster than necessary. President Johnson let it be known that he wanted the Rules Committee bypassed and a petition was circulated to discharge it from consideration of the bill. Although many frowned upon this procedure, 173 of the required 218 signatures were secured by Christmas. Judge Smith relented slowly.

He said on December 5 that the bill would be called up "reasonably soon in January." On December 18, he said hearings would begin January 9. From then on, the bill was in little danger as far as House passage was concerned. The pro-civil-rights bill majority (11 to 4) on the Rules Committee was in no mood for dilly-dallying. Even so, the inconsequential hearings and clearing the bill in that committee took three weeks; action by the House itself took only eleven days.

The House debate, which opened January 31, was marked by dignity and restraint on both sides, and the chamber acted with dispatch. One hundred and twenty-two amendments were disposed of, supporters beating down with ease every effort to weaken the bill. Of the 28 amendments accepted, one extended the life of the Civil Rights Commission for four years instead of giving it permanent status; several others tended to broaden the scope of the bill; and the remainder were minor or technical in nature. When the vote was taken February 10, the bill passed 290 to 130. Voting for it were 152 Democrats and 138 Republicans; against: 96 Democrats, 34 Republicans.

An important factor in the House action, as it was later in the Senate struggle, was the massive campaign of civil-rights, church, labor, and other organizations working for the bill.

There was opposition propaganda too. It emanated largely from a "Coordinating Committee for Fundamental American Freedoms, Incorporated." This organization was helped by segregationist groups in a number of Southern states and received some Northern support, but its funds of several hundred thousand dollars came mainly from the State Sovereignty Commissions of Mississippi and Alabama (public agencies of those two states). The John Birch Society urged its members to keep up a letter-writing and advertising campaign against the bill.

But this activity was overshadowed by the lobbying on the bill's behalf. Seventy-nine organizations participated in this. Coordinated by the Leadership Conference on Civil Rights, they included the principal civil-rights organizations, a dozen labor unions along with the AFL-CIO itself, the Americans for Democratic Action, the American Veterans' Committee, the American Civil Liberties Union, other liberal societies, and, above all, the various bodies of militant churchmen. Literally thousands of representatives of these groups poured into Washington during the House and Senate debates. Clarence Mitchell of the NAACP, Andrew Biemiller and Jack Conway of the AFL-CIO, and the Reverend James Hamilton of the National Council of Churches were key figures in the Leadership Conference.

The churches' call for justice to the Negro resounded now. Ardent Protestant, Catholic, and Jewish lobbyists were in close day-to-day contact with Congressional backers of the bill. Denominational delegations of as many as 200 persons made prayerful pilgrimages to Washington. Over 6,000 of the clergy and laity gathered in a National Interreligious Convocation on Civil Rights at Georgetown University April 28 to demonstrate support for the bill and urge prayers for its passage. President Johnson invited 150 of the leaders of this assembly to the White House the next day and told them: "It is your job, as men of God, to awaken the conscience of America." All this pressure from religious leaders had its effect. One Republican senator from the West, averse to the bill, was reported to have grumbled: "Oh, I will have to vote for it in the end because you've got those damned pastors on my neck!" Near the end of the long fight, Senator Russell complained sadly: "During the course of the debate, we have seen cardinals, bishops, elders, stated clerks, common preachers, priests and rabbis come to Washington to press for passage of this bill."

Meanwhile Negro demonstrations were still agitating many cities. Unrelated to the debate in Congress and without the guidance of the regular civil-rights leadership, some of them were taking a malignant form. Opposition was showing itself in a so-called "white backlash." Governor Wallace of Alabama, a symbol of opposition to civil rights, capriciously exploiting the "backlash," campaigned for the Democratic presidential nomination and received a substantial vote in several state primaries. Senators Humphrey and Thomas H. Kuchel of California, floor leaders for the bill in the Senate, issued a statement on April 15 warning that their efforts would be hampered by "unruly demonstrations and protests that bring hardships and unnecessary inconvenience to others." On the other hand, Negro unrest was always a reminder of the need for remedial action. Senator Jacob K. Javits of New York said early in May: "Unless the bill is passed in the next six weeks, we

will face serious disorders in many cities." On balance, the disturbances out of doors had little effect now upon the course of events
in Congress.

The debate in the Senate lasted three months and ten days. Here
the bill's proponents faced at last the dreaded filibuster—the
"Southern square," which had never yet been broken on a civil-
rights issue. The millions of words of oratory were generally ger-
mane, but they added little that was new and consequential to the
long-disputed subject. Forensics weighed less than tactical ma-
neuvers, negotiations, and the drafting of amendments. Rounding
up senators for a quorum call was often a matter of prime importance. That a majority of senators favored the bill no one doubted;
59 sure supporters could be counted from the beginning. But
would they have an opportunity to vote on it? The votes of two-
thirds of the members present, or 67 out of a possible 100, were
required to end debate and bring the bill to a vote. Until cloture
should be accomplished, opponents of the bill could prevent the
Senate from voting by merely talking and talking.

Marshaled by Senator Russell, the Southerners went into action
in three talking platoons, each in turn holding the floor while the
others rested. Nor were the pro-civil-rights forces lacking in organization. In addition to the majority and minority whips (Senator Humphrey for the Democrats and Senator Kuchel for the
Republicans), acting as floor leaders, "floor captains" were named
for various sections of the bill. A daily news letter kept all informed. Proponents also maintained constant contact with the
Leadership Conference on Civil Rights and particularly with the
militant clergy. The leaders conferred regularly with Department
of Justice officials.

Southern oratory began to flow on March 9, when the Senate
was concerned only with the routine technical question of whether
to take up the House-passed bill. It was only on March 26 that the
body was able to vote to begin formal consideration of the bill
itself. Senators Humphrey and Kuchel opened the debate March
30, explaining and defending the bill section by section. Proponents
continued to press their case, but Southerners, taking the floor in
opposition, gave no indication of allowing any votes on the bill. By
the time cloture was imposed, approximately 560 amendments had

been offered. Generally, they represented attempts of Southerners to soften or nullify provisions of the bill. Most amendments were defeated or withdrawn, but an omnibus substitute, largely the work of Senator Dirksen, was adopted.

When the measure cleared the House, President Johnson had said: "I hope the same bill will be passed in the Senate"; and Senator Humphrey had promised to resist any change in the House bill. But Senator Dirksen began even then to study the document, sentence by sentence, and formulate amendments. The astute minority leader sensed that many changes would be needed to win the necessary support of uncommitted Republicans—changes which he believed could be made without damage to the purposes of the bill. In mid-May, when Dirksen had developed some seventy amendments, bipartisan leaders and Justice Department officials worked and negotiated for a week over his handiwork. The result was virtually one more rewriting of the civil-rights bill. The substitute defined limits of government power in enforcement and provided for a certain deference to state and local agencies; otherwise the changes were largely technical or clarifying. Some liberals in both parties were unhappy over the compromise, accepting it only as a means of shutting off the filibuster. But Senator Jacob K. Javits of New York, a leading liberal, said: "no title has been emasculated, ... the fundamental bill remains." Humphrey and Kuchel and Majority Leader Mansfield praised Dirksen for his work. President Johnson said "Administration lawyers" felt that the proposed changes "generally have been helpful and would be acceptable."

The sixty-eight-year-old Senator Dirksen was to be widely hailed as the architect of the civil-rights bill. *Time* magazine, in an issue which carried his picture on the cover, said, "it is Dirksen's bill, bearing his handiwork more than anyone else's." The rare personality of the erudite and avuncular minority leader made him a favorite of television viewers and a large public. He had not been popular among Negroes; he rarely mentioned Negro grievances. He had wrestled with the civil-rights bill with an air of cynical realism. Now he quoted a line attributed to Victor Hugo: "Stronger than all the armies is an idea whose time has come."

A cloture petition was filed on June 8. Cloture would bring debate to a speedy end, allowing only one more hour of speaking time for each senator. Majority Leader Mansfield said: "the Senate now stands at the crossroads of history." The vote was taken June 10. All 100 of the senators were present. Seventy-one voted for cloture, more than enough. Of the 29 opposing votes, 23 were cast by Democrats (all but two from Southern and border states) and 6 by Republicans.

Passage of the bill was from then on a foregone conclusion, which the remaining oratory reflected. Southern senators relinquished much of the time available to them. Interest centered on the decision of Senator Barry Goldwater of Arizona, who was now the leading contender for the Republican nomination for President. Goldwater had voted against cloture, to which he had always been opposed on principle, but he had indicated that he might vote for the bill. His final decision was announced only on June 18. He declared that he was "unalterably opposed to discrimination on the basis of race, color or creed," and he recognized a federal "responsibility in the field of civil rights"; but he could not accept Titles II and VII of the bill (banning discrimination in public accommodations and in employment). "Because," he said, "I am unalterably opposed to any threats to our great system of government and the loss of our God-given liberties, I shall vote 'no' on this bill."

Senator Dirksen delivered the last speech in the eighty-three days of debate. He recalled many pieces of social and economic legislation on the statute books which opponents had denounced as in violation of the Constitution, and said there was "latitude in that document . . . to embrace within its four corners these advances for human brotherhood." He read a telegram from forty state governors in their annual meeting at Cleveland, urging enactment of the pending bill. "In the history of mankind," he said, "there is an inexorable moral force that moves us forward. No matter the resistance of people who do not understand, it will not be denied."

That evening, June 19, by a vote of 73 to 27, the Senate passed the bill. It was exactly one year after the original bill had been submitted to Congress by President Kennedy.

"This," said Senator Strom Thurmond of South Carolina, "is a sad day for America."

"This," said Senator Javits of New York, "was one of the Senate's finest hours."

Protestant, Catholic, and Jewish crusaders gathered at the Capitol in a meeting of prayer and thanksgiving. A band of theological students ended a sixty-three-day around-the-clock vigil before the Lincoln Memorial, which they had pledged to keep until the Senate passed the bill.

House approval of the final version was in little doubt. The bill fell once more into the hands of the Rules Committee, but by June 30 the committee's bipartisan majority had approved a resolution for its adoption. Fearing procrastination by Judge Smith, another member was delegated to present the rule to the Speaker—a normal function of the chairman, who declared this procedure "outrageous." Smith now saw "hordes of beatniks, misfits and agitators from the North, with the admitted aid of the Communists, streaming into the Southland mischief-bent, backed and defended by other hordes of federal marshals, federal agents and federal power." But one Southern Democrat, Representative Charles L. Weltner, of Atlanta, Georgia, changed his position of opposition to one of approval of the bill, saying: "I will add my voice to those who seek reasoned and conciliatory adjustment to the new reality. . . ."

The House approved the bill on July 2 by a vote of 289 to 126. President Johnson signed it in a White House ceremony that evening. He called on all Americans "to join in this effort to bring justice and hope to all our people—and peace to our land."

The ban on discrimination in places of public accommodation went immediately into effect, and what followed was—not a wave of defiance, which many had feared—but a wave of compliance. The historic Columbia, South Carolina, *State* said in a banner headline July 4: SOUTHERN SEGREGATION FALLS SILENTLY, WITHOUT VIOLENCE. Many hotels, motels, restaurants, and theaters ceased excluding Negroes at once. The "miracle" took place promptly even in some cities of Alabama, Mississippi, and Louisiana. In the smaller establishments in cities and in rural areas the pattern of discrimination continued with little change; intimidation was still present, and Negroes were slow to take the risk of testing their rights under the new law. Lester Maddox, a recalcitrant restaurateur in Atlanta, achieved some notoriety by his pyrotechnics, and several suits were filed in federal courts challenging the constitutionality of this section of the act. But outright resistance and public disorder were rare, and the section's constitutionality would be upheld in due course by the Supreme Court.

In signing the bill, President Johnson announced the nomination of LeRoy Collins, former governor of Florida, to be director of the Community Relations Service to be set up under the act. Governor Collins, together with Buford Ellington, former governor of Tennessee, and Luther H. Hodges, former governor of North Carolina and then Secretary of Commerce, set out promptly on a tour of visits to Southern governors to discuss ways in which the new service could help in securing voluntary compliance. Governor Collins and his quickly assembled agency were soon settling disputes—mainly, at this stage, in the desegregation of places of public accommodation.

The remaining sections of the act received little attention until after the November election; the fair employment provisions did not come into effect until July 1, 1965. The continuing racial problem manifested itself in reckless Negro demonstrations in the North and in atrocities by white Negrophobes in the Deep South. Three workers for Negro voter registration were murdered in Mississippi two days after the civil-rights bill passed the Senate; two weeks after its final enactment, a Negro lieutenant colonel was callously shot to death while motoring through Georgia. But the struggle over the civil-rights bill had at last disappeared from the front pages of newspapers. Public interest turned now to the quadrennial contest for President and the Republican National Convention opening on July 13 in San Francisco.

SEVEN

The Negro Image
1964

Much had been happening to the Negro American besides the enactment of the great Civil Rights Act.

In his first State of the Union message, January 8, 1964, President Johnson declared "unconditional war on poverty." Poverty was an enemy that held captive a far larger proportion of the nation's Negroes than of its whites, and the move was plainly a response to the Negro revolt.

"Unfortunately," the President told the Congress, "many Americans live on the outskirts of hope, some because of their poverty and some because of their color, and all too many because of both. . . . Our task is to replace their despair with opportunity."

When he cited "our failure to give our fellow citizens a fair chance to develop their own capacities, . . . a lack of education and training, . . . a lack of medical care and housing, . . . a lack of decent communities in which to live and bring up their children," he described a very large element of the Negro population. Millions of whites were similarly deprived, more in number than the Negroes; but they were a relatively small part of the total white population. Sixty per cent of the white families had annual incomes of $4,000 or more; 60 per cent of the Negro families had incomes of less—frequently much less—than that amount. Nonwhites (92 per cent of them Negroes) comprised 11.7 per cent of the nation's population, but nonwhite children made up 40 per cent of the children living in families with incomes under $3,000.

The Department of Health, Education and Welfare estimated that 60 per cent of the Negro children in America were growing up in poverty-stricken families.

And Negroes had actually been losing ground economically vis-à-vis whites in recent years. The Report of the Secretary of Labor on "Manpower Requirements, Resources, Utilization and Training," sent to Congress by the President on March 9, 1964, said: "The differences between the two racial groups have not only failed to narrow but have actually widened in such major areas as housing, income and employment. Only in education is the gap narrowing, and the full rewards of this development have yet to be reaped."

The education of Negroes still left a desperate need unfilled, particularly in the kind of training required to rescue a vast number from idleness and frustration. The emphasis in the President's project, which he submitted to Congress on March 31, was on providing the impoverished with equipment and incentive for the economic struggle. It contemplated industrial training for some 200,000 young men and women; a Job Corps which would enlist some 100,000 boys and girls to work on various projects (at $50 a month) while receiving some basic education and training; part-time employment for possibly 140,000 college students who might have to give up their studies without financial help; loans and grants to poor farm families and loans to small businesses creating jobs for the unemployed; and a variety of local antipoverty campaigns to be undertaken by community action groups, with mainly federal government financing. An Office of Economic Opportunity was to be established which would be "directly responsible" for the new programs; and, as the President announced in advance, it would be headed by Robert Sargent Shriver, Jr., a brother-in-law of the late President Kennedy, already director of the Peace Corps.

The antipoverty bill, like most other legislative business, would have to wait on the civil-rights bill; but there was little doubt that Congress would pass it—as it did the following August. The $790 million made available for the first year was approximately doubled in appropriations for the second. The program offered great promise, but many months would pass before its impact would be significantly felt. In the meantime its administrators faced staggering problems—in resisting the urge of politicians to use this government largesse for their political ends; in enlisting the cooperation of the public, establishing an understanding contact with the poor, gaining the confidence of the skeptical and embittered and awakening a desire for work and self-improvement among the army of the chronically idle; and finally in surmounting the inevitable mistakes and criticism in a process of trial and error.

The Supreme Court continued to deliver decisions upholding the constitutional rights of Negroes in a variety of situations. On May 25, 1964, it handed down an opinion reversing a court of appeals judgment and sustaining a ruling of a district court that the public schools of Prince Edward County, Virginia, "may not be closed to avoid the effect of the law of the land as interpreted by the Supreme Court while the Commonwealth of Virginia permits other public schools to remain open at the expense of the taxpayer." The high tribunal thus ended a long and painful litigation, and removed a familiar symbol of Southern resistance to school desegregation. Prince Edward was one of the original defendants in the Supreme Court's *Brown* decision of 1954. In 1959, when definitive desegregation orders appeared imminent, that county closed its public schools. They had remained closed ever since. Private schools for white children were operated by a community organization, but Negro children, who represented more than half the school population, had been left for most of this period entirely without schooling.

Referring to the court's 1955 opinion calling for public school desegregation "with all deliberate speed," the opinion said "the time for mere 'deliberate speed' has run out"—registering a frown of impatience at the South as a whole, where after almost ten years only one per cent of the Negro children were yet attending classes with whites.

In an order of March 31 the Supreme Court, by reversing a contempt judgment of Alabama courts against Miss Mary Hamilton, ruled in effect that an unmarried Negro woman must be addressed as "Miss" when appearing as a witness in court. The news of this incident struck the nation as a whole as a quaint echo of the past, yet it was still common practice in the Deep South to address Negroes by their first names in all circumstances. Elsewhere it was customary, at least in formal situations, to accord Negroes the elementary courtesies of human intercourse.

At the heart of the attitude of whites in all areas of discrimination was their conception of the Negro. In past generations most of the literature and songs and popular entertainment where Negroes appeared had presented them only in humble, comic, or despicable roles. At their kindest they had pictured faithful "darkies" singing in the moonlight or weeping at the grave of dear old "massa." In a frivolous and more damaging vein a whole school of minstrel shows, vaudeville and carnival spectacles had fostered the image of Negroes as grinning, head-scratching, watermelon-eating buffoons. The latter caricature had almost vanished from public exhibitions, but it survived as late as 1963 in the annual Mummers Parade in Philadelphia. Following a sixty-three-year-old custom, each New Year's Day was celebrated in that city by thousands of whites marching and clowning in blackface in supposed imitation of Negroes. They competed for $66,500 in prizes offered by the city. But the revolution had come since the 1963 Mummers Parade. Philadelphia Negroes were determined that they would never again suffer this "insulting, degrading humiliation."

During several weeks of agitation before the 1964 parade, blackface was first banned by nervous city authorities, then permitted again without eligibility for the prizes. The NAACP sought a court ruling against blackface makeup, but without success. Members of CORE and of the Chester Committee for Freedom then threatened to "use our bodies" as a human chain to stop the parade. Tension mounted in the City of Brotherly Love. Police Inspector Albert J. Trimmer assigned 1,500 uniformed men and 325 plainclothes men to guard against the riot which the parade seemed sure to provoke. In vain, on New Year's Eve, representatives of the three major religious faiths urged the city authorities to call off the parade. Reverend Henry N. Nichols, the Negro president of the Greater Philadelphia Council of Churches said: "I pray that the good Lord will stop the parade with a snowstorm."

The minister's prayer was answered. Sleet and freezing rain on New Year's Day forced a seventy-two-hour postponement. In the interim the problem was taken to court again, and in the face of imminent danger of public turmoil, the three-judge Common Pleas

Court granted an injunction banning both blackface parading and picketing by opponents. On January 4, the sixty-fourth annual Philadelphia Mummers Parade proceeded peacefully, in fair weather, with no faces blackened.

In contrast to the fading minstrel caricature, whites in 1964 were becoming familiar with distinguished Negroes. They had known of one distinguished Negro for the past fourteen years, but many of them had recognized *only* one. When Ralph Bunche won the Nobel Peace Prize in 1950, he became by general consent a man of distinction. Even Southern racists shared the respect for Bunche; they cited him, however, not as a symbol of the Negro potential, but as the exception that proved the rule of Negro inferiority. If all Negroes were like Ralph Bunche, many whites said, they wouldn't mind eating with Negroes or having them for neighbors, but—. Negroes were proud of the acclaim for one of their race, but as the years went by, they grew a little tired of the harping on Bunche, Bunche, Bunche—as if he were the only Negro worthy of note. There had been other distinguished Negroes all along; now there were hundreds who could not be ignored.

Negro success in sports was by now an old story. A few Negroes had long been famous in musical and literary circles and in the entertainment world; the number of these was steadily increasing. Negroes were proving capable of overcoming the barriers to the attainment of excellence in every field. For example, consider this assortment of Negro distinctions in 1964; Leslie N. Shaw, postmaster of Los Angeles, the nation's third largest city; James C. Stratton, president of the San Francisco board of education; J. Raymond Jones—incredibly a Negro sachem—presiding over New York's Tammany Hall; Edward W. Brooke, attorney general of Massachusetts, with a bright future as a Republican politician; Benjamin O. Davis, Jr., an Air Force major general, soon to be appointed chief of staff of United States forces in Korea and promoted to lieutenant general; the Reverend Elder G. Hawkins, moderator of the general assembly of the predominantly white United Presbyterian Church in the U.S.A.; George Donnell Carroll, mayor of Richmond, California (population 80,000); Dr. Vance H. Marchbanks, Jr., a moon project scientist with the United Aircraft Corporation; Reginald E. Adams, chief engineer on an ocean-going freighter; and Miss Dorothy L. Johnson, "Miss Idaho," judged one of the fifteen most beautiful young women in the United States, a contestant in the semifinals for the title of "Miss U.S.A."

Five Negroes held seats in the House of Representatives; a sixth was elected in November. Nearly a score were members of the federal judiciary. In August, 1964, Andrew F. Brimmer was appointed an assistant Secretary of Commerce. Another Negro, George L. P. Weaver, was already an Assistant Secretary of Labor. Three Negroes held the rank of ambassador in the diplomatic service. Robert C. Weaver, the Negro administrator of the Housing and Home Finance Agency, had narrowly missed elevation to the cabinet. President Kennedy had sought to have that important agency raised to the level of a department—with the well-known intention of naming Weaver Secretary of Urban Affairs; but the bill failed to pass Congress. (Both the new department and Weaver's appointment to head it came in 1966.) Carl Rowan, a journalist who had served with distinction as United States ambassador to Finland, was chosen to succeed Edward R. Murrow as director of the United States Information Agency, and became the first Negro to sit in the National Security Council.

Colored faces were rare among the nation's several hundred thousand corporation executives and directors, but even here a modest breakthrough was taking place. (The 24-billion-dollar Negro consumer market had something to do with this.) *Ebony* magazine said in its November, 1964, issue: "While there were no Negro vice presidents in major white firms five years ago, there are at least nine today and one president" (Thomas Wood, president of Decision Systems, Inc., in Teaneck, New Jersey). There were thirteen Negro members of otherwise all-white boards of directors. McCann-Erickson, Inc., Schenley Distillers Co., Pepsi Cola Co., Boston Microwaves & Associates, Davidson Brothers, Inc., Schick Safety Razor Co., and J. V. Elliott Co., were well-known firms having Negro vice presidents. (*Ebony*, an excellent monthly magazine resembling *Life* and *Look*, was itself a shining example of Negro achievement.)

In the field of literature, a few Negro writers appeared before Emancipation and by the end of the nineteenth century Negroes had produced many works of a high order, though little known to the white public. In 1964, books by Negro authors were frequently on the national best-seller lists. Gwendolyn Brooks had won the 1948 Pulitzer Prize for poetry. *The Invisible Man*, a 1952 novel by Ralph Ellison, was rated among the twenty best American works of fiction during the post-World-War-II period. The judgment was made by 200 leading writers and critics polled by *Book Week* in 1965; *The Invisible Man* was the work selected by the largest number. A Negro writer of even greater contemporary fame was thirty-eight-year-old Arthur James Baldwin. Baldwin directed no organization and led no demonstrations, but his brilliant use of the English language to expose the inhumanities of white America to its Negro minority, and the abrasiveness with which he expressed the dark realities of the racial ferment gave him a high place among the revolution's leaders.

Another Negro author should be mentioned, not for his effect upon the Negro image but as a commentary on the times. From a commercial point of view, Frank Yerby was one of the most successful writers of any race: his books were read by millions. But he was better known as the author of *Foxes of Harrow* and a dozen best-sellers than as a Negro. He even wrote romances about Southern gentry of the old slaveholding regime—a field in which Negro authorship would least be suspected. His publisher had sedulously avoided mention of the author's race, and Yerby himself had discouraged publicity on that point. Hundreds of thousands of his readers were still unaware of the fact that he was a Negro. But it did not matter now: whites who would feel contaminated by reading a Negro-authored book were rare and the popularity of the Yerby novels was too great to be affected anyway.

The theater had offered another of the earliest outlets for Negro talent. Negroes had been accepted as singers and dancers for a century. In 1919 Negro actors began to appear in serious dramatic roles in plays of Eugene O'Neill. Paul Robeson became world-famous after his performance in *The Emperor Jones*, though the prejudice he encountered in the United States turned him into an embittered expatriate. By 1964 Negroes were active and successful in every department of "show business."

Leontyne Price was an opera prima donna of world renown. Negro playwright Lorraine Hansberry (who died in 1965) won the New York critics' award of 1959 with her *A Raisin in the Sun*. *Raisin* had an all-Negro cast and it ran for nineteen months and earned $700,000. Four Broadway shows that season had racially integrated casts; in 1960-61, eight used Negro players; in 1961-62, ten; and in 1962-63, thirteen. In the 1963-64 season hardly a show opened without one or more Negroes in the cast. In rare instances light-skinned Negroes played white roles: Jane White, daughter of the former NAACP leader, starred as Helen of Troy in *The Trojan Women*. For the first time a Negro was elected president of the 11,000-member Actors Equity Association, when Frederick O'Neal succeeded Ralph Bellamy in that office.

Negro playwrights were also busy, producing what *Life* magazine called "a burst of Negro drama." As LeRoi Jones, the youthful author of *The Dutchman*, said: "The whole situation of the Negro in America is playable—it's dramatic material." James Baldwin, who contributed his *Blues for Mr. Charlie*, sensed "a tremendous ferment." "There is a whole army of people," he said, "from whom one has never heard—most of them black—who are changing our consciousness."

Nineteen sixty-four was a triumphant year for the Negro on both stage and screen. Sidney Poitier won the Oscar presented by the American Academy of Motion Picture Arts and Sciences to the best actor of the year. The award was made for his performance in *Lilies of the Field*, but he had won acclaim in a dozen performances, and the choice was almost universally applauded. The ceremony, in which the various Oscars were presented before a dazzling audience in Hollywood and televised to the nation, reflected the "in" status which the Negro had at last attained in the motion picture world. Poitier served earlier in the evening as one of the presenters of awards. The popular Negro entertainer Sammy Davis, Jr., announced the awards for musical scoring. After an inadvertent slip due to a reversal of categories in the papers handed him, Davis quipped: "Wait till the NAACP hears about this!"—and brought a roar of good-natured laughter. Poitier received his Oscar from the white actress Anne Bancroft, and obeying a natural impulse, he gave her an impressive hug. The incident, which would have been unbelievable a few years before, delighted the 1964 audience.

Poitier also won the award of the Berlin International Film Festival in June and was named chairman of the United States delegation to that meeting.

Television with its vast and constant audience was the medium that was doing most for the image of the Negro. In the area of news, its lavish coverage of developments in the civil-rights struggle served in effect as a mighty trumpet for the Negro protest; without it no one can say how the history of the era would have been written. From the standpoint of the Negro image, television newscasts presented many Negroes in a sympathetic light, and made the public familiar with Negro leaders who were at home with white scholars and statesmen. In news and public service presentations unrelated to civil rights, the public was enabled to see Negroes in many situations where they were indistinguishable from whites save by the color of their skin. In man-on-the-street interviews reporters generally made a point of questioning at least one Negro. (Each of the national networks now employed one or more Negro newscasters.) In any group of representative Americans: soldiers, students, Boy Scouts, etc., presented in connection with a fund-raising drive or otherwise, care was taken now to see that Negroes were included.

In television fiction and entertainment, with little sound of struggle or celebration of victory, a veritable revolution had taken place. Television came too late to espouse the Negro minstrel type of humor, but for years the medium had practically ignored the Negro. Only rarely did it present a Negro actor, then usually in the role of a faithful mammy or an obsequious butler. Now Negroes could be seen on television programs—as they were increasingly visible in American life—as ladies and gentlemen. Unobtrusively and routinely, here and there the part of judge or prosecuting attorney or doctor or nurse—even that of a cowboy—might be played by a Negro. On entertainment programs, Negroes performed not as crude black buffoons but as sophisticated singers or graceful and witty comics. Leslie Uggams was the regular star of the Mitch Miller show, outshining the dozen white girls on the same program.

Few noticed a little group in the March on Washington who stood before the cameras of the national networks with a banner reading: "Dogs have television shows. Negroes don't." (The dog reference was to Rin Tin Tin and Lassie.) A continuing program directed by a Negro star had not yet proven feasible. The late Nat (King) Cole had tried it, but in spite of the high quality of his weekly offering, he was unable to obtain a commercial sponsor. Nevertheless, in 1964 Cole appeared on the Danny Kaye, Jack Benny, and Garry Moore shows and was host for the American Broadcasting Company's *Hollywood Palace*. "It's been a long, slow process," Cole said, "but I don't think the sponsors and the agencies fear the dark anymore!" In 1965 a regular Negro-directed weekly program arrived in the Sammy Davis Show.

All this had not come about as a spontaneous recognition of the Negro on the part of whites, though it was partly that. The first appearances of Negroes as respectable performers on television had aroused some white resentment. Arthur Godfrey, Tennessee Ernie Ford, and others received abusive mail after the first Negroes appeared on their programs. But there were millions of Negro television viewers, and the pressure from that side was more compelling than the bawling of bigoted whites. Aided by Negro organizations, white business leaders, almost suddenly in the 1960's, discovered 20 million Negro consumers of products advertised on television. White advertising executives urged a forthright appeal to the Negro market. A statement issued by the American Federation of Television and Radio Artists in June, 1963—also signed by executives in the broadcasting and recording industries—promised that the industry would "take affirmative steps toward the end that minority group performers are cast in all types of roles so that the American scene may be portrayed realistically." A month later the NAACP in its fifty-fourth annual convention adopted a resolution calling for selective buying campaigns against "the products of those who sponsor offensive motion pictures, television and radio programs or whose programs ignore the presence and achievement of American Negroes, or who refuse to give equal employment opportunity to Negroes."

The use of Negro models in advertising in newspapers and magazines was also urged, and the public was beginning to see here and there, outside of strictly Negro publications, a handsome and smartly dressed Negro in advertisements of clothing and other products.

There were factors also which worked *against* the improvement of the Negro image. One was the squalor in which many Negroes lived—due mainly to wretched poverty, but in part also to Negro neglect and unconcern. Garbage strewn in the yard, rags stuffed in window panes, broken furniture and loose boards which could be repaired with little trouble—such conditions were to be seen even in Negro homes whose occupants were above the lowest poverty level. Comparison was rarely made with the esthetic standards of poor whites, and there were, of course, many Negroes who kept spotlessly clean and tidy homes. Yet the evidence of Negro sloven-liness was sufficient to sustain a damaging image. In the ominous problem of residential segregation, it contributed significantly to the fear among whites that once Negroes came their neighborhood would run down.

The supreme indictment of Negroes, however, was found in the statistics of crime and illegitimacy. Carleton Putnam, at the time the most conspicuous intellectual champion of racism in the United States, was able to cite reports of the National Office of Vital Statistics and the Federal Bureau of Investigation for his statement: "The American Negro on the average produces 10 times as many illegitimate children, six times as many feeble-minded adults, nine times as many robberies, seven times as many rapes and 10 times as many murders as the white man."

Official statistics, based on court convictions or jail commitments, gave an exaggerated picture of Negro crime as compared with crime among whites. Negroes were far more likely to be arrested and sent to jail than whites for similar conduct. In the South, crimes of white men against Negroes were often ignored by law enforcement authorities; a score of Negroes had been murdered in recent years apparently by white men, without a single conviction. But few denied that the actual crime rate in the nation was substantially higher among Negroes than among whites. In a *United States News and World Report* interview of October 21, 1963, Chief of Police Robert V. Murray of the District of Columbia (where Negroes represented 60 per cent of the population) was asked: "Is there any connection between the increase in the

Negro population in D.C. and the increase in crime?" Murray replied: "I would say, very frankly, that 85 per cent of the serious crimes in Washington are committed by Negroes. . . ."

In the matter of Negro children born out of wedlock, the sad facts were not exaggerated—and this evil was worsening. In 1936, 16.2 per cent of reported nonwhite births were illegitimate, compared with 2 per cent of white births; in 1940, nonwhite illegitimacy was down to 13.7 per cent. But in 1964, 24 per cent of all nonwhite births were illegitimate, while only 2.5 per cent of white children were born out of wedlock. This was not, however, a true measure of relative sexual promiscuity. Whites were more familiar with contraceptive devices and more likely to resort to abortion— or to marry—when pregnancy occurred. Many children of Negro women born out of wedlock had white fathers. Nevertheless, marital instability and the multitude of illegitimate children were there, causing distress for Negroes which went far beyond the question of the good opinion of whites.

Going a step further in an area widely considered improper for public inspection, it is to be noted that venereal disease was far more common among Negroes than among whites. The highest rate of reported venereal disease cases among the nation's larger cities was to be found in Washington, D.C.—which had the highest percentage of Negroes in its population. Among white Washingtonians venereal disease cases reported in 1964 were 21.7 per 100,-000; among nonwhite residents the rate was 107.1 per 100,000. (In New York and Baltimore the nonwhite rate was higher, but the larger proportion of white residents brought the averages down.)

Carl Rowan, a Negro in high public office in 1964, had written in 1960: "Perhaps the most serious and valid charge against Negro leaders is that they have been too 'hush-hush' where embarrassing problems like crime and delinquency are concerned. . . ." "Reform" is a word never spoken in revolutions. Every effort was being made to inspire the Negro with pride in his race, to encourage him to hold his head high and insist upon his rights. It seemed no time for Negroes to talk about Negro shortcomings. Moreover, preaching Negro self-improvement would sound like acceptance of the threadbare white excuse for discrimination: "Let Negroes wait until they have *earned* equality." Civil-rights leaders feared that efforts in this direction would destroy their effectiveness and take the fire out of the Negro revolt. No militant Negro organization was prepared to raise a banner of moral rehabilitation—unless it was the fantastic Black Muslim cult. Scorn for the white man and unbridled execration of the "white devils" protected Muslim leaders from any suspicion of weakness when they preached clean living, self-discipline, and decorum, along with thrift and hard work—as they did, with remarkable success among a small band of disciples.

In such dismaying proportions, the evils were obviously the result of generations of oppression. Just over a century earlier most American Negroes had been in a condition in which they were encouraged to multiply and were denied the luxury of marriage or monogamy. The recent increase in illegitimacy reflected the demoralizing environment of big city ghettos (where the rate was much higher than the average elsewhere). The heaviest blame was justifiably placed at the white man's door. But the evils were there. They cried out for attention, for Negro attention; and many sympathetic whites thought Negro leaders were not showing the necessary concern.

The bluntness with which the unsavory facts are reported above was rare in any but the most violently anti-Negro literature. However, the matter of Negro initiative in raising the level of the backward in all aspects, social, educational, and economic, was the subject of voluminous controversy in 1964. The exhortation came mainly from the white side; Negroes generally were on the defensive, or too full of resentment of wrongs done by whites to listen to any aspersions from white critics.

Many white writers approached the problem with careful tact. John D. Rockefeller III, whose family had made immense contributions to Negro causes, called young Negroes to "the role of the statesman who succeeds the revolutionary." In an address in ceremonies marking the eighty-third anniversary of Spelman College, he told Negro students: "Now fast-changing circumstances summon you to progress beyond protest, to capitalize upon what protest has bought, to make safe and secure what is so newly won." Daniel Bell, in the *New York Times Magazine* of May 31, referred to the high illegitimacy rate, among other problems, and urged "a new phase in which the resources of the Negro community are turned inward." John Fischer, editor of *Harper's*, incorporated in a book, *The Stupidity Problem*, his July, 1962, article in that magazine in which he urged a Negro movement "not merely to win the full rights which belong to every American, but to make sure that these rights are used—that the average Negro is willing and able to carry the full responsibilities of good citizenship."

There was perhaps no better exhibit of the diversity of white and Negro opinions on this subject than that offered by Eric Hoffer's article in the *New York Times Magazine* of November 29, 1964, entitled "The Negro Is Prejudiced Against Himself"—and the hornet's nest of reactions which it stirred. Hoffer was unmerciful. He could not think of "another instance where a minority striving for equality has been so deficient in the capacity of mutual aid and cooperation," and he leveled this cruel blow: "The Negro seems to say: 'Lift up my arms. I am an abandoned and abused child. Adopt me as your favorite son. Feed me, clothe me, educate me, love and baby me. You must do this right away or I shall set your house on fire, or rot at your doorsteps and poison the air you breathe.' "*

Two weeks later the magazine devoted four pages to letters from Hoffer readers. A majority of them, apparently from Negroes, ranged from mild dissent to foaming indignation; a few writers, including at least one Negro, applauded.

Al Capp wrote of the Hoffer article: "It says out loud what most of America is saying through clenched teeth." Another apparently white observer wrote: "If the white community persists in thinking of the Negro as a stereotype (uneducable, prone to crime . . .) it is not an image pulled out of thin air. Statistics . . . regrettably reinforce this belief." And a third: "Mr. Hoffer's important contribution would have gained much in practical usefulness if it had been infused with a little more warmth and plain sympathy for the difficult tasks facing the American Negro."

The NAACP's Roy Wilkins wrote in part:

> Treatises are pouring from the presses with the observations of white commentators who discovered the race question when the sit-ins hit the front pages in 1960 or when a James Baldwin piece shook them in 1963.
> Now comes Eric Hoffer . . . to tell 20,000,000 black Americans that

* Copyright 1964 by the New York Times Company. Reprinted by permission.

what they need is bootstrap group salvation, with a touch of Black Muslim cultism and a dash of self-segregation.

In the course of arriving at this conclusion he reveals a vast ignorance of the history of the Negro movement as well as of the social, political and economic forces which have fashioned the pattern of race relations in the United States. . . .

Oliver Leeds, a CORE official in Brooklyn, protested: "There is not a Negro community in America which does not have societies and churches which, in addition to their specific aims or religious activities, also have youth programs, day nurseries, parochial schools and even scholarship programs."

Paul Spencer, of Staten Island, N.Y., neatly divided responsibilities. "The task confronting the American Negro today," he wrote, "is that of building a cooperative, self-respecting Negro community; the task confronting the white man is to make reparation."

The following remarks in letters apparently from Negroes were also illuminating:

"Mr. Hoffer knows what he is talking about and, for the most part, says what some of us know but dare not express for fear of being called 'Uncle Tom'. . . ."

"The words and acts of the Negro leaders are and have been directed—but correctly so—to non-Negro America. When this victory is won, there will be opportunity as well as ample time, energy, funds and incentive to concentrate exclusively on bootstrapping."

"Let us build hospitals for those who need them; let us root out ghetto slums and slums everywhere; let us do all these things. But let us also ask 'mass movement analysers' like Mr. Hoffer not to preach to us through blind mouths."

The public discussion tended to overlook the fact that criminals, delinquents, and unwed mothers were after all only a small minority of the Negro Americans. Moreover, the detachment of successful Negroes from the miseries of the less fortunate, marked though it often was in the urban slums, was not a characteristic of the nationwide Negro community; and charges of leadership indifference to Negro family life and morals were unjust. No less than their white counterparts, Negro pastors preached righteousness and clean living, and ministered to the poor and afflicted. In not a few Negro neighborhoods, churchmen and others labored with solicited white help and their own modest resources to provide community centers and facilities for wholesome recreation—as in the South, half a century earlier, many had labored to provide the only Negro high schools.

In rare instances Negroes organized "clean-up" campaigns, like one in a Negro neighborhood of Hagerstown, Maryland, in July, in which 160 truckloads of debris were hauled away. The Negro organization, Harlem Youth Opportunities Unlimited (HAR-YOU), which merged in July with Associated Community Teams, Incorporated (ACT), struggled after a fashion with the problems of Harlem. At times of alarming crime waves in New York, Washington, and elsewhere—in which Negro criminals were conspicuous—Negro leaders joined others and sometimes took the lead in expressing concern. In June the Negro clergymen of the Ministers' Movement of Brooklyn and Long Island issued a statement calling for "a concerted effort on the part of the clergy and law enforcement agencies to use every resource available (except brutality) to transform the immoral image of our city into one of moral concern and mutual good will."

But the crusade was for "Freedom Now." Adam Clayton Powell said the Negro had no other responsibility now but to "quicken the white man's responsibility into action . . . —not all this business of fixing up your house," etc. Bayard Rustin's view, as he expressed it in a planning session for a report to President Johnson in November, 1965, was: "The answer to this problem is not to give the impoverished masses of the black ghetto sermons about middle-class virtues. It is to give them jobs and decent integrated housing and schools."

Martin Luther King said enough about "raising the moral and cultural climate in our Negro neighborhoods" to identify such preaching in the minds of many civil-rights workers as the King doctrine. "Even the most poverty-stricken among us," he had written, "can purchase a 10-cent bar of soap; even the most uneducated among us can have high morals." But the overriding thrust of King's mighty eloquence was a call to battle (nonviolent battle) for Negro rights. CORE and SNCC were wholly dedicated to that fight. Their members engaged in rehabilitation and educational work in preparing the more backward Negroes in the South to register and vote, but such activities were incidental.

Whitney Young summed up the objectives of the National

Urban League as "(1) to help wipe out the last vestiges and barriers of discrimination and (2) to assist Negro citizens to rise through self-qualification until they can achieve status of first-class citizenship not only in name but in fact." But now, with the revolution in full swing, the emphasis on the first of these all but obscured the second.

Assistant Director John A. Morsell of the NAACP outlined the activities and objectives of that organization in an article in the January 1965 issue of the *Annals of the American Academy of Political and Social Science*. They did not include the promotion of Negro self-help; but he noted that the Association expected to "expand its program to include active concern with problems of poverty, retraining and community orientation." He concluded with the observation that "emergence into an integrated society imposes certain demands and obligations upon a Negro community which in some respects has been ill-prepared by segregation to assume them. Here, too," he said, "the Association will find additional challenges and will seek new remedies."

EIGHT

School Boycotts
and Violence
1964

The revolution in the streets rolled on. New direct action ideas abounded, but the Negro protest found its most spectacular expression in the public school boycott. All other activities of Negro militants outside of the South were overshadowed during the early months of 1964 by the demand for a redistribution of public school pupils to accomplish racial integration. School authorities faced not only picketing, sit-ins, boycotts, and some physical obstruction from the Negro side but a rising movement of white parents who insisted that children should continue to attend the schools nearest their homes. Controversy and tension in this connection continued intermittently throughout the year.

The boycotts themselves were generally carried out in an orderly manner, but some violence erupted in the course of picketing and in attempts to stop the construction of new schools that threatened to perpetuate the segregation pattern. One such attempt produced a tragedy which added a white clergyman to the list of the revolution's martyrs. In Cleveland, Ohio, on April 7, the Reverend Bruce William Klunder, a twenty-seven-year-old Presbyterian minister, was crushed to death under a bulldozer preparing for the erection of a new school in Glenville, a predominantly Negro neighborhood. The minister had thrown himself on the ground behind the bulldozer when the machine was moving in reverse to avoid three other demonstrators who were lying in front of it, and the driver did not see him.

The school was one of three projected in Cleveland's Glenville district, where a shortage of classrooms had led to the assignment of a number of Negro children to predominantly white schools elsewhere. Since the Cleveland board of education was firmly committed to the principle of the neighborhood school, Negroes had reason to fear that Glenville school expansion was part of a plan to bring these pupils back and tighten segregation in ghetto schools. About 150 white Protestant ministers and rabbis supported the Negro protest. Earlier demonstrators had fought policemen (who arrested four of them) while trying to keep a cement mixer away from the construction site. After the Klunder tragedy a thousand demonstrators rioted, throwing stones, bottles, and other objects, until mounted policemen forced the crowd to disperse.

Public school boycotts were a form of civil disobedience. They involved wholesale violation of compulsory attendance laws and laws against inducing children to stay away from school, though little or no attempt was made to prosecute the offenders. From a practical point of view, the school boycott was the easiest means yet found to produce a massive public gesture. It was not hard to persuade school children to take a holiday, and the operation did not require adult breadwinners to take a day from their work. Then too the boycott was much more than a protest over the racial situation in schools. It was an opportunity to shake up the white power structure and let off steam over the whole matter of the Negro's inferior status. How many participants fully understood or subscribed to the boycott's specific objective is problematical. A substantial number of Negroes preferred their neighborhood schools. Among other reasons, some parents did not relish the idea of their children spending hours on school buses that could be spent, especially in the case of the older youngsters, in baby-sitting or other household chores. But the boycott was a part of the revolution, and few Negroes could refuse a call to battle for "Freedom Now."

The most spectacular of the school boycotts—helping to stimulate a rash of boycotts in other cities during the winter and spring —was that in New York on February 3, when 364,000 pupils (in addition to the 100,000 normally absent) stayed out of school for one day. The chief architect of this mammoth gesture was the Reverend Milton A. Galamison, the forty-year-old Negro pastor of a Presbyterian church in Brooklyn, who was chairman of the Citywide Committee for Integrated Schools. This irrepressible clergyman—an accomplished pianist who liked to play Chopin, an avid reader with a preference for Ibsen and T. S. Eliot, and a father who sent his own son to a private school—had made the attack upon de facto public school segregation his specialty and had ridden this wave to national prominence as a Negro leader.

The boycott was orderly and peaceful. Bayard Rustin directed operations, with the kind of efficiency that he displayed in the March on Washington. "I picked him," Galamison said, "because he is without exception the best civil-rights organizer in the country." The NAACP, CORE, the Parents' Workshop, the Harlem Parents Committee, and other groups worked together under the coordination of the Citywide Committee—with misgivings in some quarters, but in apparent harmony. Puerto Ricans also participated, rallied by a newly-formed National Association for Puerto Rican Civil Rights. (Puerto Ricans suffered much of the same kind of segregation and discrimination as Negroes, but they were cautious about identification with the Negro movement. Newspapers frequently gave them a third classification, referring to "whites," "Negroes," and "Puerto Ricans"; but by the 1960 census 97 per cent of New York's Puerto Ricans were white. Individual Puerto Ricans were able to move with less difficulty than Negroes into the mainstream.) The 2,600 pickets were courteous and disciplined; no effort was made to interfere with pupils or teachers who entered the schools; the heavily deployed police had little to do. The power of the Negro minority to disrupt a major activity of a great city was impressively demonstrated. In the opinion of many, the affair was a resounding success.

Disapproval among whites was widespread, but so was an awakening to the magnitude of Negro unrest. School authorities were spurred to give increased attention both to the integration problem and to the quality of education in Negro neighborhoods (which many considered more important). Dr. Kenneth B. Clark, professor of psychology at City College and an intellectual leader of the Negro movement, disapproved of Galamison's demands in New

York, but he said: "One must face the fact that Mr. Galamison has had more impact than all the previous years of patient, reasoned, factual study." Rustin, in a moment of elation over his accomplishment, said: "I think we are on the threshold of a new political movement—and I do not mean it in a party sense—that is going to change the face of New York in housing, in jobs and in schools."

On February 25, Chicago experienced its second public school boycott, but only 172,000 pupils stayed out of school this time, fewer than in the boycott of the previous October, when the figure was 225,000. (There were 470,000 pupils in the Chicago school system, and normal daily absenteeism accounted for 50,000.) Most of the Negro politicians in Chicago, including Representative William L. Dawson, were opposed to this boycott. The direct clash was more with the Democratic city hall machine than with the board of education. The latter commissioned a group of educators to study the problem and make recommendations, but Benjamin Willis, the general superintendent of schools, remained a symbol of the status quo, loath to make any concession to Negro demands.

Boston had its second school boycott on February 26 (its first was in June, 1963), when 25,571 pupils stayed out of school. In Boston, as in New York and Chicago, a sprinkling of white liberals participated in the boycott movement or served as teachers in so-called "Freedom Schools." It was customary on a boycott day to hold "Freedom Schools," in which small groups of children were instructed in civil rights, Negro history, and like subjects. In Boston some 1,500 whites marched from State House to City Hall, carrying placards, one of which read: "Harvard Divinity School for Boston and the Boycott." A thousand students from Wellesley College and Boston University were among the "Freedom School" teachers.

Galamison's prestige declined after the New York boycott of February 3. With his insistence upon a precipitate and chaotic reshuffling of the city's school children, he found himself increasingly isolated from national civil-rights leaders. Galamison demanded complete integration of the city's schools—high schools by the following September and elementary schools by September, 1965. He had said that if something of the sort were not done, the public school system should be destroyed. "Maybe it has run its course anyway," he said. While school authorities studied limited and gradual integration plans, Galamison set about organizing a second boycott.

The NAACP had labored long in the vineyard of public school integration in North and South; in negotiations, picketing, court action, and support of boycotts, it had moved against de facto segregation in 81 school systems in 17 states. The NAACP parted company now with Galamison's group, and the Urban League let it be known that it would not support the second boycott. CORE called for a new coordinating organization in which Galamison would be replaced. The Puerto Ricans also withheld their support. And Bayard Rustin was not available to direct the second operation. Extremists were conspicuous among those who gathered around Galamison now—including paradoxically, and embarrassingly, the Black Muslim leader Malcolm X. Congressman Adam Clayton Powell gave his "complete support." When the boycott took place on March 16, only 168,024 (in addition to the normal 100,000 absentees) responded to Galamison's call. Powell denounced "ivory tower" Negro leaders and charged James Farmer (CORE), Roy Wilkins (NAACP), and others with having "sold us out."

This agitation over de facto school segregation was frowned upon by many whites who sympathized with other phases of the Negro revolt. Representative Emanuel Celler of Brooklyn, a leader in the fight for civil-rights legislation in Congress, accused Galamison of "nihilism." He coupled him with Malcolm X as doing a "disservice" to the civil-rights movement. Politically, division on the complicated problem of de facto school segregation was on the oversimplified issue of "busing." Should children be transported by buses away from their neighborhood schools? Nearly all white politicians said no. When in the fall, Robert F. Kennedy ran against Republican incumbent Kenneth B. Keating—both conspicuous supporters of civil-rights legislation—for election to the Senate from New York, both declared their opposition to long-distance bus transportation to promote racial integration in public schools.

Among a large element of white school patrons, opposition to "busing" was intense. Many objected to any departure from the rule that children should attend the school nearest their homes. Introducing Negro children into white schools they considered bad, sending white children to Negro schools intolerable. School officials who resisted Negro pressure often found their popularity among whites enhanced. Chicago's Superintendent Willis was fortified in his intransigence by strong white support. Mrs. Louise D. Hicks, chairman of the Boston School Committee, opposed "busing" and stood fast for the neighborhood school. She had been re-elected by a handsome majority in 1963. She was re-elected again in 1965 by a landslide, and the one member of her committee who favored desegregation was defeated.

Organizations to preserve the neighborhood school began to appear in 1963; in 1964 they were to be found in virtually every city where de facto school segregation was under attack. The two largest were in New York: the Parents and Taxpayers Coordinating Council, better known at PAT, formed in September, 1963, and the Joint Council for Better Education, which came into being in January, 1964. Together they professed to represent some 160 organizations of various kinds with aggregate membership of about one million. In March they sponsored a march on the Board of Education offices and City Hall in which more than 10,000 whites braved sleet and bitter cold to protest pupil transfer plans. In July PAT presented a petition said to contain 42,749 signatures, calling for a referendum on city legislation to preserve the neighborhood school; this was rejected on grounds of miscount and invalid signatures.

White protagonists of the neighborhood school engaged in picketing and other forms of protest—even school boycotts. In a few instances, in scuffles with police, angry white parents resorted to violence. In September, a boycott promoted by the two white organizations took more pupils out of school than Galamison's second undertaking had done. The pro-neighborhood-school demonstrations were the more significant in that the white participants did not, like the Negro demonstrators, have the incitement of a whole bundle of ancient and modern grievances.

In a number of instances in various cities, white parents sought the intervention of the courts to prevent the transfer of pupils to accomplish racial integration. Although these efforts were sometimes successful on the first round, they failed on appeal to higher courts. Rulings of the latter were generally similar to that of the Court of Appeals of New York in the case of *Balaban v. Rubin,* which was upheld, in effect, by the United States Supreme Court. Parents of two white children had brought a class suit to annul a zoning determination of the New York board of education that excluded their children from the neighborhood school and placed them in a new junior high school, zoned to give it a balanced enrollment of Negroes, Puerto Ricans, and other whites. A trial court in September, 1963, granted the desired judgment on the ground that a New York law prohibited "exclusion from public schools of any child by reason of race, creed, color or national origin." The Appellate Division, to which the case came next, found in March, 1964, that such a construction of the New York law was the opposite of its purpose, and reversed the judgment. On May 7 the New York Court of Appeals, affirming the ruling of the Appellate Division, declared the issue to be simply that of: "May the schools correct racial imbalance?"—and concluded that they may. The Supreme Court in October denied *certiorari.* The high tribunal— which had indicated in the Gary, Indiana, case mentioned earlier that public school authorities were not compelled to correct racial imbalance caused by residential segregation—thus made it clear that school authorities were not *prohibited* from taking steps to that end.

An underlying embarrassment in all the argument over de facto school segregation was the fact that people were not talking about the basic problem. All of the parties to the controversy had some merit in their diverse contentions, but nearly all were dealing with an effect rather than with the cause. One of the few exceptions was Dr. Aaron Brown, the one Negro member of the New York board of education. Brown wanted a committee of city officials to "map out a plan to get rid of *de facto* segregation in *housing.*" "Until we get rid of segregated housing," he said, "the problem will be too great for us to bear."

Until Negroes should cease to be segregated in ghettos and be free to find homes wherever they could afford them, it was grotesquely unrealistic to think of distributing Negro school children more or less evenly across a big city. But there was no place in that truth for lofty assurance on either side. If Negroes were asking the impossible, whites were refusing to do what was possible and clearly right—allow Negroes to reside among them. Having no hope of escaping residential segregation in the foreseeable future, Negroes attacked the school segregation that stemmed from it— and in fact tended to perpetuate it. Segregated and generally inferior Negro schools helped to make white families avoid the ghetto. Meanwhile, public school authorities made limited but increasing concessions to Negro demands, strove to calm protesting whites, made some improvements in Negro schools, and prayed that some miracle would cause the agitation to subside.

New York's experience invites particular attention since, in the nation's largest city, and its largest concentration of Negro population, every form of agitation, every point of view, and every approach to the problem was to be found. For five years the New York school authorities had been making cautious pupil placement changes with an eye to improving racial balance, although the aggregate dent made in their million-pupil school system was small. By January, 1964, a hundred alterations had been made in district and school zones, and 16,000 Negro children had been moved to integrated situations under an Open Enrollment program.

The board of education, impatient with the planning of Superintendent Calvin E. Gross, held hearings on its own, and on January 29 (in hope of staving off the first boycott) it called for the application of the Princeton Plan to 60 schools: 30 predominantly white schools to be paired with 30 predominantly Negro schools. In each pair all the pupils in certain grades would attend one school together; those in other grades would attend the other school. On through the second boycott, in March, the board and superintendent continued studying possible plans. (The number of contemplated school pairings was shrinking, however, under pressure from white parents.)

Four days after the first boycott, the board sought guidance from State Education Commissioner James E. Allen, Jr., and the latter set up a committee of scholars and educators, including Dr. Kenneth Clark, to aid him in studying the problem. On May 12 this committee's conclusions were announced in what became known as the Allen Plan. The report was critical of the board of education: "Nothing undertaken by the New York City Board of

Education since 1954, and nothing proposed since 1963, has contributed or will contribute in any meaningful degree to desegregating the public schools of the city."

The report was also disappointing to some Negro leaders in two respects. It retreated from Allen's earlier definition of an "unbalanced" school as one with enrollment more than 50 per cent Negro or Puerto Rican, and fixed the proportion determining a "segregated" school at more than 90 per cent. It also declared flatly that "total desegregation of all schools . . . is simply not attainable in the foreseeable future and neither planning nor pressure can change that fact." But the Allen Plan delighted most Negroes. Even Galamison said it was "a giant step in the right direction." Six days later the NAACP and CORE sponsored a rally at City Hall to urge the plan's adoption.

Here was a masterly plan, though ambitious and costly, to provide better education for all the city's children. The neighborhood school concept was retained for primary schools, which would include only the first four grades; but, above the fourth grade, students would be widely redistributed and racially intermingled. "Middle schools," carrying pupils through the eighth grade, would be placed in biracial areas, and four-year comprehensive high schools would be constructed to be open to all students on a city-wide basis. As a totally new addition, the primary school experience was to be preceded by one or two years of nursery school —a particularly needed lift for children from impoverished homes. It was estimated that the changes would add $250 million to the city's $800-million school budget. As the New York *Herald Tribune* observed, all this was "obviously a long way off, even if the city, state and federal governments were willing to rush in with the money." And much of it was "perhaps impractical." But the best hope was "to reorganize and start anew for educational excellence."

On May 28 the board of education announced its plan for the school term beginning in September. It retained a remnant of the pairing program and drew cautiously on the Allen Plan. Eight schools were to be paired, involving the transfer of some 1,200 pupils. Eight junior high schools were to be rezoned to reduce the racial imbalance at three of them. Four thousand, five hundred ninth-grade children were to be taken from 10 largely Negro and

Puerto Rican high schools and distributed among 36 integrated high schools. Kindergartens were to be expanded at 18 schools and prekindergarten classes were to be established at 23.

PAT was "shocked" at this announcement, and the whole movement to stop the erosion of the neighborhood school gathered momentum. Most Negroes shared the feeling of Galamison, who now was "happy to see signs of motion at the board of education." On June 18 the seven leading organizations fighting de facto segregation agreed to support the board of education for the coming year —with an understanding that the door would be open for negotiation on future plans. For the next three months the pressure on the school board came mainly from white defenders of the status quo.

When New York's public schools opened on September 14, 1964, in the new placement pattern, 17,000 pupils, mostly Negroes and Puerto Ricans, changed schools. But arrangements were hampered for two days by a crowning gesture of protest from the champions of the neighborhood school. In a boycott sponsored by PAT and the Joint Council for Better Schools, 133,306 pupils stayed out of school on September 14, and on the next day 175,638 were absent (in addition to the 100,000 normal absentees). However, the board of education took this in its stride; Superintendent Gross said the boycott would not affect school integration plans.

Other phases of the revolution were taking a more obstreperous and irresponsible turn. Extremists moved increasingly into the limelight. The established civil-rights leaders—powerful in national political councils, trusted by Negroes in the South and influential among the Negro middle class across the country—found their influence limited in the big city slums of the North and West. In these, new leaders and more reckless tactics emerged.

In late February, in a drive to induce three Lucky food stores in San Francisco and nearby Berkeley to employ more Negroes, a new technique appeared. It was called the "shop-in." Negroes would enter the supermarket, fill shopping carts with groceries, take them to the check-out counters and allow the seeming purchases to be rung up on cash registers. Then the Negroes would walk out, leaving chaotic piles of groceries behind. The loss to the stores in manhours, spoilage, and breakage in returning the groceries to their shelves was considerable.

The shop-in ended in a few days. The store managers wisely refused to call in the police. They insisted they were employing many Negroes and said they intended to hire more. As usual in the case of extremist tactics, not only whites but many Negroes in San Francisco were displeased. The president of the Baptist Ministers Union, representing the largest Negro group in the city, threatened to break the unified civil-rights front if the shop-in continued. A local Negro newspaper, the *Bay Area Independent*, called it a "malicious idea."

About the same time, tactics in a campaign to increase employment of Negroes by San Francisco hotels were also condemned by many Negroes as well as whites. Though this affair was engineered by Negroes, whites—reflecting the propensity of California youth to demonstrate for interesting causes—were more numerous than Negroes among the participants. Twelve hundred shouting pickets linked arms and blocked all entrances to a downtown hotel; hundreds conducted a sit-in in the lobby of another. One hundred and sixty-seven were arrested before an agreement was finally reached, which a spokesman for the Hotel Employers Association said only reaffirmed "a position we have maintained over the years." However, the hotels agreed to attempt to have from 15 to 20 per cent of their staffs from minority groups by July 20.

Demonstrators, urging more state legislation banning discrimination in places of public accommodation, introduced something new in lobbying. A group in Lexington, invoking the memory of Gandhi, sat-in and fasted for several days in the Kentucky House of Representatives (which adjourned a few days later without taking the desired action). In Phoenix—Senator Goldwater's capital— a line of screaming pickets blocked the entrances to the Arizona State Senate, preventing the exit of senators until the pickets were removed by highway patrolmen.

New York saw a rash of gestures directed not at specific parties with power to deal with specific grievances, but at the general public. For instance, on March 6 thousands of New York rush-hour motorists were delayed twenty minutes by pickets who linked arms to block traffic on Triborough Bridge—until they were dispersed and half a dozen of them were arrested by police. The announced purpose of this was to call attention "to the need of better schools, housing and jobs for Negroes." Demonstrators also dumped piles of garbage on the bridge—as a symbol of conditions in Harlem.

Such performances inconvenienced not only the indifferent and the prejudiced, but liberals and friends of the Negro movement. They were frowned upon by most Negro leaders of stature, whose attitude was typified by Roy Wilkins, the staunchly level-headed leader of the NAACP. Wilkins condemned tactics "not directed at the persons responsible for conditions but at the general public," but he pointed to the national failure to move effectively against the wrongs which Negroes suffered, and said: "So the frustrated ones strike at government and the people in senseless, but understandable blows at everyone. The lesson is that, if we don't have more sense on one side, we are going to have more senselessness on the other."

The World's Fair, scheduled to open in New York on April 22, offered a tempting opportunity to make an impression on the millions watching its progress or expecting to visit it. On April 4 seventy-five pickets sitting, kneeling, and lying in the street blocked trucks making deliveries to the fair grounds, until police intervened. They said they had no quarrel with the fair, but wished to focus attention on the need for more school integration. Among those arrested was the Reverend Milton Galamison.

The Brooklyn chapter of CORE was planning a far more spectacular exploit—a "stall-in" to block major approaches to the fair on opening day. It hoped to have hundreds of autos run out of gasoline by design in the midst of congested fair-going traffic. Before that threat was fully grasped by the public, the metropolis was shocked by another proposal. On April 13 Brooklyn CORE announced a contemplated water-wasting campaign—in the event the stall-in "should fail to produce an immediate working plan on housing, schools, employment and police brutality." CORE supporters would be asked to open their faucets and let the water run. A spokesman for the Department of Water Supply, Gas and Electricity said there was "plenty of water on hand," reservoirs being at 81.5 per cent of capacity. Had the suggestion been made during the water shortage a year later, the public wrath can only be imagined. As it was, the idea met with quick condemnation nearly everywhere, and the plan was dropped before the day was over. But the stall-in project persisted.

All this was embarrassing to what might be called the Negro Establishment. Leaders like Wilkins and King had labored to fire Negroes with the revolutionary spirit, yet they wished to keep the revolution within reasonable and purposeful bounds. Galamison said: "We are not promoting violence. We are preventing violence in that if people do not have some healthy outlet to express their frustration there will be violence." That was the movement's philosophy in principle, but opinions differed sharply as to the "healthy outlet." Rebellion against the Big Five civil-rights leaders flared in many quarters. Fortunately, however, for the country and for the Negro cause, these remarkably sane and high-minded men survived with their prestige unimpaired.

Rebellion sputtered within the National Baptist Convention, but that five-million-member group remained a bulwark of Negro conservatism. At a meeting in January, attended by 600 members, its executive board overwhelmingly adopted a resolution calling for moderation and "good will," and condemning school boycotts. Its president, Dr. J. H. Jackson, said: "We must keep the struggle within the framework of law and order. . . . The atmosphere has to change, or anarchy awaits us."

Near the opposite pole was ACT (Associated Community Teams). This organization was formed in Washington in April, out of impatience with the Big Five leadership's preoccupation with the pending civil-rights bill and its "anxiety to please the white community." One of ACT's spokesmen, Nahaz Rogers, declared: "The old line of making the Negro revolution acceptable by the guide-lines of deportment and graciousness that are acceptable to the white community are gone. . . . ACT will not function in a manner that is acceptable to white people. It will do things that are acceptable to Negroes."

The idea of burning bridges of cooperation with whites had many advocates, including Adam Clayton Powell. But the regular civil-rights organizations embraced many white crusaders and leaned heavily upon white financial support. They wanted more of both. "We must speed up progress," CORE's James Farmer said, "to avoid the polarization of white and black that can only hurt our nation. Polarization would be the greatest crime of all. One-tenth of the population cannot win this fight. . . ."

Farmer was in a particularly difficult position, since he had become a symbol of intrepid defiance of racist bullies in the South and CORE was generally in the front line of Negro militancy. CORE members now were getting into all manner of extremist undertakings against his wishes and against the policy of the national organization. The Brooklyn chapter of CORE was a hotbed of rebellion. In January Brooklyn CORE had threatened to "bring New York to a complete standstill through techniques of massive civil disobedience," though this idea faded quickly under Farmer's stern disapproval. Brooklyn CORE had supported the second school boycott in defiance of its national headquarters. "In recent months," the *New York Times* reported, "Brooklyn CORE has often seemed closer to the Reverend Dr. Galamison than to its national leaders." National CORE turned thumbs down on the World's Fair stall-in, and Brooklyn CORE was suspended from the organization. At a meeting of the American Society of Newspaper Editors in Washington on April 16, not only Farmer, but Roy Wilkins of the NAACP, Whitney Young of the Urban League, and John Lewis of SNCC expressed disapproval of the stall-in—though all emphasized the Negro's desperate need and his "growing frustration, anger, militancy."

The Negro writer Louis Lomax, one of the most perceptive interpreters of the Negro revolution, addressing a group of Negro professional women in New York, declared: "Wild, new, strange voices have moved into the leadership vacuum and we are headed for bloodshed and chaos." He blamed the situation on the failure of whites to act on the more decorous Negro protests. Explaining what he meant by the "leadership vacuum," he said: "Roy Wilkins failed, James Farmer failed, Martin Luther King failed, Whitney Young failed. And Lyndon Baines Johnson failed. What must we do? To what extreme will we be pushed?"

Outbreaks of uncontrolled violence in the streets of Negro ghettos were predicted. In fact, they had been predicted so long and so often by so many Negro leaders that the general surprise when they came in July and August to New York, Rochester, Philadelphia, and other cities—and a year later to Los Angeles—was an indication of how few whites were listening to what Negroes were saying.

The World's Fair stall-in proved a failure. But for a week it held the attention of the nation as no other civil-rights demonstration since the March on Washington. New York awaited the fair's open-

ing day, Wednesday, April 22, with extraordinary apprehension.
For a few days the threat of chaotic turmoil in the streets overshadowed all other news of the great exposition. "CORE's 2,800
CARS FOR WEDNESDAY," the *Herald Tribune* headlined, and the
Times: "TIE-UP ON SUBWAY AND TICKET LINES AT FAIR PLANNED."
The project expanded. Sit-ins and lie-ins were scheduled as additional obstructions on bridge, tunnel, and expressway. Emergency
cords were to be pulled to stop subway trains. Visiting stall-in
motorists were "expected" from cities as far away as San Francisco.

But it all came to naught, or nearly so. The reasons can be
summed up in the storm of public disapproval, the negative pressure of CORE leadership, a court restraining order, and the heaviest concentration of traffic policemen in New York's history—900
on foot, 200 on motorcycles. Police cars and tow trucks waited
at frequent intervals along Grand Central Parkway and at every
80 yards on Triborough Bridge. A rainy day tended to further
dampen stall-in ardor. Only twelve cars reported for stall-in duty,
and only one or two actually got into car trouble. With a few
scattered exceptions, the other traffic harassments also failed to
materialize.

Incidentally, the fiasco represented a victory of CORE regulars
over the rebels. A serious schism had developed over the stall-in
initiative, for it appealed not only to the Brooklyn chapter, but to
many CORE members throughout the city. In proof of its own un-
faltering militancy, the national CORE leadership scheduled conventional demonstrations inside the fair grounds—at the federal
pavilion and at the pavilions of some states regarded as hostile to
Negro aspirations. These demonstrators were boisterous to a degree
that aroused much criticism. Pickets shouting "Freedom now!"
almost drowned out the voice of the President of the United States
in his dedicatory address at the federal pavilion. They were demonstrating, James Farmer said, "to point up the contrast between
the glittering world of fantasy and the real world of brutality, bigotry and poverty that our people have faced in the hundred years
since slavery."

Farmer's personal image as a fearless crusader had also to be
preserved, and this consummate performer met the challenge.
Wired for sound by a television network (a small microphone on
his chest), he sprawled on the sidewalk with his back against one

of the New York City pavilion's entrance doors. It was symbolic, he explained repeatedly, of the way Negroes were blocked from jobs, houses, etc. When the police finally decided to arrest him, he refused a request of detective Chief William Kimmons that he stand up, saying he could not "voluntarily cooperate with . . . injustice." So he was carried bodily to the patrol wagon by police. "Be as gentle with him as you can, men," the chief said. Admiring young CORE members sang:

> Farmer is our leader;
> We shall not be moved.

The cry of "police brutality" was heard after virtually every clash of civil-rights demonstrators with law enforcement. It was a routine complaint of the movement at all levels. Civil-rights leaders urged the appointment of civilian boards to investigate charges of police brutality. Police authorities generally opposed this kind of interference, preferring their own complaint and investigation procedures. The subject gave rise to heated controversy, particularly in New York. Philadelphia, Rochester, Indianapolis, and Trenton had set up such boards—with indifferent success.

Police brutality well described, or understated, the treatment met by Negroes at the hands of the myrmidons of white supremacy in some sections of the South. But elsewhere the charges were often undeserved. Denunciations are all too common and words of praise too rare for these men who daily risk life and limb in the protection of society. According to the Uniform Crime Report, 88 policemen were killed in the line of duty in the United States in 1964; 18,001 were assaulted, 9.9 assaults per 100 officers, and the assaults resulting in injuries totaled 7,738. The months of racial turmoil had placed a heavy new burden on police. They raised baffling problems of how to deal with civil disobedience and demonstrator excesses, and preserve indispensable public order. In recent years the police of every city with a large Negro population had been given special instruction in the racial aspects of law enforcement, with stern cautions against discrimination. A substantial number of Negroes were in police uniform. Police force administrators generally strove to eliminate racial bias. Their attitudes ranged from the unimaginative "toughness" of Los Angeles Chief of Police William H. Parker to the wisdom and restraint of New York's Police Commissioner Michael J. Murphy.

But the old pattern of one set of rules for handling Negroes and another for dealing with whites was not soon to be lived down—or, in fact eradicated. Police brutality, though an image imbedded in the consciousness of many Negroes since childhood, was largely a memory of the past. But it was still, in too many cases, an experience of the present. Many white policemen deepdown harbored vestiges of the old feeling about Negroes. Civil-rights demonstrations, moreover, brought on disturbances which tested both the energies and the tempers of the police. Many policemen had sustained injuries in not so nonviolent encounters. Most Negroes hated and distrusted the police (notwithstanding there were many Negroes in police uniform now). The police were the Negro's principal contact with government and white-ruled society, which had mistreated him from time immemorial. Bad blood between Negroes and police was to play a large part in the angry rioting which blazed in eastern cities in the summer of 1964, more frightfully in Los Angeles in August, 1965, and in many cities in subsequent years.

On July 16 a fifteen-year-old Negro boy, James Powell, was shot to death on a Harlem street by an off-duty white police lieutenant, Thomas R. Gilligan. The boy reportedly had lunged at Gilligan with a knife. There was doubt about the judgment of a 200-pound policeman in shooting to kill a 122-pound Negro boy, even if the latter had a knife; but a grand jury, after six weeks of hearings, concluded that Gilligan was not criminally liable for Powell's death. In the meantime Negroes had rioted in seven cities.

Those riots were mild in comparison with the wild rebellion in Los Angeles a year later. The estimates of property damage in the seven cities added up to about $6 million, and five people lost their lives (including three persons killed when a helicopter, in which a civil-defense official was observing the rioting in Rochester, hit the roof of a Negro tenement). In Los Angeles' week of turbulence, the property damage was conservatively estimated at $35 million and the death toll was thirty-four. But the riots of the summer of 1964 shocked the nation and gave concern to a watching world.

Some called them a "setback" for the Negro movement. But they drew urgent attention, for the first time in many quarters, to the intolerable miseries of Negroes in Northern city ghettos. Negroes might say with some truth, "The only way we can make people listen to us is by starting a riot."

The turmoil in Harlem began Saturday night, July 18, following an indignation meeting over the killing of Powell. Within seven hours, Negro mobs were thrashing back and forth through the center of the ghetto, breaking windows, smashing storefronts, looting, and harassing any white civilian in sight. Police swung their night sticks furiously, and fired so many shots into the air that more ammunition had to be rushed from the police pistol range in the Bronx. Something like this went on intermittently for four days. Bricks, bottles, garbage can tops, and other missiles were aimed at police from upper-story windows and roofs. One missile-hurler on a rooftop was shot dead by a policeman—the only fatality; 35 policemen and 81 civilians were seriously injured. The riots elsewhere followed a more or less similar pattern.

Those in Rochester, Paterson, and Philadelphia were also touched off by police-Negro incidents. In all the riots, the police were the rioters' adversaries. Negroes damaged and looted the property of white merchants (few business establishments were owned by Negroes) and manhandled some whites. But, except through the police, the white man did not strike back—a circumstance that distinguished this modern turmoil significantly from the race riots of old, when white mobs wreaked bloody vengeance upon resisting Negroes. These were not melees of white against black. They were simply desperate Negroes on the rampage, with only the police to subdue them at last.

In the predawn hours of July 21 the Harlem violence leaped over the East River to rage intermittently for three days in the Bedford-Stuyvesant ghetto of Brooklyn. This was touched off by a midnight rally of Brooklyn CORE.

Four days later the fiercest rioting of all broke out 378 miles away in the Negro ghetto of Rochester—a New York state city of 318,000—35,000 of them Negroes. In three tumultuous days in Rochester, 350 persons were injured and nearly 1,000 arrested; one white man was killed by Negro youths. Four hundred state troopers reinforced local police and a 1,200-man detachment of the National Guard made a show of force. A curfew was imposed; tear gas and high-pressure hoses were used.

While Rochester was still cleaning up the debris, violence flared across the Hudson from New York in New Jersey—in Jersey City on August 2 and 3, in Elizabeth and Paterson in mid-August. Also in mid-August, rioting came to Chicago, in the suburb of Dixmoor. These were smaller and sooner quelled than the New York and Rochester riots.

Criminal elements were present in all of this turmoil. Semirespectable people could be seen among the looters in the confusion and hysteria, but professional criminals became increasingly aware of the bonanza that riots offered. In the Philadelphia riot, the last of the series, criminals appeared to have a significant hand. The night-long bedlam there on August 28-29 resembled that in Harlem, but the looting was more thorough and lasted many hours after other violence subsided. The Philadelphia police, thanks to planning and study of the riots elsewhere, moved with notable efficiency when their city's riot came. As Mayor James H. J. Tate observed with pride, order was restored on the second day without loss of life and without the use of horses, dogs, tear gas, or firearms. But 248 people, including 66 policemen, had been injured; 289 had been arrested.

In Philadelphia, unlike the other riot cities, local Negro leaders praised the police performance and did not heap blame on white officials. "This was not a spontaneous riot," said the Reverend William H. Gray, a leading Negro minister and executive director of the Police Advisory Board. Cecil B. Moore, president of the Philadelphia branch of the NAACP, said: "I think the police exercised a remarkable degree of restraint."

(It is an interesting commentary on the times that Philadelphia faced a problem that did not immediately confront the other riot-torn cities. Philadelphia was awaiting a visit three days later of the Beatles. Those famous English crooners had a devastating effect upon American young ladies, which often required the attention of hundreds of police. Had the rioting continued, few Philadelphia policemen could have been spared for Beatle duty.)

Civil-rights leaders everywhere deplored the rioting. Roy Wilkins, vacationing in Wyoming when the Harlem violence erupted, said: "I don't care how angry Negroes are . . . , we can't leave [our cause] to the bottle-droppers and rock-throwers"—and hurried back to confer with other leaders in New York. After Rochester, Dr. Eugene T. Reed, president of the New York State NAACP, telegraphed all sixty-one of its local branches, urging action to prevent outbreaks in their communities. Virtually all of the well-known figures in the civil-rights movement condemned the rioting. But most of these leaders were strangers to the typical denizen of a Northern Negro ghetto—or suspect because of their amicable association with powerful whites. Their nonviolent methods had not brought any perceptible relief to ghetto agony. Even James Farmer and Bayard Rustin, who strove tirelessly to calm tempers in Harlem, found themselves in a hostile atmosphere.

Many whites, whose study of the Negro problem was limited to the first paragraphs of sensational newspaper stories, concluded instinctively that the riots were Communist-inspired. In Harlem three radical organizations suspected of riot incitement—the Progressive Labor Movement, the Harlem Defense Council, and the Community Council on Housing—were placed under a court restraining order. The first of these tended to follow the Chinese Communist line. Leaders of the feeble Communist party of the U.S.A. (Russian line) disclaimed any connection with the riots; they said the leaders of the Progressive Labor Movement—"parasites on the Negro freedom movement"—had been expelled from the Communist party. None of these organizations, nor all of them together, were a decisive factor in the Harlem uprising; and investigations failed to reveal systematic Communist stimulation in the others. There were false rumors and inflammatory talk and printed leaflets—traditional riot ingredients, but not underlying causes. Communists, Black Muslims, and miscellaneous extremists had a hand in this mischief.

The whole body of rioters was only a tiny fraction of the Negro population in each instance. Most Negroes watched the excitement from a distance or stayed at home; some went to church and prayed. But a multitude shared the feelings that the few vented in violence.

Only a handful of Frenchmen participated in the storming of the Bastille.

NINE

Revolution in Mississippi
1964

It was still in the South that the revolution had its greatest impact. Until 1963 nearly all the turmoil had been in the South. The 1954 Supreme Court ruling against segregation ushered in a period, varying in duration among the eleven former Confederate states, in which not Negroes only, but civilization suffered. In addition to intensified persecution of Negroes, those years saw history, anthropology, and Christian doctrine distorted to support the segregationist position, electoral contests reduced to competitions in appeals to race prejudice, defiant bravado on the part of politicians, and challenges to the authority of the government of the United States. In most of the South that fever had run its course by 1964; little by little, crisis by crisis, state by state, moderate elements had risen to ascendancy, and the area of the miasma had been reduced to sections of South Carolina, Georgia, Florida, and Louisiana and the states of Alabama and Mississippi. But intolerance, violence, and resistance to change were fiercer than ever as they fell back upon these narrower confines. This area presented a problem unlike any other in the national spectrum.

The "Black Belt" has long been a useful designation for the zone of most stubborn race prejudice. This is the name given to a belt of low-lying country extending in an arc from eastern Virginia through the Carolinas, Georgia, Alabama, Mississippi, and Louisiana to northeast Texas. In an earlier era it had been the location of most of the great multi-slave plantations, and it remained the area of heaviest concentration of Negro population. Whites in the

Black Belt—in 134 counties a minority of the inhabitants—for generations had been reared in the almost religious conviction that the Negroes must be kept down, segregated, and under control. Resistance to change had abated in the upper reaches of the Black Belt with the onward march of the Upper South states, but in the Deep South the Black Belt was still a reliable guide to the most difficult sections.

"Deep South" had become a psychological rather than a strictly geographical designation. Southwestern Texas and southern Florida were deeper south, but no one identified those relatively liberal sections, of small Negro population, with the "Deep South." South Carolina, next to Mississippi the state with the largest proportion of Negroes in its population (39 per cent), had been emphatically "Deep South" in the 1950's, but under a moderate state administration and with industry booming, South Carolina had cleared a number of desegregation hurdles peacefully and—partly because of the lethargy of its Negro leaders—was not now to be classed among the most troublesome states. Georgia, with a population 31 per cent Negro, was a state in which enlightenment and courageous leadership, though in the ascendancy, existed side by side with elements of darkest fanaticism. The incumbent Governor Carl E. Sanders was a liberal, in the Southern sense, and notable strides had been made in breaking down segregation; but large sections of Georgia were still in the grip of prejudice and tension and the state was shamed by the outrages of a flourishing Ku Klux Klan. Louisiana (33 per cent Negro) was more nearly dominated by extremists, though voices of moderation were heard in that state and extensive desegregation has been accomplished in the New Orleans and Baton Rouge areas.

The contiguous states of Alabama and Mississippi formed a special trouble zone. Much of Alabama lay in a particularly backward sector of the Black Belt, though the state had a row of progressive cities across its northern end and relatively tolerant Mobile at its southern extremity. Alabama might have avoided being paired with Mississippi as one of the most difficult states, and might have escaped much distress, were it not for the two recklessly inflammatory governors with whom it had been afflicted since 1958: John Patterson until January, 1963, and, since then, George Wallace. Mississippi (42 per cent Negro) was of all states the most completely in the grip of white supremacy fanaticism.

These Black Belt-Deep South communities were a muddy back-water from the main currents of American thought. What passed for public opinion on the race problem there was a rancid stew of prejudice, misinformation, hate, and paranoia. It started with the premise that Negroes were inferior creatures, who could not be allowed to associate with whites as equals without both racial debasement and danger to public safety. It envisioned white citizens with backs to the wall in defense of "racial integrity" (an expression now preferred to white supremacy) against not only unruly Negroes, but the Supreme Court, the federal government, the national press and television, and national religious leadership—all of which were believed to be dominated by sinister influences, especially Communism. Friendship for Negroes on the part of whites had a suggestion here of immorality, advocacy of equal rights for them an odor of treason. Terrorists charged with revolting crimes against Negroes and white champions of the Negro met with sympathy rather than condemnation from most of the populace.

Whites who dissented from this phantasmagoria suffered in many ways. They were shunned by their neighbors; those in business lost customers and credit facilities; some found life unbearable for themselves or their families and moved away. Nonconformists were under constant surveillance—by miscellaneous busybodies, by the Ku Klux Klan, and by local officials. Alabama and Mississippi had state agencies, called State Sovereignty Commissions, dedicated to the perpetuation of the status quo: state intelligence services spied upon persons showing an interest in the civil-rights movement, whether white or colored, and kept voluminous files.

The scales of justice were weighted heavily on the side of racial intolerance. The prevailing theory of law enforcement, accepted even by intelligent officials, held it to be vital to public peace that Negroes should not be allowed to "provoke the whites." Police activities were directed toward restraining not white assailants, but Negro victims of white attack. Police, while conniving at anti-Negro outrages, were alert to suppress Negro demonstrations. They harassed peaceful civil-rights workers and made wholesale arrests on minor, false, or frivolous charges such as parading without a permit, violation of traffic laws, vagrancy, and immorality. The state and local courts, cooperating routinely, dealt brusquely with Negroes and sent thousands of them to jail. Whites who molested Negroes, if they got into court at all, were seldom punished.

Though many Negroes were known to have been killed by whites, no white man had been convicted of the murder of a Negro in Alabama or Missisippi in the memory of man. For Negroes the "law" was not a source of protection but an instrument of persecution and intimidation.

The sickness in this substantial corner of the nation was worse than most Americans imagined. Frank Trippett, a Mississippi-born associate editor of *Newsweek*, visiting his home state, found himself handicapped in giving the picture because, he said, "the truth about Mississippi lacks credibility." Life in these two states was sometimes compared to that in a totalitarian society like that of Soviet Russia or Germany under Hitler. As under those regimes, a large and noisy element approved of what was going on, and another large element conformed because conformity was safer and more comfortable than dissent. True, this was only a single-track variety of totalitarianism. It was not dictatorship; the state administrations did not command uniform obedience in other matters or discipline fractious politicians. But racism itself was unifying and supreme.

Nevertheless the picture painted in general terms would do an injustice to the white populace of those two states if mention were not made of the brave, sometimes heroic efforts of men and women of conscience to stem the evil tide. They were but a faint leaven, yet a traveler visiting a selected list of addresses could gain the impression that a numerous element of whites deplored the existing state of affairs. The prestige of some of these was sufficient to enable them to make cautious gestures on the side of moderation and survive; others spoke out boldly until they were more or less forced to leave; a few tough liberals braved all and joined the ranks of civil-rights crusaders. Some silent officials would have welcomed a change in public policy. Two hopefully moderate candidates had actually won election to state office, William F. Winter as state treasurer of Mississippi and Richmond Flowers as attorney general of Alabama. A score of legislators in the two states had spoken out in recent years against reckless white supremacy legislation, though nearly all of these had been returned to private life as a result.

Among those who persevered in the good fight at home some of the most effective were newspaper editors. Courageous moderation was not characteristic of the press as a whole. The large metropolitan newspapers more often than not had fostered prejudice and hysteria. Several of those in Alabama in 1964 had begun to adopt a more constructive tone, but in Mississippi nothing was doing more to poison the public mind than the stuff that appeared daily in Jackson's two papers, the *Clarion Ledger* and the *Daily News*. A third Jackson paper, the *State Times*, which deviated cautiously from the anti-Negro line, had been forced to go out of business at the end of 1961. In the next echelon of daily papers, however, and among weekly papers a dozen editors were still trying to awaken their readers to the tragic folly of what was going on. A few such had been ousted when their papers were bought out with racist money. Yet the daily *Delta Democrat Times* of Greenville, edited by Hodding Carter, Jr., did very well financially and was the strongest voice of moderation in Mississippi; Neil Davis of the *Lee County Bulletin* in Alabama was appealing for sanity in cogent editorials and still making a business success. J. Oliver Emmerich, editor of the *Enterprise Journal* in turbulent McComb, Mississippi—repeatedly threatened, bombed, and beaten in his long struggle to restore decency and order to that community—was to be classed among the heroes. A Mississippi woman, the unconquerable Mrs. Hazel Brannon Smith, editor of the *Lexington Advertiser*, survived ruthless economic pressure and physical harassment and won the 1964 Pulitzer Prize for her fearless editorials.

Two men who in different situations had labored manfully, but with repressed feelings, for sanity in race relations—one in Alabama, the other in Mississippi—banished all inhibitions in the fall of 1963. Each spoke out in a resounding public speech, and each went to work immediately to tell more in a book.

Charles Morgan, Jr., was a Birmingham attorney active in the Democratic party and known to nearly everybody in town. Tough, sophisticated, gregarious, he might have gone far in Alabama politics had he been willing to acquiesce in the racial insanity, but he chose otherwise. His speech to the city's Young Business Men's Club on September 17, 1963—two days after four Negro children were killed in a terrorist bombing—was perforce his Birmingham valedictory. In a blistering indictment, Morgan charged that all white Alabamians—officials, businessmen, editors, clergymen, "all of us"—had a share of the blame for the revolting crime. "We are ten years of lawless preachments; ten years of criticism of law, of the courts, of our fellow men; a decade of telling school children the opposite of what the civic books say. We are a mass of intolerance and bigotry. . . ." Morgan's book, published in May, 1964 (by Harper & Row), was entitled *A Time to Speak*—from Ecclesiastes III, 7: "a time to keep silence, and a time to speak." The author is now a regional director of the American Civil Liberties Union.

An even greater sensation was caused by a speech, followed by a book, by James W. Silver, who for twenty-seven years had been a professor of history at the University of Mississippi. Professor Silver had talked sense on the race question for years among faculty colleagues and students and a few others around the state. He had befriended James Meredith, the lonely first Negro student, throughout the latter's stay at "Ole Miss." When Silver was elected president of the Southern Historical Society in 1962, he resolved to use his inaugural address the following year to give that society and the world a true picture of what was going on in his state. His address, prepared with meticulous research and consultation over a period of months, was delivered at the Society's annual convention in Asheville, North Carolina, on November 7, 1963. With the scholarship and authority of a respected historian, he told how Mississippi had "been on the defensive against inevitable social change for more than a century," and said:

> In committing itself to the defense of the biracial system, Mississippi has erected a totalitarian society which to the present moment has eliminated the ordinary processes by which change may be channeled. Through its police power coercion and force prevail, instead of accommodation, and the result is social paralysis. Thus, the Mississippian who prides himself on his individuality in reality lives in a climate where nonconformity is forbidden, where the white man is not free, where he does not dare to express a deviating opinion without looking over his shoulder.
>
> And yet, in spite of all that has been presented in this paper, it seems inescapable that Mississippians one day will drop the mockery of the late Confederacy and resume their obligations as Americans. There is small reason to believe that they will somehow develop the

capability to do it themselves, to do it, as Faulkner says, in time. If not, the closed society will become the open society with the massive aid of the country as a whole, backed by the power and authority of the Federal Government.

Silver's book, *Mississippi: The Closed Society*, was published (by Harcourt, Brace & World) in 1964. The author left Mississippi about the same time for an assignment at the University of Notre Dame, but he remained on leave of absence from "Ole Miss" and returned to it briefly before severing his connection in 1966.

Of these two rebellious states, Alabama would furnish more turmoil and crises in 1965; in 1964, Mississippi held the spotlight. Mississippi had a larger proportion of Negroes in its population than any other state, but the Negro protest had been feebler in Mississippi because it was more sternly repressed there. The state became a storm center, however, in 1964, when an army of outside crusaders, organized in a "Mississippi Summer Freedom Project," came in to arouse Mississippi Negroes and inform them of their rights.

Mississippi was the most backward state in the Union, its people the poorest and most ignorant. That is, of course, a generalization. The state was not without affluent and polished gentry. The capital city of Jackson harbored an unusual concentration of wealthy aristocrats and business magnates; in Greenville one could meet more urbane and cultivated people than in the average city of its size elsewhere in the country. The median family income of whites was $4,209 a year, that of Negroes $1,444. Mississippi's 916,000 Negroes were the crudest and most retarded in the United States—a result of white oppression, but a circumstance which nourished the myth of racial inferiority so deeply imbedded in the Mississippi mind. Here too the generalization could be misleading: there were a number of Negroes of talent, education, and refinement in the state; after Faulkner the most distinguished contemporary Mississippian was probably Leontyne Price, the Negro prima donna. But thousands of the state's most energetic and ambitious Negroes had been in effect driven away year after year. Negroes, now 42 per cent of the population, had been a majority until the 1930's. Only the bravest Negroes in the most tolerant communities were able to, or dared to, exercise the franchise. More than 70 per cent of the whites—but less than 7 per cent of the Negroes—were registered.

The state legislature, from which the tiny moderate element had been virtually eliminated in the last several elections, was regarded by a widely respected Mississippi writer as "probably the lowest common denominator of any political assembly in the United States."* In the governor's chair, the blustering Ross Barnett had been succeeded by the more temperate Paul Johnson, who made a sensationally conciliatory speech upon his inauguration in January; but in his campaign for election Governor Johnson had outdone the other contenders in promises to maintain the status quo and he showed no signs of any significant departure from these promises. Ku Klux Klansmen had been organized for the first time in modern times in Mississippi early in 1964, this field having been monopolized previously by the Citizens' Councils. The Mississippi Klan, a new order called the White Knights of the Ku Klux Klan, was one of the most vicious and the most secretive of the white supremacy groups. It was growing fast, along with a strident new organization of similar propensities called "Americans for the Preservation of the White Race." The calmly analytical Southern Regional Council in a report of July 14, 1964, said of Mississippi: "Here every datum of economics and every fact and twist of history have conspired to keep its white people deeply and ofttimes harshly resistant to change and its Negro people ill-equipped for it." In 1964, emboldened and instructed by the visiting crusaders, Mississippi Negroes were at last awakening; the white government and public were united in a desperate effort to stop that awakening.

The Voter Education Project, which we discussed earlier, had withdrawn from Mississippi, except in two special local situations, in November, 1963. In the other ten Southern states it had added many thousands of Negroes to the voter lists, but it despaired of making significant headway in Mississippi because of the harassment and terrorism in that state. "Until that is knocked out," its director said, "you are not going to get any meaningful registration there." The response of SNCC and CORE exemplified the

---

* Hodding Carter III in *New York Times Magazine*, June 23, 1963.

revolution's strategic rule to meet rebuff only with massive new attack. The time had come for an all-out drive to arouse, inform, and organize the Negroes of Mississippi. Thus the Mississippi Summer Freedom Project of 1964.

The Council of Federated Organizations (COFO), which since 1962 had coordinated the efforts of the various civil-rights groups in Mississippi in the earlier voter registration drive, was the organizational nucleus for the bigger and bolder initiative. This was not supervised by the Southern Regional Council but was dominated by the daring Student Nonviolent Coordinating Committee. Planning started early in 1964 with announcements from both SNCC and CORE of a coming all-out drive in Mississippi, and the call went out for student volunteers. The National Council of Churches came forward with active support, seeking both to encourage the move and to keep it on a high plane. In May systematic recruitment got under way. Efforts were made to screen out the immature and emotionally unstable. Applicants were required to complete questionnaires; they had to be at least eighteen years of age, and those under twenty-one were required to obtain the permission of their parents. The project was an invitation to self-sacrifice. Those accepted were obliged to furnish their own transportation to and from Mississippi and pay their own living costs. They were to be housed with Negro families (in the case of white workers a scandalous detail from the Mississippi point of view). Overshadowing these hard conditions was the obvious danger, which no one tried to minimize. But students responded with enthusiasm.

They came from Swarthmore, Cornell, Yale, Harvard, Pennsylvania, and a dozen other universities and colleges in the East, including women's colleges—Mount Holyoke, Bryn Mawr, Smith, and others; they came from Colorado, Stanford, the University of California, and from colleges in the Middle West. Many white Mississippians envisioned a horde of Communists and beatniks coming to rape and pillage. As a matter of fact, the screening efforts did not eliminate all the dubious characters. There were eccentrics and radicals among them, and others were radicalized by their Mississippi experience. But the majority were from the American mainstream, youths with high religious and political ideals. Yet they were after all exceptional—"oddballs," some called them. A Mississippi Negro leader accepted that description: "They ain't nothing but oddballs," he said—"coming down here to get scared to death and shot at just to help us Negroes!" A typical student volunteer expressed their commitment thus: "Mississippi is the last stronghold of the old Confederacy and feelings are bitter, but those who are going there have made their decisions rationally. We know there is a chance of being hurt, of being jailed, or being killed, but we still believe in the cause so strongly that we must go."

A training school was set up by the National Council of Churches in the Western College for Women at Oxford, Ohio. In two-weeks courses there volunteers were instructed on conditions in Mississippi and on the nature of their mission. Warned of the hardships and danger ahead, they were trained in techniques for taking beatings with minimum bodily injury—and, of course, without retaliation.

Mississippi prepared angrily for the "invasion." The state legislature passed a spate of new laws to preserve public order—or in other words, to keep Negroes and white crusaders under control. The State Highway Patrol was increased from 275 to 475 men, municipalities were given new authority to restrain movements of individuals and to pool police forces and equipment, penalties for violating city ordinances were increased, and heavy fines were prescribed for refusal to comply with police commands in nine circumstances relating specifically to the tactics of civil-rights demonstrators. A fear seized thousands of Mississippi whites not unlike the ancient terror of a slave uprising. Talk of "killing niggers" was more common than before. Unpunished crimes against Negroes multiplied; in the state's southwest corner five Negroes were reported slain in six months. On the night of April 24 crosses were burned in 64 of the state's 82 counties. Half a dozen Negro churches were burned in June. (Ten more would be burned in July, six in August, and five in September.)

Meanwhile the Summer Freedom Project aroused anxiety in many quarters outside of Mississippi. The results of a nationwide Louis Harris poll, published on July 6, showed only 31 per cent approving of the dangerous enterprise; 57 per cent disapproved and 12 per cent had no opinion. The *Washington Post*, in a leading editorial of June 25, voiced deep concern. It paid high tribute to "this breathtakingly admirable group of youngsters—their idealism, their decency and their courage." But it saw a danger that "tragedy could grow into holocaust, murder into massacre," and reminded that "the federal government cannot guard every hoodlum, Klansman and racist."

By mid-June, 175 of the young people had already arrived in Mississippi and several hundred more were completing their training. Countless insults and harassments had been suffered, and one appalling tragedy. But the crusaders kept coming. At the summer's end they numbered over 1,000: about 700 student volunteers together with 100 regular civil-rights workers, 100 clergymen, and 150 lawyers. Sharing with the NAACP Legal Defense Fund the heavy burden of providing legal counsel were three groups largely of volunteers: the Lawyers Constitutional Defense Committee, the National Lawyers Guild, and the Lawyers Committee for Civil Rights under Law. Of the regular workers about three-fourths were from SNCC and one-fourth from CORE. Aaron E. Henry, president of the Mississippi conference of the NAACP, was chairman of COFO, but otherwise the NAACP and SCLC participated only nominally in the project. Operations were directed from COFO headquarters in Jackson by Robert Parris Moses, a Negro scholar (with a master's degree from Harvard) and a veteran of three years of the SNCC struggle in Mississippi.

A COFO report on the project for the four months ending October 31 showed 3 persons killed, 80 beaten, 3 wounded by gunfire in 35 shootings, and more than 1,000 arrested; 35 churches burned, 30 homes and other buildings bombed. Unsolved mystery surrounded the deaths of other Negroes—like a fourteen-year-old youth, wearing a CORE T-shirt, whose body was found floating on the Big Black River and two adults whose bodies were recovered from a backwater of the Mississippi. It was easy for cynics to say that all this distress had accomplished nothing. Tangible results indeed were few. In the registration of Negro voters, the chief ostensible objective, only meager progress had been made (about 1,200 new registrations in the state). But Mississippi would never be the same again. The monolithic fortress of white supremacy had been breached, not broadly, but beyond repair.

COFO had established forty-seven small schools, scattered over the state, where illiterate and near-illiterate Negroes were taught reading and writing—and more besides, including how to register for voting. Nearly an equal number of community centers were established. About 150 volunteers, staying on after the summer project, and 200 staff members of SNCC and CORE were continuing the work in more than half of these. The morale of Mississippi Negroes had received a tremendous lift. Many had been made to feel the dignity and joy of manly protest; new leaders had come forward. A political consciousness had been awakened, out of proportion to the handful of Negroes then on the voting list (28,500).

The new Negro political initiative found expression in a "Mississippi Freedom Democratic Party." The MFDP sought to register the will of the large element of disfranchised citizens and, with some justification, claimed as much legality as the regular state electoral processes, from which most Negroes were illegally excluded. The idea began in 1963 when an improvised "Freedom Election" was held simultaneously with the regular November election. In the "Freedom Election," which was open to all citizens of voting age, 80,000 votes were cast for the NAACP's Aaron Henry for governor and the Reverend Edwin King, the white chaplain of nearly all-Negro Tougaloo College, for lieutenant governor.

The Freedom Democratic party, organized in the spring of 1964, sought not only to demonstrate but to exercise real political power. Before the Democratic National Convention in August, it held its own precinct and county meetings and state convention and elected a delegation which it claimed to be more nearly legal than the delegation chosen exclusively by whites. An embarrassing hassle occurred at Atlantic City, which will be described in the next chapter. The MFDP delegation was given only token recognition, but the incident dramatized the injustice of the Mississippi situation and resulted in positive gains for the Negro cause. The MFDP also put forward candidates for the United States Senate and three seats in the House of Representatives subject to the November election. When the State Election Commission found that they did not meet legal requirements for inclusion on the regular ballot, an MFDP election was carried out independently. This was carefully planned and supervised. Additional civil-rights workers came to Mississippi to help. Voters were registered on forms calling for the same information as the official registration forms but omitting the Constitution-interpreting requirement. Two hundred voting places were set up in the state. Sixty-nine thousand voted in the MFDP election, favoring, with near unanimity, not only the MFDP nominees for Senate and House, but the Johnson-Humphrey ticket (while Mississippi was going 7 to 1 for Goldwater in the regular election). An effort to seat the candidates thus "elected" to Congress aroused much national sympathy and received substantial, though insufficient, Congressional support in 1965.

The "long, hot summer" in Mississippi drew nationwide, even worldwide, attention to the Mississippi problem. It brought a new awareness and a faint sense of shame to that state. Civil-rights activities would be a little safer there in the future. The dominant organization of businessmen, the 2,500-member Mississippi Economic Council, issued a memorable call for acceptance of the law of the land, communication between the races, and extension of the franchise to all. Twenty-three Protestant, Catholic, and Jewish leaders formed a "Committee of Concern" and set about collecting funds to rebuild the burned-out churches. In two areas historic advances had been made. These could not be called COFO accomplishments, but the fact that the steps were taken and taken without serious disturbance reflected a new awareness of the realities of the times, which the Summer Project shared in bringing about. A few days after the signing of the Civil Rights Act of 1964 Negroes for the first time entered and were served at a number of previously "white-only" restaurants, including those in Jackson's two leading hotels. In September Mississippi took the first steps of compliance with what had been the law of the land since the Supreme Court's *Brown* decision of 1954. Fifty-eight Negro children entered the first grade in 13 previously all-white public schools in three districts: 39 in Jackson, 18 in Biloxi, and one in Carthage.

The atrocity that overshadowed all others in the Mississippi Summer Project was the killing of three COFO workers in Neshoba County in east-central Mississippi on June 21. Two of the murder victims were white: Michael Schwerner, aged twenty-four, a former New York social worker on the staff of CORE, and Andrew Goodman, twenty, son of a New York building contractor and a junior at Queens College. The third was James Chaney, a twenty-one-year-old Negro youth of Meridian, Mississippi. Schwerner and his wife had come to Meridian six months earlier to set up a community center, which included a 10,000-book library donated by Northern students. Mrs. Schwerner taught reading and citizenship and instructed Negro women in the operation of sewing machines, while Schwerner pushed voter registration. Chaney was their assistant. Both Schwerner and Chaney served as instructors in the training school for volunteers at Oxford, Ohio, and they met Goodman there.

On Saturday, June 20, these three gathered five other crusaders in a CORE-owned station wagon and drove south to Meridian. There they learned that fifty miles northwest in Neshoba County Mount Zion Baptist Church, a meeting place for civil-rights workers and the prospective location of a Freedom School, had been burned to the ground on the night of the 16th. On Sunday, June 21, Schwerner, Chaney, and Goodman set out in the station wagon to inspect the ruins. There a Negro lay leader told them that on the night of the fire he was dragged from his car in the churchyard and clubbed unconscious by a white mob. Returning through the town of Philadelphia (population 5,500), the county seat of Neshoba, at about 4 P.M., the three were arrested by Deputy Sheriff Cecil Price on a charge of speeding. Released at about 10:30 P.M., after Chaney paid a fine of $20, they drove off into the night. They never saw Meridian again.

On Monday anxiety for the three men began to grow. Neshoba County Sheriff Lawrence Rainey said he saw no cause for alarm. "If they're missing," he said, "they just hid somewhere, trying to get a lot of publicity." That was a common white reaction to racist outrages in the Deep South. The claim was almost routine that incidents were contrived by publicity-seeking civil-rights workers. It was predicted that these three men would eventually turn up unharmed, probably in the North, possibly in Cuba.

But the grim likelihood that they had been done to death occurred to knowledgeable observers throughout the nation. In Washington on Tuesday Attorney General Kennedy postponed a scheduled trip to Europe and ordered the FBI to investigate. President Johnson ordered the use of military helicopters to help in the search for the missing men. Then came news that the station wagon had been found, burned out in a Neshoba County bog. On Wednesday the President sent Allen Dulles, the former director of the CIA, to confer with Governor Johnson and others in Jackson. The next day he ordered out 200 sailors from the naval air station at Meridian to aid in the search. (Mississippians seemed more resentful of all this federal activity in their state than distressed over the apparent tragedy.)

On August 4, six weeks after the search began, FBI agents uncovered the bodies of the three young men—buried deep in the red clay of an earthen dam under construction at a farm five miles southwest of Philadelphia. The Negro Chaney had been savagely beaten and shot once in the head, twice in the body. Schwerner and Goodman had each been killed by a single shot in the head. Evidently specific directions had led the FBI to the spot. Rumor had it that an informer had been paid $25,000. (Many Mississippians speculated more over who the informer might have been than over the identity of the assassins, and were less shocked by the crime than over the thought that the FBI might have paid for the tip.)

It was in bringing to justice the perpetrators of racist crimes in the Deep South that the impotence of the federal government under our federal system was most distressingly apparent. In some less publicized killings of Negroes no arrests were made, or cases were dismissed when a justice of the peace declared the killing an act of self-defense or a coroner's jury found death accidental. In glaring cases, the Federal Bureau of Investigation intervened energetically up to the point of trial. FBI agents worked diligently and with the efficiency for which they are famous—only to see their efforts frustrated by state courts or by segregationist local district judges and juries in federal court. There was no federal law against murder, except on federal property.

There was the assassination of Medgar Evers in Jackson, Mississippi, in June, 1963. This Negro leader, a World War II veteran, was buried in Arlington National Cemetery, and a galaxy of high government officials attended the ceremony. In the meantime FBI agents were making a round-the-clock search for the killer. A collection of evidence, including a fingerprint on the murder weapon, pointed to an outspoken racist named Byron De La Beckwith, and Beckwith was arrested. He went on trial on January 27, 1964. In the three-day process of seating a jury, some white veniremen, when asked if they thought it "a crime for a white man to kill a nigger in Mississippi," gave evasive or qualified replies. They were excused. The jury finally chosen, however, was all-white. Beckwith admitted in court having written a letter to the National Rifle Association saying in part: "We are going to have to do a lot of shooting to protect our wives and children from bad niggers." He had written many letters during his seven months in jail. The prosecution brought out that in none of the more than 150 examined did the defendant deny having killed Evers. Beckwith agreed that he represented himself "as making a sacrifice for the cause."

The jury reported on February 7 that it had been unable to reach a verdict. A new trial was called. A second jury having failed to reach a verdict, another mistrial was declared on April 17, and Beckwith was freed.

The case of the murder of Lemuel A. Penn in Georgia on July 11, 1964, was similarly dismaying. Penn was a Negro who had quietly pursued his career as an educator; he was director of adult and vocational training in the District of Columbia public schools. He also held the rank of lieutenant colonel in the United States Army Reserve. He had not been conspicuous in civil-rights activity. To his assassins—who shot him as he drove along a Georgia highway with two other Negro officers, all in uniform, returning from annual training at Fort Benning—Colonel Penn was apparently just a Negro who had not "kept in his place."

On presidential orders the FBI went to work and arrested four Ku Klux Klansmen. One of them had confessed and implicated the others, though he later repudiated his statement. Two Klansmen were finally brought to trial for the murder in September before an all-white jury. The defense attorney denounced the "horde of federal agents in our midst" and harangued: "Never let it be said that a jury . . . of Anglo-Saxon men will convert the electric chair of this state into a sacrificial altar to satisfy the savage appetite of the clamoring mob." The jury deliberated slightly more than three hours and reached a verdict of acquittal.

The ugly tradition of immunity for racist killers was sustained once more in the Neshoba County case. Only one of the three victims was a Negro, but his two white comrades—"nigger lovers" and "traitors to their race"—were regarded by racists with equal hatred and contempt. A Neshoba County grand jury "investigated" the slaying for three days and made no charges.

The FBI, working independently of state courts, sought to establish guilt on the milder charges possible under federal law. The Department of Justice could act only under two old Reconstruction era statutes against depriving individuals of their civil rights. One of these (Section 241 of the United States Code) was aimed at conspiracies and the other (Section 242) at acts under the color of law. The maximum penalty under the former was ten years imprisonment and a $5,000 fine; under the latter it was a year in prison and a fine of $1,000.

On December 4 FBI agents arrested twenty-one white men, including Sheriff Lawrence Rainey of Neshoba County, Deputy Sheriff Price, and several leaders of the Ku Klux Klan. Nineteen were charged with violating the civil rights of the murdered youths, two with being accessories to the crime. The FBI complaint said the killings were plotted by the KKK, that Price arrested the three on a fictitious speeding charge and then released them so that he and the other conspirators would intercept them and kill them.

At a preliminary hearing for the nineteen before United States Commissioner Esther Carter in Meridian on December 10 an FBI agent testified that he had obtained a signed confession from one of the two defendants who were not present. Miss Carter, a Mississippi woman, ruled this testimony hearsay and incompetent, and dismissed the charges against all nineteen.

Indicted by a federal grand jury in January, 1965, seventeen of the defendants were at last brought to trial in federal court in February. The presiding federal judge was William Harold Cox, one of those segregationist judges whom President Kennedy had appointed. Judge Cox threw out the indictment. "The indictment surely states a heinous crime against the state of Mississippi," he said, "—but not a crime against the United States."

The Negro Revolution in the Presidential Election 1964

The Negro revolution overhung the 1964 presidential race—from the early skirmishing of Republican hopefuls to the Democratic landslide in November. Theodore H. White found that factor of sufficient importance to fill two of the thirteen chapters in his *The Making of the President 1964* and to receive frequent mention in the remainder of the book. From fear of its explosive possibilities, the subject was approached with caution and campaign oratory was addressed mainly to other matters; but the attitude of the candidates on civil rights was never absent from political calculations and it had a massive effect upon the election.

Of the four serious contenders for the Republican nomination, three, Governor Nelson A. Rockefeller of New York, Ambassador Henry Cabot Lodge, and Governor William W. Scranton of Pennsylvania, had shown conspicuous support for civil rights. So had Governor George Romney of Michigan, who was much in the picture though not a declared candidate. Only one, Senator Barry Goldwater, who became the Republican nominee, took an unsympathetic view of the Negro movement. Goldwater was not a racist: he insisted upon his opposition to racial discrimination and his earlier record was not to the contrary. Yet he had voted against the Civil Rights Act of 1964 and it was abundantly evident that he would "go slow" on civil rights. So the Republican candidate was anathema to Negroes, and he became the rallying point for opposition to the civil-rights movement at all levels of prejudice down to the angriest Negrophobes.

The expression "backlash" came into vogue early in the year. It represented a hope of Southern segregationists and later of Goldwater partisans that whites, resenting the tactics of civil-rights crusaders and alarmed over Negro rioting, would lash back at Negroes at the polls—not only in the South but all across the land. A Louis Harris survey, published on August 17, found that "fully 87 per cent of the American people" felt "that the recent riots in New York, Rochester and Jersey City hurt the Negro cause." But, except insofar as it referred to the old prejudice of Southerners, the "backlash" failed to materialize as a major factor in the presidential election.

It was to mobilize the "backlash" that Alabama's Governor Wallace set out in the spring on his anomalous campaign for President. Campaigning in the North, Wallace put aside the violent demagoguery that had made him a symbol of racism in Alabama. But his reputation was enough to attract Negro-haters, while many of the less prejudiced were impressed by his now disarming plea for state rights and individual liberty. Entering Democratic primaries in three states, Wallace received 34 per cent of the vote in Wisconsin, 30 per cent in Indiana, and 43 per cent in Maryland. Then the Republican National Convention offered Wallace supporters a conservative candidate with a much more impressive chance of election. Four days after Goldwater's nomination, the Alabama governor, having covered himself with glory in the eyes of the Deep South, retired from the race.

Troubled over the possibility that a "backlash" would throw votes to Goldwater, the leaders of the Big Five civil-rights organizations and A. Philip Randolph met in New York on July 29, and after three hours of debate issued a call to their followers "to observe a broad curtailment, if not total moratorium, of all mass marches, mass picketing and mass demonstrations until after Election Day." Wilkins, King, Young, and Randolph signed the statement before it was promulgated. James Farmer of CORE and John Lewis of SNCC had first to consult their national offices and, under pressure from militant associates, they finally rejected it. Nevertheless, the "moratorium" was generally observed. Several big city riots were still to come, but that was a different matter, beyond the control of civil-rights leadership. Organized, large-scale demonstrations virtually ceased, not to be resumed again until the following winter.

When it came to the voting in November, the "backlash" was hard to find: Goldwater carried five Deep South states, but he won in no other state except his own Arizona.

At the Democratic National Convention the Negro revolution, represented by the Mississippi Freedom Democratic party, furnished nearly all the excitement there was. When that body began to assemble in Atlantic City for the meeting, which opened on August 24, sixty-eight delegates and alternates from the MFDP (all but four of them Negroes) were on hand demanding to be seated as the representatives of Mississippi. This would have meant exclusion of the delegation of whites chosen by the state's regular Democratic party machinery, in which Negroes, as usual, had had no part.

An undoubted majority of the convention's 5,260 delegates and alternates would have liked to administer a rebuke to Mississippi white supremacists. The blatant exclusion of Negroes from the state's electoral processes, passionately exposed before the convention's credentials committee, was a monumental scandal. Moreover the regular Mississippi delegates could not be relied upon to support the party's nominees; some were already giving aid and comfort to the enemy. Yet their status was technically more nearly legal than that of the MFDP delegation, and to allow an improvisation like the latter to participate in national convention decisions might have set a dangerous precedent. Party leaders wrestled with the problem for three days amid emotional scenes and conflicting pressures and decided upon a compromise. The credentials committee ruling, approved by the convention, read that no delegate from the regular group could sit unless he pledged allegiance to the party's ticket; and that two of the MFDP delegates, Aaron Henry and the Reverend Edward King (white), would sit with full right of vote, while the others would have the status of "honored guests." Of greater significance in the long run, the ruling also provided that at future conventions of the Democratic party no delegations would be admitted from states in which the party process deprived citizens of the right to vote because of their race or color.

In all the circumstances, this was a triumph for the Mississippi Freedom Democratic party and for the Negro cause. But it did not satisfy the MFDP contingent. Against the advice of Martin Luther King and some other national Negro leaders, angry MFDP delegates rejected the compromise, invaded the convention floor with purloined passes and badges and insisted on taking the seats allotted to Mississippi. When after three hours, order was restored, they had lost much of the public sympathy which their original gesture had aroused. All but three members of the regular delegation bolted the convention rather than promise support of the party's nominees.

The problem of the Negro protruded in continual crises during the summer. When the Republican National Convention met in San Francisco in July, Colonel Penn had just been assassinated in Georgia and the search was under way for the bodies of Chaney, Goodman, and Schwerner, murdered in Mississippi. On the day the Republican Convention adjourned, the shooting of James Powell in Harlem precipitated the series of riots in northern cities that ended with the upheaval in Philadelphia the weekend after the Democratic National Convention.

The Republican candidate was constantly concerned over the danger of arousing passions on this issue. On July 24, while Harlem and Bedford-Stuyvesant were simmering, he expressed his concern to President Johnson in a sixteen-minute conference at the White House. A laconic joint statement issued afterward said: "Senator Goldwater expressed his position, which was that racial tensions should be avoided. Both agreed on this position." The Goldwater organization produced a campaign movie, a twenty-eight-minute documentary, exhibiting girls in topless bathing suits, stripteasers, delinquent youths, and other evidences of immorality—of which the candidate made a campaign issue—but also dealing at considerable length with Negro riots and looting. It cost $65,000 and 200 copies were sold throughout the country. But when Goldwater saw the film he was horrified, especially at the anti-Negro material. "It is nothing but a racist film," he said, and he ordered its showing canceled

Yet Goldwater bore down heavily in campaign speeches on the "growing menace in our country . . . to personal safety, to life, to limb and property, in homes, in churches, on playgrounds and places of business, particularly in our great cities"—and preached law and order as "the most elementary and fundamental purpose of any government." He made little mention of the causes of Negro unrest. In contrast, President Johnson said, for instance, after the Harlem outbreak: "In the preservation of law and order there can be no compromise—just as there can be no compromise in securing equal and exact justice for all Americans." Goldwater's voluble concern over the rights of states also tended to identify him with the segregationist South and aroused the kind of ire that Roy Wilkins voiced when he said: "Goldwater says he is not opposed to Negro ambitions, but believes in leaving these matters to the states. That is like the Roman emperors not being opposed to Christians but leaving them to the lions."

The candidates for Vice President did not alter the division on the civil-rights issue. The Republican nominee, Representative William E. Miller of New York, was an ineffectual echo of Goldwater. The President's running mate, Senator Hubert H. Humphrey of Minnesota, had led the Democratic fight for the Civil Rights Act and had long been a champion of the Negro cause.

The Negro rejection of Goldwater in November was almost unanimous: President Johnson received an estimated 96 per cent of the Negro vote. And the Negro vote was far more telling than it had ever been before. In the nation as a whole, the NAACP estimated that 6 million Negroes were registered to vote. In the South, the voter registration campaign had raised Negro registration from 1,386,654 in 1962 to 2,164,000. Four of the six states carried by the Democratic party would have gone Republican had it not been for Negro voters. In each of those states—Arkansas, Florida, Tennessee, and Virginia—the number of Negro votes clearly exceeded the margin of Johnson over Goldwater; a majority of the white voters cast their votes for the Republican candidate. The five Southern states that Goldwater carried—Alabama, Georgia, Louisiana, Mississippi, and South Carolina—were those in which less than 45 per cent of the eligible Negroes were registered to vote. In Mississippi, where less than 28,500 Negroes were registered, Goldwater received 359,693 votes, 87 per cent of the total; Johnson was favored by only 52,618 Mississippi voters, an estimated 21,200 of them Negroes.

Many Negroes were elected to public offices, generally minor ones. This was not unusual in the North and West, but a few won election in the South. In the nation as a whole 18 Negro state senators and 76 Negro representatives were elected or re-elected to serve in 24 state legislatures. These included a second Negro state senator in Georgia and a Negro member of the House of Representatives in Tennessee. In one Alabama county with a preponderance of Negroes a revolutionary change occurred: in Macon County, the home of Tuskegee Institute, after a long and painful struggle, enough Negroes were now exercising the franchise to elect two justices of the peace, a member of the school board, and a member of the board of revenue. In Arkansas the Negro vote was responsible for the adoption of a constitutional amendment eliminating the poll tax. In Massachusetts, Attorney General Edward W. Brooke, the highest elected Negro official in the country, accomplished a remarkable political feat. Brooke, a Republican, won re-election by more than 900,000 votes while Johnson was defeating the Republican candidate for President in that state by a margin of over 1,200,000. The election of John L. Congers (Democrat) of Detroit and the re-election of five incumbents increased the number of Negroes in the House of Representatives to six.

That the Negro question was the controlling factor in the South was an inescapable conclusion. Historically, the Republican party had been the friend of the Negro; the "Solid South," having largely disfranchised the Negro, was for generations regarded as a secure Democratic party asset. Following a trend of recent years, a majority of Southern whites in this election had entered the Republican fold because the old party attitudes toward the Negro seemed to be more or less reversed. The Kennedy and Johnson administrations had been moving dramatically toward equal citizenship for Negroes; the Republican party under Goldwater raised hopes of a retreat from that policy. With the exception once of Louisiana, the Southern states that went Republican in 1964 had not voted for a Republican presidential candidate before since Reconstruction.

The three states in which Governor Wallace had campaigned

showed up comfortably in the Democratic column. But in another state and apart from the presidential race, a white "backlash" indeed appeared—and caused a setback in the supremely difficult problem of segregated housing. In California, an enactment of 1963 called the Rumford Act had made it unlawful to discriminate with respect to race, color, creed, or national origin in the sale of about 70 per cent of the dwellings in that state. Before the voters on Election Day was a proposed constitutional amendment, called Proposition 14, which would invalidate the Rumford Act and prohibit the state or any of its subdivisions from infringing on the right of any property-owner (excluding owners of hotels and other lodgings) to sell or rent to anyone "in his absolute discretion." The California Real Estate Association had drafted the amendment and promoted a vigorous campaign for its adoption. In spite of the opposition of not only Negroes but Governor Edmund G. Brown and other moderate leaders of both parties, Proposition 14 was adopted by a majority of more than two to one. Governor Brown said this would not be "the end of California's fight against discrimination and segregation in housing," and civil-rights leaders planned an attack upon the constitutionality of Proposition 14.

In the general excitement, little note was taken of a four-day mock election which the Mississippi Freedom Democratic party had conducted in that state. Ballot boxes for the "freedom vote" had been set up in barber shops, restaurants, cleaning establishments, churches, and even in automobiles to reach backwoods areas. In this fashion 63,000 Negroes cast votes for President Johnson (and 17 for Goldwater). In four of Mississippi's five congressional districts, Negroes gave votes to Negro candidates for the House of Representatives: Aaron Henry, 36,792; Mrs. Fannie Lou Hamer, 18,450; Mrs. Annie Devine, 2,805; and Mrs. Virginia Gray, 7,450.

Contending that 450,000 Negro citizens were "systematically and deliberately prevented from voting" in the regular election in Mississippi, the MFDP challenged the seating of the state's five members of the House of Representatives and urged seating of the three women chosen in the mock election. The first of these objectives aroused considerable support across the nation. In December the Commission on Religion and Race of the National Council of Churches urged the House to "conduct a thorough investigation into the election of the five prospective congressmen and to take actions needed to secure the right of every qualified citizen of Mississippi to vote in federal elections." But the Commission voiced the feeling of most MFDP sympathizers when it said of the second objective: "Their attempt, we feel, clouds the clear issue of the present election system in that state." The Big Five civil-rights organizations all endorsed the first of the MFDP objectives, but the NAACP and the Urban League withheld support of the second. Aaron Henry, president of the Mississippi NAACP, had not attempted to be seated. When the new Congress opened on January 4, 1965, the three women contestants were quietly turned away from the House chamber, and the five of the regular Mississippi delegation were seated. But more than one-third of the members of the House wanted to reject the regular delegation; the vote was 276 to 148. The challenge persisted until it was finally dismissed by the House on September 17, 1965, by a vote of 228 to 143.

With the election behind him, President Johnson's determination to press on in the fight against racial injustice was given emphatic and eloquent expression on December 10. Speaking to an assembly sponsored by the National Urban League, he said:

> It is more than a hundred years since Abraham Lincoln charged the living to dedicate themselves to the unfinished work of the dead at Gettysburg.
> Even Lincoln, with his deep sense of man's imperfections, could not know that a century later we would still be striving to abolish racial injustice.
> No task is more deeply rooted in the complexities of American life. Poverty and tradition, fear and ignorance, the structure of our society and the workings of our economy, all converge on this enormous wrong which has troubled the American conscience from the beginning. Its just solution is essential, not only to give the full blessings of freedom to Negroes, but to liberate all of us.
> There are those who say: It has taken us a century to move this far. It will take another hundred years to finish the job.
> I do not agree.

Great social change tends to come rapidly, in periods of intense activity and progress before the impulse slows. I believe we are in the midst of such a period of change.

It is our task to carry forward nothing less than the full assimilation of more than 20,000,000 Negroes into American life. This is not to be assimilation of bland conformity. Our object is not to make all people alike. It is, as it has always been, to allow ready access to every blessing of liberty, while permitting each to keep his sense of identity with a culture and tradition. In this way we enlarge our freedom and enrich our nation.

Turning to the Civil Rights Act of 1964, the President noted "widespread support, in all parts of the country, of the public accommodations title"—in which he saw "proof of the educational value of law, and the reservoir of good will among Americans." Compliance with this section banning discrimination in restaurants, hotels, and other places of public accommodation (Title II) had not been greatly affected by the fact that its constitutionality had been challenged in the courts and a Supreme Court judgment on the question was still pending. Four days after the President spoke, the high tribunal rendered its decision, unanimously upholding those provisions of the Act.

Two cases had been brought to the Supreme Court on appeal from lower court rulings. In the first, which was started by the Heart of Atlanta Motel in Atlanta, a three-judge federal district court had upheld the law and enjoined the motel from practicing discrimination. In the second case, that of Ollie's Barbecue in Birmingham, another three-judge federal court had held Title II unconstitutional. All nine justices of the Supreme Court agreed that the section was valid under the commerce clause of the Constitution. "In framing Title II of this act," the court said, "Congress was also dealing with what it considered a moral problem. But that fact does not detract from the overwhelming evidence of the disruptive effect that racial discrimination has on commercial intercourse." Two days after the decision five Negroes were served at Ollie's Barbecue.

The Community Relations Service—whose discreet mediation had already helped in some of the more difficult situations—conducted a survey in October in 53 cities with populations over 50,000 in nineteen states which had no public accommodations statutes. It found, in virtually all of these cities, that desegregation had been accomplished in more than two-thirds of the hotels, motels, chain restaurants, theaters, and sports facilities—as well as public parks and libraries. Even in the South most of the larger restaurants and hotels were no longer refusing to serve Negroes. But some of these establishments made Negroes unwelcome in subtle ways which no law could prevent. A number of restaurants evaded the desegregation requirement by becoming private clubs, with nominal membership fees. In many small towns, especially in the Deep South, the Civil Rights Act had made no change in the pattern of segregated eating places; intimidation prevented most Negroes from challenging it. Here and there Negro leaders made a point of visiting still segregated restaurants to prove their right under the law, but the performance involved unpleasantness and risk which few wanted to encounter often. The general elimination of discrimination in the South would have to wait for further erosion of racial prejudice. Nevertheless a mighty advance had been made. Thousands of Southerners were becoming accustomed to seeing Negroes in restaurants, theaters, and motels that formerly excluded them. Custom lagged behind law, but not as far behind as many had expected, and the gap continued to narrow.

Apart from Title II, implementation of the Civil Rights Act had scarcely begun. Under Title VI, the Administration was laying the groundwork for the elimination of discrimination in federally-financed programs. The President said in his Urban League speech on December 10: "Last week I approved the first set of regulations to implement that principle." No action had been taken under the provisions in Title VII to end discrimination in employment. These would not begin to take effect until July 1, 1965, but the body that was to administer them, the Equal Employment Opportunity Commission, needed to organize and plan for its responsibilities in advance of that date. The setting-up of this commission would be long delayed.

Many arms of the federal government were already engaged in activities related to the Negro revolution; with the implementation of the Civil Rights Act they were expanded and their number increased. "With so many groups in a single field," the President said, "there is always the danger of duplication, overlap or unnecessary delay." He therefore announced the appointment of

Vice President Humphrey "to take responsibility for working with all these groups, assisting in coordination of their efforts, and guiding them toward energetic pursuit of equal opportunity for all." To assist the Vice President in this task, a new cabinet-level Council on Equal Opportunity was set up on February 6, with Wiley A. Branton, who had headed the Voter Education Project in the South, as its executive director. This was not, however, the final solution of the problem of coordination. In September, 1965, the Council on Equal Opportunity was dissolved, and much of its activity was concentrated in the Department of Justice.

That department was headed now by Nicholas de Belleville Katzenbach, with the title of Acting Attorney General until he was appointed Attorney General in January, 1965. Robert F. Kennedy had resigned in September to run for senator from New York, and had been elected to that office in November. On December 19, 1964, in the resignation of Assistant Attorney General Burke Marshall, the Department of Justice lost an official who had long been a key figure in the federal government's civil-rights activities. To succeed Marshall as Assistant Attorney General in charge of the Civil Rights Division, the President appointed John Doar, a veteran of four years in the work of the division. Doar, also noted for his quiet efficiency and tact, had shown conspicuous courage in a number of situations of physical danger in the South.

ELEVEN

Selma

1965

The lull in demonstrations signaled by the moratorium agreement of July, 1964, continued through the turn of 1965. Civil-rights leaders took stock of the postelection situation, planned strategy for coming months, and gave vent to disagreement and feelings of rivalry among themselves. Thoughts turned toward the scandalous denial of the vote to Negroes in the Deep South, with particular attention to Alabama, where crusaders of the Student Nonviolent Coordinating Committee had been struggling for Negro voter registration since 1962. Martin Luther King, visiting Selma on January 2, 1965, told about 800 Negroes gathered in Brown Chapel Methodist Church that he was coming back to assist in "a march on the ballot boxes throughout Alabama."

The chief source of dissension within the civil-rights movement was the perennial argument between the cautious and the bold. Should prudence move on in more or less orderly fashion to break down the barriers to Negro advancement by degrees, or should audacity try to crash through them all pell-mell? It was in large part a conflict between the old and the young. Negroes of middle age and older had been reared in an era when cringing was a way of life, when adapting to the wishes of whites was the key to almost any kind of attainable success. But in a generation born not long before the 1954 *Brown* decision, and come to manhood since the 1960 wave of sit-ins, there were thousands whose minds had been formed in a different mold. These viewed the whole structure of second-class citizenship as an unmitigated outrage and wanted to see it demolished without delay. Such youths were to be found in all the civil-rights organizations; they were an element of ferment even in the venerable NAACP. In SNCC virtually all were of this generation and this outlook; there were no old heads.

Many Negroes chafed under the rule of nonviolence, but the leadership of the Big Five, including SNCC and CORE, still adhered to that principle. "Nonviolent" was of course a part of the name of the Student Nonviolent Coordinating Committee. CORE at that time required of each member: "He will meet the anger of any individual or group in the spirit of good will; he will submit to assault and will not retaliate in kind either by act or word." But many Negroes were getting tired of turning the other cheek. In Jonesboro, a small town in a Ku-Klux-Klan-infested area of northern Louisiana, Negroes had armed themselves and formed an organization called the "Deacons for Defense and Justice." Though Deacons patrolled the Jonesboro headquarters of CORE, CORE officials, like other civil-rights leaders, expressed sympathy but avoided identification with them. By the summer of 1965 Bogalusa, Louisiana, had become the center of Deacon strength and a score of chapters had sprung up more or less secretly in Louisiana and Mississippi. How many members there were nobody knew. The Deacons claimed their only purpose in carrying arms was to provide protection against the Ku Klux Klan and other racist ruffians. Their guns were in fact almost never brought into play, but armed Deacons had a sobering effect on the essentially cowardly Klansmen.

Most Negroes gave a cold shoulder to the Communists who turned up at civil-rights gatherings here and there. SNCC made no effort to screen its field workers for Communist sympathies. One Snick leader remarked: "When they get mixed up with us, a Communist dies and a person develops. They're not subverting us, we're subverting them. We're more revolutionary than the Communists." CORE director James Farmer quipped, "A Negro finds it tough enough to be black, without being black and red."

The Black Muslims continued to exercise considerable influence. Several developments had tended to keep the cult in the public eye. One was its espousal by the temperamental heavyweight boxing champion Cassius Clay. A more serious matter was a split and feud between its foremost leaders, Elijah Muhammad and Malcolm X. These two men, the mystical Messenger of Allah and his voluble spokesman, were more than mere charlatans. Despite their doctrine of hate and their theological and political fantasies, there was depth in some of their thinking and an element of positive good in their ministrations. Within a small inner circle they had been able, as James Baldwin wrote, "to heal and redeem drunkards and junkies, to convert people who have come out of prison and keep them out, to make men chaste and women virtuous. . . ." Robert Penn Warren found Malcolm X "a man of great talents and magnetism."

Nine days after the assassination of President Kennedy, Malcolm X spoke of the fallen President with derision, saying his death was a case of "the chickens coming home to roost." Elijah Muhammad—apparently welcoming the opportunity to be rid of a rival—promptly suspended Malcolm X from his position in the brotherhood. "With the rest of the world," the Messenger of Allah said, "we are very shocked at the assassination of our President."

For over a year afterward Malcolm X, with an irregular following, agitated independently. He urged extension of Muslim activity to the broad Negro struggle and gave evidence of moving toward cooperation with civil-rights leaders. He embraced the orthodox Moslem faith and made a pilgrimage to Mecca. In Harlem, on February 20, 1965, while addressing a meeting of the Organization for Afro-American Unity, which he had formed, Malcolm X was assassinated, felled by a shotgun and two revolvers. A week of tension followed. The four-story Muslim center in New York was burned to the ground. Heavy police guards patrolled various Black Muslim installations, including the mansion of Elijah Muhammad in Chicago and the Harlem funeral home where Malcolm's body lay exposed before a stream of visitors.

On Sunday, one week after the assassination, Malcolm X was buried after orthodox Moslem rites in a Christian church in Harlem. Some regular civil-rights leaders attended the funeral; conspicuous among them were James Farmer of CORE, James Forman of SNCC, Bayard Rustin, and Dick Gregory. Negro playwright Ossie Davis, who delivered the eulogy, said Malcolm X was "a prince—our own shining prince—who did not hesitate to die, because he loved us so."

The publicity lavished on the firebrands, the extremists, and the eccentrics tended to obscure the center of gravity in the Negro movement. Considerably more Negroes were enrolled in the National Association for the Advancement of Colored People than in all the other civil-rights and Negro protest groups combined. The most influential individual by far (thousands knew the name of no other national Negro leader) was Martin Luther King. King's unceasing eloquence, his high moral tone, and his dedication to fearless nonviolent action had won him not only a vast following among both Negroes and whites in the United States, but international renown.

One morning in late October, 1964, King awoke to learn from a radio announcement that he had been awarded—"for the furtherance of brotherhood among men"—the Nobel Peace Prize. At thirty-six, he was the youngest man and the twelfth American ever to receive that honor. He announced promptly that the prize (about $54,000) would be used to finance civil-rights activities. He called the award "a tribute to the discipline, wise restraint, and majestic courage of the millions of gallant Negroes and white persons of good will who have followed a nonviolent course in seeking to establish a reign of justice and a rule of love across this nation of ours."

The Negro leader carried his new distinction with dignity. In London, on his way to Norway for the presentation, he was invited to preach on Sunday, December 6, at St. Paul's Cathedral. It was the first time a non-Anglican had ever delivered the evensong sermon in that edifice. His scholarly religious message, interspersed with quotations from philosophers and poets as well as the Bible, was heard by 4,000 admiring Britons, nearly all of them white. In Oslo, on December 10, he received the award in the traditional ceremony, in the presence of the King and the Crown Prince of Norway. The next day he delivered the traditional address to the students of Oslo University. While the civil-rights movement in the United States was "a special phenomenon which must be understood in the light of American history," he said it was "a relatively small part of a world development."

Something within has reminded the Negro of his birthright of freedom, and something without has reminded him that it can be gained. Consciously or unconsciously, he has been caught up by the Zeitgeist, and with his black brothers of Africa and his brown and yellow brothers in Asia, South America and the Caribbean, the

United States Negro is moving with a sense of great urgency toward the promised land of racial justice.

Returning to America, Dr. King received the Medallion of Honor of the City of New York and was honored at a series of functions in which Vice President Humphrey, Mayor Wagner, and Governor Rockefeller were conspicuous. Especially significant was his reception in Atlanta, Georgia, in the heart of the South. Nearly 1,500 Atlantans, a majority of them white, leading citizens among them, gathered at a dinner in his honor. The scene was the Dinkler Plaza Hotel, which until the previous summer had refused to admit Negroes. This Negro was now presented with a specially commissioned Steuben glass bowl, etched with Atlanta's symbolic dogwood blossom and bearing the inscription: "To Dr. Martin Luther King, Jr., Citizen of Atlanta, Recipient of the 1964 Nobel Peace Prize, with respect and admiration, January 27, 1965." The meeting closed with everyone singing "We Shall Overcome."

Five days later the Nobel Prize winner was in a Selma, Alabama, jail. He had taken time out for the Atlanta ovation from the voter registration campaign which he had promised in his January 2 speech in Brown Chapel. Fifteen hundred Negroes were arrested in Selma the week of February 1, bringing the total arrested since mid-January to 3,300. King spent four days in jail—duly dramatizing the incident—before posting $200 bond and securing his release. The campaign continued and gathered momentum until it reached a climax six weeks later which riveted the attention of the nation and the world. King and his organization were energetically assisted (and often criticized) by the Student Nonviolent Coordinating Committee. Lawyers of the NAACP Legal Defense Fund were strenuously involved and rendered invaluable aid. Nearly everyone and every group of prominence in the civil-rights movement and 6,000 religious leaders joined in the grand finale. But the leadership and inspiration were King's. It was his greatest triumph.

The number of Negroes registered to vote in Alabama had increased from 6,000 in 1947 to 110,000 in November, 1964. Yet 370,000 Negroes of voting age, approximately 70 per cent of the total, still were not registered. In the Black Belt hardly any progress had been made. In Dallas County, of which Selma is the seat,

Negroes comprise 57 per cent of the total population, but at the beginning of 1965 only 335 Negroes were registered to vote. In contrast, 9,543 whites were on the voting list. In neighboring Lowndes and Wilcox counties, where Negroes outnumber whites approximately four to one, not a single Negro was registered.

Selma, sometimes called the "capital of the Black Belt," was a city of approximately 30,000 population situated on the right bank of the Alabama River a little south of the center of the state. Its hostility to pro-Negro influences had ancient roots. A century before the climax of Martin Luther King's "invasion," Selma—then a Confederate arsenal and munitions manufacturing center—had been burned and laid waste by a Union army, which included a Negro regiment. In the intervening years Selma had rebuilt and grown and progressed in many ways, but the attitude of Selma whites toward Negroes and their fear of agitation of the Negro question had changed but little. One needs to realize the intense hatred of "agitators" among these Black Belt whites to understand their incredible behavior during the winter and spring of 1965. Dallas County Sheriff James G. Clark expressed no more than the prevailing view when in January he roared to Snick leader John Lewis: "You're an agitator, and that's the lowest form of humanity!"

The main purposes of King and his associates were to embolden Alabama Negroes to demand their rights, and to bring their grievances to the attention of the nation. In the objective of placing Negroes immediately on Alabama voting lists, little was expected and less accomplished. In Selma, in addition to the familiar tactics of obstruction and delay, the registrar functioned only two days a month (although as a concession to King's campaign, applicants on other days were allowed to sign an "appearance sheet" to get into line for next attention). King wrote in the *New York Times Magazine* of March 14: "Selma has succeeded in limiting Negro registration to the snail's pace of about 145 persons a year. At this rate it would take 103 years to register the 15,000 eligible Negro voters of Dallas County. . . ." But denial of the vote to Negroes was the discrimination that the American people were most nearly united in condemning, and this was an area in which the hypocrisy, immorality, and illegality of Black Belt practice were visible to all who looked in that direction.

From early January on, a typical day in Selma saw Negroes from city and farm converging on the campaign headquarters at Brown Chapel and marching to the court house, there to be barred by Sheriff Clark and his helmeted posse and ordered to disperse. The Negroes would chant, sing, and pray and submit to arrest by the hundreds. (With jails overflowing, most of those arrested were held only briefly.) Dallas County's swaggering, quick-tempered sheriff had established himself as the symbol of Selma police brutality much as Commissioner "Bull" Connor (a native of Selma, by the way) had been the chief villain of the piece in Birmingham in 1963. The scale of the demonstrations steadily increased as more local Negroes rallied and sympathizers gathered from afar. The campaign spread into neighboring counties. On February 18, in Marion, seat of Perry County, twenty-five miles from Selma, it registered its first martyr. Jimmy Lee Jackson, a Negro laborer, was fatally shot and ten other persons, including three newsmen, were beaten in a clash with state troopers.

As usual in the Negro movement a strong religious note permeated the campaign in Selma. Negroes often knelt on the street in prayer, led by one of the many clergymen among them; they prayed even for Sheriff Clark. They sang hymns and they sang "We Shall Overcome" and all the familiar civil-rights songs. Some new songs developed in Selma, like this one:

> Police cars are the Berlin Wall,
>   Berlin Wall, Berlin Wall,
> Police cars are the Berlin Wall,
>   In Selma, Alabama.
> We're going to stand here till it falls,
>   till it falls, till it falls,
> We're going to stand here till it falls,
>   In Selma, Alabama.
> Love is the thing that'll make it fall,
>   make it fall, make it fall,
> Love is the thing that'll make it fall,
>   In Selma, Alabama.

A small band of Alabama whites who hated injustice to Negroes also made an appearance in Selma. All honor must be paid them; their action required a special kind of intestinal fortitude.

"Concerned White Citizens of Alabama" they called themselves—
some sixty professors, businessmen, school teachers, housewives
and others, led by the Reverend Joseph Ellwanger, of St. Paul's
Lutheran Church in Birmingham. They staged a one-and-a-
quarter-mile march to the Dallas County Court House on March 6.
Tears trickled down the cheeks of some of the women among them
as crowds of Selma whites cursed, insulted, and jeered them.

Beginning with "Bloody Sunday," March 7, the Selma struggle
was at the top of the news in the nation for three weeks (yielding
the spot only briefly to the first space flight in the Gemini series).
King was determined to crown the campaign with a march east-
ward through fifty miles of Black Belt country infested with Ku
Klux Klansmen and other hostile whites, to Montgomery, the state
capital. He announced the plan on February 2, and later fixed
March 7 as the day. Governor Wallace in a news conference on
March 6 pointed to the "additional hazard placed on highway
travel by any such action" and said: "Such a march cannot and will
not be tolerated."

Nevertheless, on Sunday, March 7, 500 Negroes, including
young boys and old women, set out down U.S. Route 80 for
Montgomery, most of them carrying satchels and bedrolls. After
marching about 300 yards they found the highway barred by 100
of Sheriff Clark's possemen, 15 of them mounted, and 50 state
troopers equipped with gas masks and under orders from the Governor to stop the march. The possemen, who figured prominently
in these Alabama disturbances, were tough white men who volunteered with the zest of huntsmen for the duty of chastening Negroes. The marchers were given "two minutes to turn around and
go back." When they failed to budge, the police moved in with
tear-gas bombs and night sticks—the horsemen mounting what resembled a Cossack charge—and drove them back into Selma.

Governor Wallace said if the Negroes had gone on they would
have been attacked by angry whites. "We saved their lives by
stopping the march."

But across the nation the incident set off an uproar the like of
which had not been seen before in the history of the civil-rights
movement. Clergymen, governors, state legislatures, and labor
unions thundered denunciations. Governor George Romney and
Mayor Jerome P. Cavanagh led 10,000 in an indignation march in

Detroit. In New York 15,000 marched through Harlem. Demonstrators snarled traffic in Chicago, Los Angeles, and Washington. University campuses seethed. Even in the South Mayor Leonard Rogers of Knoxville, Tennessee, called citizens to a prayer meeting for the Selma Negroes. Fourteen youths contrived, for the first time in history, a sit-in in the corridors of the White House itself. (They were ejected and arrested after seven hours, and the White House let it be known that nothing of the sort would be permitted again.) Episcopal Bishop James A. Pike of California declared that the 400,000 ministers, priests, and rabbis in the United States should converge on Selma if the federal government failed to act. Over 400 of them headed for Selma anyway. Walter Lippmann said in his newspaper column: "Unless Selma is expunged by a mighty national act of repentance and reparation, how shall Americans look themselves in the face when they get up in the morning?"

The Negroes appealed to the federal district court at Montgomery to enjoin Governor Wallace and Alabama police authorities from further interfering with the projected march. The Department of Justice entered the case on their behalf. The injunction would be granted in due course, but pending hearings on the suit, Judge Frank M. Johnson, Jr., issued an order restraining the group from again undertaking the march.

Nevertheless on Tuesday, March 9, a second attempt was made. This came to a tame anticlimax with some embarrassment for King. About 1,000 Negroes, joined now by 450 white sympathizers from the North, set out toward Montgomery. Four hundred yards down the highway stood the same police cordon as before. King said the marchers wanted to kneel and pray, and permission was granted. After praying, the column turned and headed back. The turnabout was the subject of vociferous controversy; some Negroes said they had been "betrayed." The decision to desist had been reached in last-minute negotiations in which Governor Collins, director of the federal Community Relations Service, who had arrived by jet plane, had had a part. But the undertaking was only postponed. There would yet be a march on Montgomery, King said, "in numbers that no one can count."

That night three white clergymen who had come to Selma to aid the Negro cause were attacked on the street by white hoodlums. One of them, the Reverend James J. Reeb, a Unitarian minister from Boston, was taken to a hospital with multiple fractures of the skull. Two days later, in the words of Dr. King, Reeb joined "the ranks of those martyred heroes who have died in the struggle for freedom and human dignity."

The surge of indignation in the North was kindled anew by Reeb's death. A procession in Chicago carried a coffin, symbolizing the minister's bier. In the ecumenical spirit of the day Cardinal Spellman donated $10,000 toward a memorial to the martyred Unitarian minister. Led by Washington clergymen, a crowd of 15,000 gathered in Lafayette Park, across from the White House, to demand federal intervention in Alabama. From Maine to California more clergymen and miscellaneous idealists began making the pilgrimage to Selma. Archbishop Iakovas, primate of the Greek Orthodox church, was one of them. Half a dozen Roman Catholic nuns from St. Louis had appeared there while Reeb was dying; more came now from Chicago, Detroit, and elsewhere—to make a picturesque addition to protest demonstrations.

Governor Wallace flew to Washington on Saturday for a conference, at his own urgent request, with the President. It was apparent from subsequent comment of each that there had been no meeting of the minds, but they talked for more than three hours. The President in his news conference mentioned several obvious steps that he had urged in the interest of racial justice and peace and said: "I told the Governor that the brutality in Selma last Sunday just must not be repeated."

On Monday evening, March 15, the President delivered a televised address to a joint session of the Congress. The speech, with a strongly personal ring and delivered with visible emotion, was widely considered the most eloquent of his career. It was in preparation for a drastic new voting rights bill to be submitted two days later. President Johnson's only previous personal appearances before joint sessions were his two State of the Union messages and his speech following the assassination of President Kennedy. He said now in part:

> At times history and fate meet at a single time in a single place to shape a turning point in man's unending search for freedom. So it was at Lexington and Concord. So it was a century ago at Appomattox. So it was last week in Selma, Alabama.
>
> There, long-suffering men and women peacefully protested the

denial of their rights as Americans. Many were brutally assaulted. One good man—a man of God—was killed.

Many of the issues of civil rights are complex and difficult. But about this there can be no argument. Every American citizen must have an equal right to vote. There is no reason which can excuse the denial of that right. There is no duty which weighs more heavily on us than the duty to ensure that right.

Even if we pass this bill, the battle will not be over. What happened in Selma is part of a far larger movement which reaches into every section and state of America. It is the effort of American Negroes to secure for themselves the full blessings of American life.

Their cause must be our cause too. It is not just Negroes, but all of us, who must overcome the crippling legacy of bigotry and injustice. And we shall overcome.

He uttered the words from the anthem of the Negro revolution with slow, firm emphasis: "And we *shall* overcome."

In Montgomery on Tuesday, March 16, James Forman of SNCC led about 600 students, who, having been refused permission to present a petition to the Governor, staged a sit-down in the street. They were dispersed by police with spectacular brutality. Mounted possemen clubbed and flailed them until eight of their number required hospitalization.

History has recorded the many instances of the repression of a struggling people by a ruthless gendarmerie in the past only in writing or, in recent times, with but a few lucky photographic shots. Modern techniques and a swarm of alert cameramen placed the Selma drama upon a stage before the eyes of the world. The public not only read but *saw* it daily on television and in the press. The following sampling of captions under published photos will give an idea of how the drama was carried into the homes of many millions of people: "Alabama state troopers, wearing helmets and gas masks, drag off a demonstrator after breaking up the vote march in Selma yesterday"; "One demonstrator (left) falls to her knees while another (foreground) is clubbed by a state trooper in Selma, Ala."; "State troopers using clubs, whips and tear gas broke up effort by civil-rights demonstrators to march to Montgomery"; and (under a two-page spread in *Life*): "Alabama's Answer. Flailing their heavy canes, mounted sheriff's possemen and state troopers charge without warning into a packed mass of demonstrators at Montgomery the day after the President's speech. At left above, horsemen drive demonstrators to a sheltering porch. Then (center above) a girl tries to dive behind a tree but is clubbed down. At right above, Paul Clemson, an angry student from Penn State, kneels by a wounded boy. . . ."

Many Negroes in the simmering urban ghettos of the North and West tended to identify "Bull" Connor, of Birmingham fame, the law enforcement officers of Neshoba County, Mississippi (where three civil-rights workers were murdered in 1964), and now Jim Clark and his men, of Selma, with policemen everywhere. The ferocity of the police in these Deep South crises encouraged a feeling that law and established authority were instruments of white oppression. "Selma!" was one of the cries heard in the Los Angeles rioting in August 1965.

In Montgomery, Judge Johnson (a native Alabamian) was weighing the appeal from Governor Wallace's ban on the Selma-Montgomery march. On Wednesday, March 17, he issued his ruling. He warned of the danger in making the long march in the existing atmosphere of tension, but he declared that "in this case the wrongs are enormous" and the march should be permitted. He ordered the Governor not to interfere, and to give the marchers full protection. Governor Wallace promptly went before a joint session of the Alabama legislature to excoriate the ruling. But he said "we will obey."

Sunday, March 21, was set as the date for the march to begin. Friday, the 19th, Wallace wired the President that Alabama could not afford the expense of calling out the 6,000 National Guardsmen estimated to be needed to protect the marchers. President Johnson commented at a news conference the next day: "It has been rare in our history for the governor and the legislature of a sovereign state to decline to exercise their responsibility." However, in the early hours of Saturday he had signed documents placing the Alabama National Guard under federal control and directing the Secretary of Defense to use whatever federal forces he might find necessary to deal with "domestic violence." In Brown Chapel committees worked late Saturday night preparing food hampers, camping instructions, and first-aid kits.

On Sunday morning 3,200 Negroes and white sympathizers—students, clergymen, nuns, and the rest—gathered in a festive mood in front of Brown Chapel. The goal now was not only justice for Negroes in the Selma area but a "change in the climate" on a national scale. "Walk together, children," King told the crowd, ". . . and Alabama will be a new Alabama, and America will be a new America."

Observation planes circled overhead as they set out and marched through countryside deserted except for soldiers, passing cars, and a few white hecklers. Another song had been added to their repertoire:

> Oh, Wallace, you know you can't jail us all.
> Oh, Wallace, segregation's bound to fall.

Seven miles out of Selma, where the four-lane highway narrows to two lanes, 2,900 marchers turned back, in accordance with Judge Johnson's instructions that only 300 should march along the narrower road. The smaller band continued, camping three nights along the way. Before they arrived at their appointed overnight bivouacs a thin line of soldiers swept cautiously across each field to check against mines, bombs, or booby traps. Assistant Attorney General John Doar, who now headed the Justice Department's civil-rights division, was on hand—as he had been in every major crisis in the South—to see that federal court orders were obeyed. He tramped with the marchers or drove his own car nearly all the way.

Wednesday when the bedraggled marchers reached the outskirts of Montgomery they met 10,000 fresh allies, who had flown in by chartered planes. That night on an improvised stage in a ball park Harry Belafonte, Leonard Bernstein, Sammy Davis, and a score of other famous artists and entertainers performed for the multitude in an exuberant extravaganza. Thursday morning an army of 25,000 took up where the little band had left off. They marched triumphantly the last three and a half miles and massed before the Alabama state capitol—where the delegates of six states met in 1861 to form the Southern Confederacy, and on whose steps Jefferson Davis took the oath of office as its president.

Governor Wallace refused to see a delegation bringing a petition for Negroes to be allowed to vote in Alabama. But that did not matter now. The crowd sang and listened patiently for two hours while a series of civil-rights celebrities spoke; then the man arose whom everyone—including the nation's television viewers—wanted to hear.

"We have walked on meandering highways and rested our bodies on rocky byways," said Martin Luther King. "They told us we wouldn't get here. And there were those who said that we would get here only over their dead bodies. But all the world today knows that we are here, and that we are standing before the forces of power in the state of Alabama, saying 'we ain't goin' let nobody turn us around.' "

He called for more marches everywhere—on segregated schools, on poverty, and on "ballot boxes until race baiters disappear from the political arena." He lifted the crowd to a peak of emotion with a rhythmic chant: "I know you are asking today. 'How long will it take?' I come to say to you this afternoon however difficult the moment, however frustrating the hour, it will not be long, because truth crushed to the earth will rise again. How long? Not long, because no lie can live forever. How long? Not long, because you still reap what you sow. Not long, because the arm of the moral universe is long but it bends toward justice."

In a concluding crescendo he quoted from the Battle Hymn of the Republic and boomed to the ecstatic crowd: "His truth is marching on! Glory hallelujah! Glory hallelujah! Glory hallelujah!"

The historic march on Montgomery had been accomplished without the bloodshed that so many had feared. But Thursday night tragedy struck. Mrs. Viola Gregg Liuzzo, a white lady, the wife of a labor union official and mother of five children, had come to Selma from Detroit, because, as her husband related, "she said it was everybody's business, she had to go." Mrs. Liuzzo had walked with the marchers on the first and last days, spending the remaining time shuttling demonstrators along the highway in her car. On Thursday night she joined the group of other volunteer motorists who were carrying demonstrators back from Montgomery to Selma, and had started back for another load. About twenty miles out of Selma a car drew alongside and a bullet smashed through the window, striking her in the temple. LeRoy Moton, a young Negro

SCLC worker in the car with Mrs. Liuzzo, huddled on the floor until the gunmen's car raced away. Then he seized the steering wheel, but the car hurtled off the highway into a pasture. The youth hitchhiked back to Selma and informed the police. By the time the latter reached her car Mrs. Liuzzo was dead.

President Johnson went on television only sixteen hours later. Speaking with obvious anger to an angry public, he announced that the FBI had already arrested four Ku Klux Klansmen charged with the murder, and he scorchingly denounced those "enemies of justice who for decades have used the rope and the gun and the tar to terrorize their neighbors." Vice President Humphrey, conveying the sympathy of the President and himself, was among the many dignitaries who visited the bereaved family. Governor Romney declared two days of official mourning in the state of Michigan for a woman "who made the supreme sacrifice in the unending cause of securing for all of her fellow American citizens those unalienable rights endowed . . . by our Creator."

The Legislative Accomplishment 1965

Sympathy with the Negro struggle was never more fervent or more general than at the conclusion of the great Selma-Montgomery march. The Negro novelist Ralph Ellison described it as "a moment of apocalyptic vision." But the glow of a sensational episode fades quickly in the broad march of events. Selma dropped out of national news at the end of March, and the old patterns of prejudice and discrimination were not long in reasserting themselves. Popular feeling for the Negro suffered a sharp reverse in August with wild Negro rioting in Los Angeles. But permanent gains had been made. Above all, Selma had produced, and led Congress to enact, an epochal bill to put an end to Negro disfranchisement.

Nothing was more impressive in the Selma episode than the mobilization in the nation of a church militant. Some of the ministers were coldly received when they returned to their congregations; a few were reproached by their superiors though more were commended. But, in the words of the Reverend Robert W. Spike, director of the National Council of Churches Commission on Religion and Race: "The church reached a turning point when its messengers on U.S. 80 showed with their feet that racism runs against the morality of any faith." The evangelist Reverend Billy Graham canceled engagements in Europe to "see if we can't bring the healing message of the Gospel" to the Deep South. Graham had been criticized for his attitude of detachment from the burning problem of race relations. Now he said: "I have never felt that we should attain our rights by illegal means, yet I must confess that the demonstrations have aroused the conscience of the world."

The interfaith comradeship that developed in Selma was an interesting by-product. One minister called it "ecumenically fantastic." Methodist Bishop John Wesley Lord said: "Once you have walked not only side by side but heart to heart in a common effort you can never return to your separateness again." Roman Catholic Father Geno Baroni said: "We got a new and healthy respect for each other on that highway out of Selma"; and the Reverend William A. Wendt (Episcopalian) went further: "I would say that there is joy in Heaven, and that Pope John is leading the rejoicing."

What was the effect of it all upon Alabama? An observer from a distance might have expected the massive display of national disapproval of Alabama behavior and the witness of this multitude of religious leaders to the justice of the Negro's cause to have opened the eyes of Black Belt whites, even to have brought some feeling of shame. But few who knew the Black Belt had such hopes. The effect of the demonstrations was in fact largely nullified locally by the boundless racist talent for vilification. The instinctive racist response to any message of justice to the Negro was to vilify the messenger.

"Scum" was the favorite term of natives for the visitors to Alabama from across the nation—though thousands of them belonged to what might better have been called the *cream* of the American public: clergymen, professors, writers, and officials—eminent figures among them—and students of highly respectable background. Marching close to Dr. King on the road to Montgomery were another winner of the Nobel Peace Prize, Dr. Ralph J. Bunche, undersecretary of the United Nations, and New York city council president, Paul R. Screvane. It is true that most of the marchers were dusty and ill-kempt; there were bearded men and trousered women, who invariably aroused suspicion among rural Black Belt folk; and, as is to be expected when 25,000 people are drawn to an exciting situation, there was an element of something like scum. Racist sleuths may have seen some instances of sexual immorality; they invented many. Some of the stories they circulated were incredibly revolting. Not even the nuns or Mrs. Liuzzo were spared. A relatively mild version of the filth was heard in Congress. Alabama's Representative William L. Dickinson described the marchers as in large part "human flotsam—adventurers, beatniks, prostitutes and similar rabble," among whom "drunkenness and sex orgies" were "the order of the day."

An Episcopal minister polled some eighty fellow clergymen who had been active participants in the demonstrations. They said they could not have observed every incident but not one of them had witnessed sex scenes or heavy drinking. The out-of-state newsmen, of whom there were about 400, said they saw nothing resembling the racist canards. Nevertheless a large element of Alabamians—who never saw out-of-state publications—were led to believe that the magnificent gesture of conscience was an outrageous invasion by a vicious and sinister mob.

Some leading Alabama churchmen condemned the Selma-Montgomery march. Catholic Archbishop Thomas J. Toolen said it was "a great injustice to the state of Alabama," and the place for priests and nuns was "at home." Methodist Bishop Kenneth Goodson called the march "a great disservice to human freedom," which was "delaying reconciliation."

Yet Alabama *had* been moved in some degree. The faint voice of liberalism in the state, even among politicians, began to take a stronger tone. Some newspapers were shocked into positions of resistance to racist insanity from which they would not retreat. In the northeast Alabama city of Anniston, 500 citizens, including bank presidents, industrialists, clergymen, and a city commissioner, signed a statement published as a full-page advertisement in the Anniston *Star* three days after the Selma-Montgomery march, urging a "responsible, realistic and thoughtful response" to Negro aspirations. Three weeks later twenty-two of the state's top business leaders signed a similar statement and had it published as a front-page advertisement in the major Alabama newspapers and in the *Wall Street Journal*.

The prestigious Birmingham *News*, in a two-column, front-page editorial on March 28, reviewed the recent disgraceful events in the state and called for action to convince the world "that Alabama is at work in a positive, constructive manner correcting past ills and facing up to realities of the Negro insistence on further redress." The paper concluded:

> This state has been described by one angered non-Alabamian as a place that ought to have a fence built around it, which ought to be isolated. It is a tragic, offensive description of bitterness. But that's

the way a great many people ARE thinking of us—and they don't separate the bed-sheet brutes from decent, churchgoing, law-abiding folk.

THE PEOPLE who can do something about this know who they are. If elected leaders don't put us on a better, more effective, more convincing course, then these other Alabama leaders must do something about it. They'd better do it soon or you can really put up a headstone over this entire commonwealth that will forever read "Here We Rest."

The city of Selma settled down to a truculent calm. The mayor and city council began holding weekly conferences with Negro leaders, but Negroes saw no significant improvement in their condition and continued to boycott local merchants. On April 16 a three-judge district court at Mobile enjoined Sheriff Clark from using the hated possemen and ordered him to protect Negroes participating in peaceful demonstrations. The Hammermill Paper Company, since the previous summer, had contemplated building a $25-million-dollar pulp mill near Selma. Civil-rights groups picketed the company's offices in Erie, Pennsylvania, for some weeks, demanding that the project be suspended. The pickets finally withdrew on May 12, when the company declared "its intention to use its full influence as a corporate citizen of Dallas County to secure the full protection of the law for all rights, including equal employment opportunity and the right to register and vote freely and without discrimination or intimidation."

After the slaying of Mrs. Liuzzo, Martin Luther King made one of the impulsive mistakes with which his great achievements were interspersed: he proposed a national boycott of Alabama products, the withdrawal of investment and federal funds from Alabama banks and suspension by the nation's business community of all plant expansion and location in Alabama. The plan was endorsed by King's own SCLC, but it was coldly received by most civil-rights leaders and organizations. It was pointed out that, even if an effective economic boycott of the state were possible, it would work a hardship on friend and foe alike and would cause Alabama Negroes to suffer. The plan was soon abandoned.

Rarely has momentous legislation been enacted so directly in response to one spectacular upheaval as the Voting Rights Act of 1965.

President Johnson had for several months contemplated offering a voting rights bill in this session of Congress. His intention to do so was announced on February 6, but the nature and timing of the bill had not then been decided. No one was more aware of the need for a drastic measure than Attorney General Katzenbach and men like John Doar in the Justice Department, but it is unlikely that the Administration would have felt it possible to go as far as it did in this bill without the unwitting help of Sheriff Clark, Governor Wallace, and company—and the bonfire lit by SNCC and Martin Luther King.

A month earlier it would have been hard to conceive of Congress welcoming the President's proposals of March 17 to "strike down restrictions to voting in all elections—federal, state and local —which have been used to deny Negroes the right to vote." Recommendations of President Kennedy in 1962 and 1963, going further than the voting provisions of the Civil Rights Act of 1957, 1960, and 1964, but milder than these of President Johnson, had gone unheeded. But, after Selma's Bloody Sunday, an overwhelming majority in Congress was eager to go all the way.

Yet it was not an angry or a hasty law that emerged. Compared to the year-long struggle over the Civil Rights Act of 1964, enactment proceeded with dispatch; but four and a half months elapsed between the bill's introduction and its final approval by the Senate on August 4. Every provision was meticulously gone over; proposed changes were debated and some adopted. The Southern concept of state rights lost another round, but the bill was drawn with meticulous care to keep federal encroachments to a minimum.

Like the Civil Rights Act of 1964, the Voting Rights Act of 1965 was a bipartisan achievement. Republicans in Congress were anxious to restore the historic image, obliterated in the Goldwater presidential campaign, of the Republican party as the Negro's friend. They began early to prod President Johnson for a strong voting rights recommendation, and several House Republicans introduced a bill of their own. On February 23, 31 Republican leaders—5 governors, 4 senators, and 23 representatives—signed a statement urging the President to "move and move promptly" on voting rights legislation (chiding him also on his delay in appointing the members of the Equal Employment Opportunity Commission created by the Civil Rights Act of 1964). When the Administration bill reached Congress on March 17, Minority Leader Dirksen took hold much as he had done in the 1964 civil-rights battle. The opposition from Southerners in Congress was feeble this time. Senator Russell, their leader in the fight against the Civil Rights Act of 1964, was ill and away from the Senate. Senator Albert Gore of Tennessee, an opponent of the 1964 Act, supported the 1965 bill, as did twenty-two Southerners in the House of Representatives.

A number of minor changes were made to clarify provisions of the bill and to fortify it against arguments of unconstitutionality. The greatest controversy, and four weeks of delay, were caused by an effort led by freshman Democratic Senator Edward M. Kennedy of Massachusetts to ban the poll tax in state and local elections. The poll tax had already been banned in federal elections by Amendment XXIV of the Constitution, ratified in 1964, but four states—Alabama, Mississippi, Texas, and Virginia—still imposed the tax as a voter qualification in other elections. Attorney General Katzenbach and the Administration questioned the constitutionality of a statutory ban on the poll tax in state elections and strongly opposed its inclusion in the bill. But on the floor of the Senate, Kennedy staged a spectacular and almost successful fight, which established the youngest brother of the late President as a political figure to be reckoned with. The poll tax ban amendment was defeated, but only by the bare majority of 49 to 45. Meanwhile Kennedy's fight encouraged supporters of the poll tax ban in the House and it was included in the bill passed by that body. It was eliminated in the House-Senate conference report. Nevertheless the bill as finally passed declared the finding of Congress that the poll tax abridged the constitutional right of citizens to vote and directed the Attorney General to seek its invalidation through the courts. The Supreme Court eliminated the poll tax completely in a decision nine months later.

The Act was drawn with painful ingenuity to deal drastically only with those sections of the country where Negro disfranchisement was practiced—in the words of Senator Dirksen, "only to send the fire wagon where the fire is." The use of the tests and other devices that had so often been used to deny registration to Negroes was banned in those states and political subdivisions in which a literacy test or similar qualifying device was in force on November 4, 1964, and where fewer than 50 per cent of the population voted, or were registered to vote, in the 1964 presidential election. The states and subdivisions thus affected were Alabama, Alaska, Georgia, Louisiana, Mississippi, South Carolina, Virginia, twenty-six counties in North Carolina, and one county in Arizona. Those states and counties could no longer require, as a prerequisite to voting, demonstration of educational achievement, knowledge of any particular subject, or ability to interpret any given material; they could not require proof of good moral character or the endorsement of some already registered voter. All of these devices lent themselves to discriminatory use by anti-Negro registrars. Wherever local officials balked or delayed, federal examiners could be sent in to do the job.

In signing the bill into law on August 6, President Johnson recalled that Negroes had come to these shores originally "in darkness and in chains," and said: "Today we strike away the last major shackle of those fierce and ancient bonds. Today the Negro story and the American story fuse and blend." Implementation of the new law proceeded with extraordinary dispatch. The President announced at the signing on Friday August 6:

> Tomorrow at 1 P.M. the Attorney General, at my direction, will file a lawsuit challenging the constitutionality of the poll tax in Mississippi. This will begin the legal process which, I confidently believe, will very soon prohibit any state from requiring the payment of money in order to vote.
>
> And also by tomorrow the Justice Department, through publication in the Federal Register, will have officially certified the states where discrimination exists.
>
> I have, in addition, requested the Justice Department to work all this weekend so that on Monday morning they can designate any counties where past experience shows federal action to be necessary. And by Tuesday trained federal examiners will be at work registering men and women in 10 to 15 counties.

That schedule was punctually followed. Scores of Justice Department employees worked through the weekend. Forty-five federal examiners—some of them Negroes—had already been trained in a special course by the Civil Service Commission. Eighteen of these were dispatched Monday, two each, to nine hard-core segregationist counties in Alabama, Louisiana, and Mississippi. Twenty-seven others awaited assignment to additional counties in those states and in Georgia and South Carolina.

Prospective Negro voters promptly jammed federal examiners' offices in the Black Belt. On Tuesday, hundreds turned out to register in Selma; in Canton, Mississippi, the examiners were unable to cope with the crowd in a single day; long lines of Negroes sought registration in three Louisiana parishes. A Justice Department survey showed that in the first two months 110,000 Negroes were registered by local officials in the affected states, and, by October 25, 56,000 additional Negroes had been registered by federal examiners. The pace slackened somewhat in September, reflecting lingering fear of white reprisals and apathy, but Negroes continued to register. By August 6, 1966, one year after the signing of the Voting Rights Act, the number of Negroes registered to vote in the six Southern states affected was estimated at 1,289,000, or nearly 46 per cent of those of voting age. A year earlier the number had been just over 870,000. In Alabama the number of Negroes on the voting lists more than doubled, increasing from 113,493 to 248,000, or 51.5 per cent of the Negro voting-age population. In Mississippi, Negro registration increased from 25,265 to an estimated 139,000—though this was still only 32.9 per cent of the Negroes of voting age in that state.

The federal examiners had proved their worth. They received applicants with a friendly courtesy to which Negroes were little accustomed in the Black Belt; some Negroes heard themselves addressed as "Mr." or "Mrs." by a white official for the first time in their lives. The presence of federal examiners was also a reminder of the futility of obstructionist tactics and stimulated unprecedented activity by local registrars. Federal examiners themselves, who were then functioning in forty-two counties, had registered 123,981 persons.*

While this new law in the field of voting rights was moving toward enactment, broad implementation of the Civil Rights Act of 1964 was at last getting under way. There was delay in the field of employment, where the ban on discrimination would not come into effect until July 2, 1965, but the Act's other provisions for stamping out racial segregation and discrimination had produced a massive activity in the federal establishment. By the fall of 1965

* Statistics from August 5, 1966, press release, Southern Regional Council.

it would be possible to say that the Civil Rights Act of 1964 had prompted more desegregation than all the laws, court decisions, and executive orders of the previous decade. The mere fact that Congress had declared discrimination unlawful accelerated the trend toward equal treatment before enforcement pressures were brought to bear. Yet, measured against the Act's whole undertaking, the progress that had been made was only a tiny beginning.

The Civil Rights Act of 1964 was intended to rescue the Negro from inferior status, no less. But society and the national economy were so permeated with situations of discrimination against the Negro that the more the evil was attacked, the more of it was exposed and the farther its complete eradication seemed to recede into the future. And there was truth in the warning of Monsignor Edward D. Head in a 1964 Labor Day sermon in New York's St. Patrick's Cathedral: "We are prudent and experienced enough to remember that the passage of the law will no more of itself obliterate racial inequality and injustice than did the striking of the Ten Commandments by God himself obliterate sin or establish a community of grace and justice." Nevertheless the vigor of the Administration's efforts and the public response in the first half of 1965 augured well for the great enterprise. Burke Marshall, after his resignation as Assistant Attorney General, assisted Vice President Humphrey for several months in the gearing-up for implementation of the Act, when regulations were issued by twenty-one federal departments and agencies. "The thing that the Act reaches," Marshall said, "is the official caste system in this country. Our experience shows that we are going to get rid of it. It may take ten more years, but it won't take more than that."

The Act was divided into eleven sections, or titles, of which the most important were Titles II, IV, V, VI, VII, and X. Other sections included a feeble attack upon voter discrimination, strengthened the hand of the Attorney General in court action against discrimination, and called for surveys by the Department of Commerce to determine the extent of the participation of citizens in elections by race, color, and national origin. Still other sections gave the right of trial by jury in most criminal cases under the Act, authorized the necessary appropriations, and preserved the right of states to enact legislation in this area not inconsistent with the Act. It was Title VI (Nondiscrimination in Federally Assisted

Programs)—affecting nearly 200 programs which received over $18 billion of federal aid annually—that placed the heaviest burden of work upon the national administration. This invocation of financial sanctions was to prove the most effective instrument yet found for the elimination of racial discrimination. It is time to examine more closely the titles mentioned and see what was happening under each.

Title II (Public Accommodations), as we have already observed, began to do its work as soon as the bill was signed into law on July 2, 1964, and compliance with it had gone steadily forward—with much less difficulty than had been generally expected. After twelve months virtually all the previously segregated hotels, restaurants, and other places of public accommodation in the larger cities and the vast majority of those in cities of 10,000 population or more had opened their doors to Negroes—even if they did not welcome them.

Title IV (Public Education) authorized the Commissioner of Education (1) to conduct a survey and report on the lack of equal educational opportunity for minority groups, (2) to offer technical assistance to states, political subdivisions, and school districts in the process of desegregation, (3) to arrange training institutes for school personnel in dealing with desegregation problems, and (4) to make grants to school boards for the employment of specialists in such training. This title also authorized the Attorney General to file suits seeking to compel desegregation of public schools and colleges, although for the most part this would be accomplished by the funds cut-off provisions of Title VI without the necessity for court action. In fact Title VI would have a far greater effect upon public education and would place greater responsibilities upon the Commissioner of Education than this section.

The initial introduction of Negro pupils into a previously all-white school, or vice versa, involved many psychological, educational, and administrative problems. The provisions of Title IV empowering the Commissioner of Education to give technical and financial assistance to school districts faced with these problems were designed, in the words of Attorney General Kennedy, to "smooth the path upon which the nation was set by the Brown decision." The help offered by the Office of Education was also an inducement to integrate schools; hostile segregationists had called it a "bribe." But the provisions of Title VI were making desegregation inevitable anyway, and this was a needed service that local school boards were rarely able, or disposed, to provide for themselves. The Office of Education supported institutes, 56 in the first year and 58 in the second, for counseling school administrators and teachers and school board attorneys. It also made grants to state and local school administrations, 27 in the first year, 43 in the second, to conduct similar activities. The appropriation of approximately $8 million for this Title IV activity in 1965-1966 was repeated for fiscal 1967, forecasting its continuance on a similar scale.

About one-fourth of this activity in 1966 was in areas of the North and West where public schools had long been desegregated. De facto segregation existed there, but the Civil Rights Act expressly forbade the use of federal funds to help achieve "racial balance." The Office of Education sought to help nevertheless in solving various problems arising there in the operation of integrated schools.

Title V (Commission on Civil Rights) strengthened that agency, broadened its scope, and extended its life until January 31, 1968. Congress also increased its appropriation from $985,000 in the 1964 fiscal year to $1,280,000 for fiscal 1965. The Commission's staff, reorganized and increased from 76 to 101 members, moved into vigorous activity under William L. Taylor, formerly its general counsel, who was appointed staff director. In the winter of 1965 the Commission was engaged in many activities in connection with the implementation of the Civil Rights Act of 1964—various titles of which it explained to the public in a series of handy pamphlets. It assisted federal departments in the development of regulations and procedures under Title VI and provided staff assistance to the Vice President in his task of coordinating the federal civil-rights program.

As the Commission stated in its preface to the pamphlet, "Title VI—One Year After": "When, by July 1965, it became apparent that formal procedures for the enforcement of Title VI had been completed, the Commission turned its attention to an appraisal of whether those procedures were being effective at the local level in areas where the most overt and simple discriminatory practices had previously been widespread in federally assisted programs." The Commission thus became a watchdog over the implementation of this far-reaching section of the Act—a valuable function, which sometimes aroused the ire, however, of the departments and agencies concerned.

Title VII (Equal Employment Opportunity), dealing with hiring and promotions, labor union practices, and many intricate details of the treatment of workers, took up almost as much of the text of the Act as all the other titles combined. Its gist was a command to employers, labor unions, and employment agencies to treat all persons without regard to their race, color, religion, sex, or national origin. This applied to employers and labor unions with 100 or more workers from July 2, 1965, and coverage was to be extended each year until July 2, 1968, when those with 25 workers would be covered.

In its enforcement, however, this title was replete with sources of frustration and delay. It required that complaints of discrimination should be referred to state and local fair employment practices commissions or officials where such existed. (Thirty-five of the fifty states and the District of Columbia had their own fair employment practices laws or commissions.) These would have as much as 60 days (120 days during the first year) in which to deal with the cases before they would fall within the jurisdiction of the Equal Employment Opportunity Commission, which was created to administer the law. In the cases within its jurisdiction the Commission was to investigate and seek voluntary compliance with the law through mediation and conciliation. It had no enforcement authority. If voluntary compliance failed, the complainant could file suit in federal court or the Commission could recommend that the Attorney General bring suit, but relief could be obtained only through the cumbersome process of litigation.

The five-member Commission also suffered from the delay in setting it up—a delay which appeared to be due to difficulty on the part of the President in finding a suitable man to head it. Although the ban on employment discrimination came into effect only on

July 2, 1965, the members of the Commission could have been appointed at any time after the signing of the Act, and it would have been desirable to give the Commission reasonable time in which to arrange quarters, recruit staff, study its problems, and plan the work. It was not until May 10, 1965, however, that President Johnson announced the appointment of the Commission.

The post of chairman was not easy to fill. It called for a person of such ability and prestige as to make up in part for the weakness of the law, and it was not an attractive job. It promised disappointments and criticism and little opportunity for shining accomplishment. The appointment finally went to Franklin D. Roosevelt, Jr., bearer of an illustrious name and then Under Secretary of Commerce. (Incidentally, his father as President during World War II had initiated the first federal effort in this field by setting up a Fair Employment Practices Commission, which lasted until 1948.)

When the Commission opened its doors on July 2, it was working with only a partial staff in temporary quarters, with policies yet to be formulated and many questions yet to be decided. (Among the latter was the ticklish matter of what constituted sex discrimination!) The Commission was not in full operation until October. By that time it had received 1,383 complaints, of which 966 appeared to come within its jurisdiction. The complaints, largely spurred by the NAACP, were more than it had expected or was prepared to handle. During the first year the number exceeded 8,000. Roosevelt resigned in May 1966 (feeling the call of New York state politics). The Commission remained without a chairman until August 31, when the position was filled by Stephen N. Shulman, general counsel of the Air Force and a former member of the President's Committee on Equal Employment Opportunity.

The duty of seeing to the elimination of employment discrimination on the part of firms holding contracts with the government was transferred from the former President's Committee on Equal Employment Opportunity, which President Kennedy had set up, to a new Office of Federal Contract Compliance, established by executive order in the Department of Labor.

Title X (Community Relations Service) created a conciliation agency, which contributed significantly to the successful implementation of Title II, which banned segregation in places of public accommodation. Former Governor LeRoy Collins of Florida went to work as its director immediately after the signing of the Act on July 2, 1964. He was assisted in the launching of the Community Relations Service by Harold C. Fleming, executive vice president of the Potomac Institute and a veteran of race relations work, who served as deputy director during the first five months. Collins, earlier a defender of segregation, now an ardent apostle of interracial brotherhood, was a man of tact and personal charm, and his background as a former Southern governor was an additional asset in his work of smoothing the path of desegregation in the South. He resigned in June, 1965, to accept the post vacated by Roosevelt as Under Secretary of Commerce.

Calvin Kytle, then deputy director, served as acting director of the Community Relations Service until December, 1965, when Assistant Director Roger W. Wilkins, a thirty-three-year-old nephew of the NAACP's Roy Wilkins, was appointed director. Former Congressman Brooks Hays served as associate director for a few months before resigning to run unsuccessfully for governor of Arkansas. In April, 1966, Congress approved the transfer of the Service from the Department of Commerce, under which it had been placed originally, to the Department of Justice. This move, prompted by the President's desire to concentrate civil-rights activities in the latter department, was opposed in many quarters on the ground that a mingling of conciliation and prosecuting functions would impair the Service's effectiveness.

The role of the Community Relations Service had become somewhat uncertain. Conciliation of contending parties in the civil-rights struggle was obviously a massive need, but specific disputes which might lend themselves to useful mediation by a federal agency were rare. The Service had broadened its activities in promoting interracial harmony beyond the function given it by the Civil Rights Act, "to provide assistance to communities and persons therein in resolving disputes, disagreements, or difficulties relating to discriminatory practices based on race, color or national origin. . . ." It set up a Division of Community Action to assist "in developing both official and voluntary programs to end discrimination and correct inequities, and in upgrading or forming effective human relations commissions." A Division of Media Relations worked "with the local and national news media in interpreting civil-rights events," and developed "pamphlets, brochures and audio-visual material aimed at improving race relations."*

Title VI (Nondiscrimination in Federally Assisted Programs) was the veritable dynamo in the Civil Rights Act of 1964. It contained this sweeping command:

> Section 601. No person in the United States shall, on the ground of race, color or national origin, be excluded from participation in, be denied the benefits of, or be subjected to discrimination under any program or activity receiving Federal financial assistance.

Enforcement of this section was provided for in the powerful language of dollars and cents. Federal departments and agencies were empowered to effect compliance "by the termination of, or refusal to grant or to continue assistance under such program or activity to any recipient as to whom there has been an express finding on the record, after opportunity for hearing, of a failure to comply...."

A large part of national life was affected by this title. It covered the whole spectrum of programs, public works, and institutions which received any amount of federal support. Activities in the basic fields of education, economic opportunity, agriculture, business, housing, health care, and welfare—such diverse services as school lunches, airport construction, maternity and infant care, nurses' training, and forest protection—were involved. And the law forbade not only exclusion of Negroes, but also details of discrimination such as "White" and "Colored" signs, separate facilities for withdrawing library books, or separate hours for the use of a hospital recreation room by patients of one race.

The National Guard units of the several states receive heavy federal financial support, yet as late as 1962, ten Southern states had no Negro National Guardsman of any rank. As a result of increasing pressure, which was capped by the Civil Rights Act, Negroes were enrolled in each of these states by the end of 1964. The elimination of lingering discrimination in the recruitment, assignment, and promotion of Guardsmen would be a much longer process.

---

* *Catalog of Federal Programs for Individual and Community Improvement*, Office of Economic Opportunity, December 15, 1965.

Every applicant for new or continued federal assistance was required to submit a statement that it was, or would immediately begin, complying with the law and the regulations issued under it. More than 100,000 such assurances of compliance were received before the end of the first year. But progress reports were required, inspection tours by several hundred federal investigators would be necessary, and it would be many months, in fact years, before the elimination of discrimination would be complete.

Of the ten departments and twelve agencies of the federal government concerned, the heaviest burden of Title VI fell upon the Department of Health, Education and Welfare. HEW's vast allocations of federal funds included many situations in which racial discrimination was deeply entrenched. Complaints poured in to that department; in the first half of 1965, seven hundred complaints charged discrimination in schools, 350 in hospitals, receiving federal aid. The Office of Education disbursed $2 billion a year in aid to schools, and it faced a challenge which had baffled all efforts for a decade—that of putting an end to public school segregation in the South.

The new responsibilities necessitated some reorganization and expansion of the already huge aggregation of bureaus and offices that made up HEW. Commissioner of Education Francis Keppel was elevated to the rank of Assistant Secretary and Harold Howe II was appointed to succeed him as head of the Office of Education. A unit was established called the Equal Educational Opportunity Program, which was put in the charge of David S. Seeley, a former Peace Corps official. Directly attached to the Secretary's office, an office was set up to be headed by a Special Assistant for Civil Rights—a post later to be filled by F. Peter Libassi, then deputy staff director of the Commission on Civil Rights. In July, 1965, President Johnson named John W. Gardner, president of the Carnegie Corporation and a leading figure in American education—strongly committed to end discrimination—to succeed Anthony J. Celebrezze as Secretary of HEW.

Most of the affected institutions and activities across the nation were able to establish the absence of discrimination from the start, or took prompt steps to end the discriminatory practices that existed. But in many cases, particularly in the South, compliance could be obtained only after haggling and struggle. In April, 1966, Secretary Gardner reported that returns from a questionnaire sent to 8,250 hospitals showed that 4,000 were in compliance with the guidelines, 400 definitely not. Other returns were being processed or were under negotiation. In the recalcitrant school districts of the former Confederate states the Office of Education guidelines called for a good faith start on desegregation forthwith—usually the desegregation of four grades—and complete desegregation by the fall of 1967. Though evasion and subterfuge were still practiced, by October, 1965, 97 per cent of the 4,946 school districts in Southern and border states had had their desegregation plans approved. Desegregation proceeded promptly in some districts where resistance was most expected. In Neshoba County, Mississippi, the scene of the murder of three civil-rights workers the year before, ten Negro pupils had been admitted to classes with white children. But 97 districts offered unacceptable plans, and 69 refused to submit any desegregation plan at all.

At the other end of the squeeze that caught recalcitrant Southern school districts, the Department of Justice pushed dozens of suits to compel desegregation by court order.

Negro leaders charged that HEW was accepting only "paper compliance," resulting in only token desegregation, and complained of the gradualism in all this. Equality should be established at once and let the white-supremacists get used to it as gradually as they pleased. But many whites thought the Office of Education was "moving too fast," and a storm of protest rose. Commissioner Howe became the chief scapegoat for Title VI and anathema to the segregationists of the Deep South. In September, 1966, he was attacked with vituperation by Southerners in Congress. But the tall, square-jawed, 200-pound Commissioner—who had been a school superintendent and had commanded a Navy mine sweeper in World War II—never flinched.

Before 1964, Southern defiance of the Supreme Court's express command that public school segregation must end had been a national scandal. Ten years after the Supreme Court's decision only 34,110 of the South's 2,894,563 Negro school children had been integrated with whites. That was 1.18 per cent of the total. In the fall of 1964 the percentage nearly doubled; in 1965 it rose to 5.2 per cent; and in 1966 it doubled again. Public school segregation in the South had not ended, but—excepting the de facto variety—it was at last inescapably on its way out.

The reduction in the number of all-Negro classes and the dispersal of Negro pupils among previously all-white schools frequently resulted in the removal, on one pretext or another, of Negro teachers. Many Southern whites were unwilling to entrust their children to them. The National Education Association and other groups were active in finding openings for these teachers elsewhere. New York Commissioner of Education James E. Allen urged school superintendents in that state to hire qualified Negro teachers from the South. An NEA survey found that 668 Negro teachers in Southern and border states had been displaced or downgraded for reasons related to school integration from May through September, 1965; 85 per cent of these had found teaching posts elsewhere, or other employment. Accurate figures on the whole picture are not available but the number of Negro teachers affected probably reached 5,000 by the end of 1966—out of over 110,000 in Southern and border states.

Another source of some embarrassment was the shift of white children in the South from racially mixed public schools to burgeoning private schools, where segregation could be continued. But this failed to reach critical proportions. Earlier, a general flight to private schools had been widely predicted. However, in South Carolina and Mississippi, where the movement had made most headway, private schools at the end of 1966 had enrolled only about 4,500 and 2,000 pupils respectively. This compared with approximately 660,000 pupils in the public schools of each state. Four states extended subsidies to private schools in the form of tuition grants to their pupils, but this, as a device for evading desegregation, was under attack in federal courts. Discrimination against Negro teachers was also under legal attack.

From the introduction in July, 1963, of what became the Civil Rights Act of 1964, to the enactment of the Voting Rights Act of 1965, Congress, under Administration pressure, had rounded out an impressive achievement in the civil-rights field. Implementation of the new legislation still left much to be desired, but—as historian C. Vann Woodward observed in the *New York Times Magazine* of August 29, 1965—Congress had "put more teeth into law and more law on the books than . . . in the whole period since 1875."

THIRTEEN

The Problem of Rehabilitation
1965

The problem of the disintegrating Negro family received much attention in 1965—surreptitiously in large part, but boldly in a memorable speech by the President of the United States. It was, as we noted in Chapter 7, a touchy subject.

Controversy centered early in the year around a mysterious Department of Labor document called the "Moynihan report." Compiled for the President, this was originally intended for use within the Administration and was considered confidential, but its contents leaked to the press bit by bit. Before the end of the year the report, entitled "The Negro Family: The Case for National Action," could be had in a 78-page brochure at the Government Printing Office for 45 cents. Its principal author was Assistant Secretary of Labor Daniel Patrick Moynihan. Moynihan was warmly sympathetic with the Negro movement, but he grappled with this problem with unprecedented boldness. (Moynihan resigned in July to run unsuccessfully for president of the New York City Council.)

The report began with a penetrating analysis of the "Negro American revolution," which, it said, "is rightly regarded as the most important domestic event of the postwar period in the United States." It saw also "profound international implications."

It was in no way a matter of chance that the nonviolent tactics and philosophy of the movement, as it began in the South, were consciously adapted from the techniques by which the Congress Party undertook to free the Indian nation from British colonial rule. It was not a matter of chance that the Negro movement caught fire in

America at just that moment when the nations of Africa were gaining their freedom. Nor is it merely incidental that the world should have fastened its attention on events in the United States at a time when the possibility that the nations of the world will divide along color lines seems suddenly not only possible, but even imminent.

The report reviewed events in the areas of law and public administration which made it possible to say that "the demand of Negro Americans for full recognition of their civil rights" had been met, but that the nation now faced "a different set of challenges, which may prove more difficult to meet. . . ." For it found "a considerable body of evidence to support the conclusion that Negro social structure, in particular the Negro family, battered and harassed by discrimination, injustice and uprooting, is in the deepest trouble." Among the Negro middle class, family stability was as great as, or greater than, among the white middle class. But "the emergence and increasing visibility of a Negro middle-class may beguile the nation into supposing that the circumstances of the remainder of the Negro community are equally prosperous, whereas just the opposite is true. . . ."

The report presented conclusive statistics to bear out such statements as these:

> Nearly a quarter of Negro women living in cities who have ever married are divorced, separated, or living apart from their husbands.
> Nearly one-quarter of Negro births are now illegitimate.

This theme was further developed by President Johnson in his speech of June 4, 1965, of which the "Moynihan report" was the chief source and inspiration. The speech, delivered appropriately at Howard University, was historic in its frank recognition by an American President of "white America's" responsibility for the Negro's "long years of degradation and discrimination," and his call "to end the one huge wrong of the American nation." It was illuminating in its succinct portrayal of the Negro revolution, than which, the President said, "nothing in any country touches us more profoundly and nothing is more freighted with meaning for our own destiny." Leslie W. Dunbar, one of the most perceptive observers of that revolution, said of his speech: "Since its delivery there is little anyone can add or needs to add to draw attention to the severity of the national problems and the widespread misery of

Negro Americans." We would be remiss if we failed to quote extensively from that speech here.

"The American Negro," the President said, "acting with impressive restraint, has peacefully protested and marched, entered the courtrooms and the seats of government, demanding a justice that has long been denied." And his protest had met with a massive response. "It is a tribute to America that, once aroused, the courts and the Congress, the President and most of the people, have been the allies of progress."

> Thus we have seen the high court of the country declare that discrimination based on race was repugnant to the Constitution, and therefore void. We have seen in 1957, 1960, and again in 1964, the first civil rights legislation in this Nation in almost an entire century.

But he realized that the revolution had still a long way to go.

> The voting rights bill will be the latest, and among the most important, in a long series of victories. But this victory—as Winston Churchill said of another triumph for freedom—"is not the end. It is not even the beginning of the end. But it is, perhaps, the end of the beginning."
>
> That beginning is freedom. And the barriers to that freedom are tumbling down. Freedom is the right to share fully and equally in American society—to vote, to hold a job, to enter a public place, to go to school. It is the right to be treated in every part of our national life as a person equal in dignity and promise to all others.
>
> But freedom is not enough. You do not wipe away the scars of centuries by saying: Now you are free to go where you want, do as you desire, and choose the leaders you please.
>
> You do not take a person who, for years, has been hobbled by chains and liberate him, bring him up to the starting line of a race and then say, "you are free to compete with all the others," and still justly believe that you have been completely fair. . . .
>
> Thus it is not enough just to open the gates of opportunity. All our citizens must have the ability to walk through those gates.
>
> This is the next and more profound stage of the battle for civil rights. . . .

In spite of great progress among a minority, the lot of most Negroes in recent years had actually worsened in relation to that of whites.

The number of Negroes in schools of higher learning has almost doubled in 15 years. The number of nonwhite professional workers has more than doubled in 10 years. The median income of Negro college women exceeds that of white college women. And there are also the enormous accomplishments of distinguished individual Negroes, many of them graduates of this institution....

These are proud and impressive achievements. But they tell only the story of a growing middle-class minority steadily narrowing the gap between them and their white counterparts.

But for the great majority of Negro Americans—the poor, the unemployed, the uprooted and the dispossessed—there is a much grimmer story. They still are another nation. Despite the court orders and the laws, despite the legislative victories and the speeches, for them the walls are rising and the gulf is widening.

Here are some of the facts of this American failure.

Thirty-five years ago the rate of unemployment for Negroes and whites was about the same. Today the Negro rate is twice as high.

In 1948 the 8 percent unemployment rate for Negro teen-age boys was actually less than that of whites. By last year the rate had grown to 23 percent, as against 13 percent for whites.

Between 1949 and 1959, the income of Negro men relative to white men declined in every section of this country. From 1952 to 1963 the median income of Negro families compared to white actually dropped from 57 percent to 53 percent....

The infant mortality of nonwhites in 1940 was 70 percent greater than whites. Twenty-two years later it was 90 percent greater.

Moreover, the isolation of Negro from white communities is increasing, rather than decreasing, as Negroes crowd into the central cities and become a city within a city.

Of course Negro Americans as well as white Americans have shared in our rising national abundance. But the harsh fact of the matter is that in the battle for true equality too many are losing ground every day.

Why did this situation exist? Not all the answers were clear, but we did know "the two broad basic reasons." First, there was poverty, and the lack of training and medical care. Beyond this was a "cause much more difficult to explain": disabilities which other ethnic groups had not had to combat—"the devastating heritage of long years of slavery; and a century of oppression, hatred and injustice."

We are not completely sure why this is. The causes are complex and subtle. But we do know the two broad basic reasons. And we do know that we have to act.

First, Negroes are trapped—as many whites are trapped—in inherited, gateless poverty. They lack training and skills. They are shut in slums, without decent medical care. Private and public poverty combine to cripple their capacities.

We are trying to attack these evils through our poverty program, through our education program, through our medical care and our other health programs and a dozen more of the Great Society programs that are aimed at the root causes of this poverty.

We will increase, and accelerate, and broaden this attack in years to come until this most enduring of foes finally yields to our unyielding will. But there is a second cause—much more difficult to explain, more deeply grounded, more desperate in its force. It is the devastating heritage of long years of slavery; and a century of oppression, hatred and injustice.

For Negro poverty is not white poverty. Many of its causes and many of its cures are the same. But there are differences—deep, corrosive, obstinate differences—radiating painful roots into the community, the family, and the nature of the individual.

These differences are not racial differences. They are solely and simply the consequence of ancient brutality, past injustice, and present prejudice. They are anguishing to observe. For the Negro they are a constant reminder of oppression. For the white they are a constant reminder of guilt. But they must be faced and dealt with and overcome, if we are ever to reach the time when the only difference between Negroes and whites is the color of their skin.

Nor can we find a complete answer in the experience of other American minorities. They made a valiant and a largely successful effort to emerge from poverty and prejudice. The Negro, like these others, will have to rely mostly on his own efforts. But he just cannot do it alone. For they did not have the heritage of centuries to overcome. They did not have a cultural tradition which had been twisted and battered by endless years of hatred and hopelessness. Nor were they excluded because of race or color—a feeling whose dark intensity is matched by no other prejudice in our society.

Nor can these differences be understood as isolated infirmities. They are a seamless web. They cause each other. They result from each other. They reinforce each other. Much of the Negro community is buried under a blanket of history and circumstance. It is not a lasting solution to lift just one corner of that blanket. We must stand on all sides and raise the entire cover if we are to liberate our fellow citizens.

He pictured the intolerable condition of Negroes in big-city ghettos (one of which would explode ten weeks later in more frightful rioting than any yet seen).

One of the differences is the increased concentration of Negroes in our cities. More than 73 percent of all Negroes live in urban areas compared with less than 70 percent of the whites. Most of these Negroes live in slums. Most of them live together—a separated people. Men are shaped by their world. When it is a world of decay, ringed by an invisible wall—when escape is arduous and uncertain, and the saving pressures of a more hopeful society are unknown—it can cripple the youth and desolate the man.

There is also the burden that a dark skin can add to the search for a productive place in society. Unemployment strikes most swiftly and broadly at the Negro. This burden erodes hope. Blighted hope breeds despair. Despair brings indifference to the learning which offers a way out. And despair, coupled with indifference, is often the source of destructive rebellion against the fabric of society.

There is also the lacerating hurt of early collision with white hatred or prejudice, distaste, or condescension. Other groups have felt similar intolerance. But success and achievement could wipe it away. They do not change the color of a man's skin. . . .

It was, significantly, before this predominantly Negro audience that the President discussed the breakdown of the Negro family. But this was a curse for which "most of all, white America must accept responsibility." There was no "easy answer," though it called for greater efforts in the fields of education, employment, public welfare, social and health programs—and especially "an understanding heart by all Americans."

Perhaps most important—its influence radiating to every part of life—is the breakdown of the Negro family structure. For this, most of all, white America must accept responsibility. It flows from centuries of oppression and persecution of the Negro man. It flows from long years of degradation and discrimination, which have attacked his dignity and assaulted his ability to provide for his family.

This, too, is not pleasant to look upon. But it must be faced by those whose serious intent is to improve the life of all Americans.

Only a minority—less than half—of all Negro children reach the age of 18 having lived all their lives with both of their parents. At this moment little less than two-thirds are living with both of their parents. Probably a majority of all Negro children receive federally aided public assistance sometime during their childhood.

The family is the cornerstone of our society. More than any other force it shapes the attitude, the hopes, the ambitions, and the values of the child. When the family collapses it is the children that are usually damaged. When it happens on a massive scale the community itself is crippled.

So, unless we work to strengthen the family, to create conditions under which most parents will stay together—all the rest: schools and playgrounds, public assistance and private concern, will never be enough to cut completely the circle of despair and deprivation.

There is no single easy answer to all of these problems.

Jobs are part of the answer. They bring the income which permits a man to provide for his family.

Decent homes in decent surroundings, and a chance to learn—an equal chance to learn—are part of the answer.

Welfare and social programs, better designed to hold families together are part of the answer.

Care of the sick is part of the answer.

An understanding heart by all Americans is also a large part of the answer.

The President announced his intention to call in the fall a conference of leaders and scholars both in and out of government. Its purpose would not be to advance the cause in a strict sense of civil rights, which the Negro was "finally about to secure." It would be to seek ways of helping the Negro "to fulfill these rights"—"to move beyond opportunity to achievement."

But there are other answers that are still to be found. Nor do we fully understand all of the problems. Therefore, I want to announce tonight that this fall I intend to call a White House conference of scholars, and experts, and outstanding Negro leaders—men of both races—and officials of government at every level.

This White House conference's theme and title will be "To Fulfill These Rights."

Its object will be to help the American Negro fulfill the rights which, after the long time of injustice, he is finally about to secure.

To move beyond opportunity to achievement.

To shatter forever not only the barriers of law and public practice, but the walls which bound the condition of man by the color of his skin.

To dissolve as best we can, the antique enmities of the heart which diminish the holder, divide the great democracy, and do wrong—great wrong—to the children of God.

What was being done in mid-1965 to help the Negro to rise? The War on Poverty was aimed at that in large part. Its purpose was to rehabilitate the poor and backward, both white and Negro, and by the $3,000-income rule poverty afflicted one-half of the Negro population, 20 per cent of the white. The Economic Opportunity Act of 1964 declared it to be "the policy of the United States to eliminate the paradox in the midst of plenty in this Nation by opening to everyone the opportunity to live in decency and dignity." That was an undertaking of staggering magnitude. The economist Leon Keyserling told a House committee, after additional funds were appropriated later in the year, that the program could accomplish no more than a fraction, maybe 7 per cent, of its goal. It was nevertheless a groping, stumbling, heroic move in that direction.

There were federal programs for the rehabilitation of communities and the poor antedating the Economic Opportunity Act, with which the War on Poverty was mainly identified, notably the Manpower Development and Training Act of 1962 and the Area Development Act of 1961. There had long been church, philanthropic, and other private groups working in this field, though their scope was meager in proportion to the total need. The Ford Foundation had given some $21 million in three years to programs helping deprived families—largely, though not exclusively, Negro —to improve their environments in a number of cities. The work of Dr. Saul Alinsky and his Industrial Area Foundation in Chicago and elsewhere received much publicity. Dr. Alinsky was a pugnaciously independent individual who bitterly opposed the government's antipoverty program, but he had shown exceptional talent for organizing and stimulating the poor.

Among Negroes the emphasis was still on protest and militancy, but there was more stirring in the field of self-help than heretofore. The *Wall Street Journal* of August 10 described a CORE project in Tallulah, Louisiana, for sprucing up Negro homes and neighborhoods, getting better jobs, reducing school dropouts, and the like. It said a proliferation of such programs indicated "that self-help may eventually replace 'Freedom Now' as the major emphasis in civil-rights activities." More or less similar projects were noted in Washington, D.C., Tulsa, Jacksonville, Hartford, Atlanta, and elsewhere. In a 1,500-member Southern Consumers' Cooperative in Louisiana, Negro savings were being used to provide credit for Negro business enterprises. The NAACP and the National Urban League were jointly sponsoring a job-training program in Cleveland. Gloster Current, the NAACP's director of branches, was quoted as saying: "Once civil-rights groups like ours get over the burden of competing for news space with the more dramatic activities, we can turn our attention to the less dramatic but important things like self-help."

In the great experiment of the federal government, as June 30 brought fiscal 1965 to an end, the Office of Economic Opportunity (OEO), set up to administer the Economic Opportunity Act, had disbursed $195 million of its $790-million appropriation; nearly all of the remainder had been obligated. The OEO had been strenuously busy—organizing, assembling personnel, opening offices, planning, issuing attractive brochures on its various offerings, enrolling applicants in a dozen programs and otherwise getting on with the massive task of preparation. Some help had been extended to the poor, but, generally speaking, the wheels of operation were just beginning to turn.

However, the War on Poverty was already beset with difficulties and hounded with criticism and complaints. In an enterprise so new in human experience it could hardly have been otherwise. For this was not an effort directly to feed and clothe the hungry and destitute—as some of the poor imagined—but a program to change men and women. And the poor were not a mass of docile suppliants eager to labor and learn, but an infinite variety of deprived human beings whose psychology, rivalries, resentments, suspicions, propensities, and aspirations were still only dimly understood. To give the poor a bright future of self-supporting citizenship had to be a process of trial and error, and it would take a long time—five, ten years, maybe a generation. "Criticism, experimentation, and even mistakes," said OEO's undaunted director, "are what makes democracy work." The question was: would Sargent Shriver, OEO, and the nation persevere?

It is not said in a derisive sense that Shriver's idealism, his dedication, and his handsome face fitted him for the image of a Galahad leveling his lance at the enemies of the poor. He was a man of boundless energy, an able, imaginative administrator and a cogent spokesman for the undertaking. He commanded respect for his universally applauded achievement in launching the Peace Corps. Unfortunately Shriver continued to direct the Peace Corps along with his exacting task at OEO, and did not relinquish the former post until the beginning of 1966. Politics, which would plague the War on Poverty increasingly, had, in its inception, deprived it of a uniquely valuable leader. Adam Yarmolinsky had been its chief planner and was expected to be Shriver's right-hand man. He was sacrificed to Southern Congressmen, who found him too liberal and forced his removal as the price for their voting for the poverty bill.

Shriver succeeded in surrounding himself with men of exceptional ability, though necessarily lacking in experience or expertise in this new field. Some 500 "consultants" were employed at fees ranging from $35 to $100 a day; half a dozen of these served as top executives. As of June 30, 1965, 616 persons had been appointed to permanent positions, drawing annual salaries of from $9,500 to $25,000. The seemingly lavish pay scale aroused some of the noisiest criticism of the War on Poverty.

The major programs of OEO were divided into three categories, those directed at youth, those for adults, and those for communities, and a fourth, related to all three of these, called Volunteers in Service to America, or VISTA. VISTA was a kind of domestic version of the Peace Corps, with a similar appeal to the unfailing reservoir of American idealism. Its unsalaried volunteers were to go into slums and backwoods communities and perform services similar to those of Peace Corpsmen in underdeveloped countries abroad. Twenty thousand volunteers had applied, 851 were in training, and 202 were in the field.

Poverty-blighted youth—whose redemption was so much to be desired—furnished the toughest customers for OEO. Many in this category were undisciplined, intractable, and indolent, not a few had vicious habits and criminal tendencies. Embarrassing incidents occurred and these received inordinate publicity. Shriver was to say five months later: "To read some newspapers one would believe that the Job Corps is characterized by riots, fights, violence and mismanagement. The facts, however, reveal that: (1) There are 17,000 young men and women in Job Corps today. Out of these 17,000 less than 1 per cent have ever been involved in any disturbance of any significance. (2) There are 70 Job Corps centers in operation today. Most people have never heard of 95 per cent of them because 'nothing' ever happens there—'nothing,' that is except education, work, and rehabilitation of youngsters formerly out of work and out of school." The Job Corps was one of three youth projects; it had enrolled 10,241 at mid-year. It was to prove one of the most expensive of OEO operations, the cost reaching $4,500 per enrollee for nine months of training.

A Neighborhood Youth Corps provided work near home, largely part-time, together with counseling and some remedial education, for school dropouts, problem students, delinquents, and others. It sought to get these to stay in school or return to school. Two hundred and seventy-eight thousand had enrolled in this. A College Work-Study program arranged part-time work on and off campus to enable needy students to remain in college. It was aiding some 40,000 students.

For adults, an Adult Basic Education program had enrolled 37,991 persons, and the number increased to 195,000 by the end of the year. Rural Family Loans and Small Business Loans had loaned some $21 million to needy farmers and small enterprises. A Work Experience program was helping 88,700 unemployed adults obtain basic education, skills, and work experience.

The Community Action programs were, in Shriver's words, "at the heart of the War on Poverty," and they took about one-third of its funds. They embraced a great variety of activities carried on by a variety of organizations. Other antipoverty programs were spelled out in some detail in the Economic Opportunity Act. Under this head the OEO was authorized to cover "part or all of the costs" of community programs which provided "services . . . of sufficient scope and size to give promise of progress toward elimination of poverty or a cause or causes of poverty through developing employment opportunities, improving human performance, motivation and productivity, or bettering the conditions under which people live and work." By June 30 local groups had launched Community Action programs in 415 communities and had received 3,222 grants from OEO, totaling $237 million.

The Community Action programs represented, according to

OEO's first annual report, "a unique partnership between local communities and the federal government." But in practice a harmonious partnership was proving exceedingly hard to bring about. The operations involved jobs and federal money, which are everywhere related to politics. The problem was accentuated by a stipulation in the Economic Opportunity Act that programs should be "developed, conducted and administered with the maximum feasible participation of residents of the areas and members of the groups served." In other words, a share of the jobs and of the authority had to be given to representatives of the poor themselves. That share was generally fixed by OEO at from one-fourth to one-third. The arrangement was designed to give greater confidence and dignity to the poor and to provide a channel of communication with them. But it was highly disturbing to politicians who were themselves accustomed to distribute city jobs and control jobholders. Political friction delayed the launching of Community Action programs in some of the cities—Los Angeles was a tragic example—where such help was most urgently needed.

Nevertheless most Community Action programs were proceeding smoothly, apart from the troubles to be expected in activities so innovative and so largely experimental. One program, "Head Start," was winning nearly universal praise. Under Head Start, poor children four and five years of age were given eight weeks of intensive training and general care to enable them to begin their educational careers more nearly on a par with children from middle-class homes. They were given a nourishing lunch every day, received proper attention from physicians and dentists, and by specially trained teachers were led gently into the world of books, pictures, music, and classroom activity. This project, originally planned for 100,000, by June 30 had enrolled over 560,000 children in 13,400 classrooms in 2,400 communities. Mrs. Johnson, the First Lady, was honorary chairman.

FOURTEEN

Watts

1965

The Los Angeles riots of August 11-17, 1965 (one week after the signing of the Voting Rights Act) came as a bewildering surprise—an indication of how little was yet known of the condition and temper of Negroes in the big-city ghettos. A surprise the rioting plainly was—to Los Angeles, to California, and to the nation. The Council on Human Relations and representatives of federal civil-rights agencies in Los Angeles had predicted trouble if the problems of the Negroes continued to be neglected, but their warnings were less emphatic here than in most other large cities. Commentators shook their heads wisely after the event and said it was evident that it had to come. But nobody had foreseen this conflagration—nobody except possibly Howard H. Jewel. Jewel, who was then serving as an assistant to California Attorney General Stanley Mosk, had written a memorandum to his chief on May 24, 1964, in which he said that Los Angeles police and Negroes were "embarked upon a course of conflict. . . . If violence erupts, millions in property damage may ensue, untold lives may be lost. . . ." The Jewel report was dug out of the files and made public after the upheaval was over.

United States Assistant Attorney General John Doar remarked in June 1965 that "racial trouble" during the coming summer was "somewhat less likely than last summer." Many other observers did see ghetto disturbances impending—but in New York, Chicago, Philadelphia, or some other city than Los Angeles. The *Reader's Digest* had published an article in its October, 1964, number entitled, "How Los Angeles Eases Racial Tensions." Eulogizing the

Los Angeles County Commission on Human Relations, the authors (Patricia and Ronald M. Deutsch) said: "African and Asian representatives have been brought there to see how Americans can deal with the civil-rights struggle. CHR's files are full of letters of thanks and admiration from other cities." Theodore H. White wrote in *The Making of the President 1960:* "Los Angeles is that city of the United States where the Negro probably receives the most decent treatment and has the best opportunity for decent housing." The city had received mildly favorable notice from Negro observers. A "statistical portrait" drawn in 1964 by the National Urban League, rating American cities in terms of housing, employment, and other basic aspects of Negro life, ranked Los Angeles first among the sixty-eight cities examined. The pre-eminent Negro magazine *Ebony*, in its March, 1965, issue, listed Los Angeles among the "10 best cities for Negro employment," noting: "In October 1964 the city's overall unemployment rate was 5.2 per cent, equalling the national figure. Unemployment among its half million Negroes during the same period was 7.9 per cent, high but not double the overall figure as is the case nationally."

Negroes were much in evidence in downtown Los Angeles, particularly in and about city, county, state, and federal office buildings. They held 25 per cent of the county government jobs. Negroes also held three of the 15 seats on the Los Angeles city council. Two of the city's state assemblymen, the city's postmaster, and one Congressman from Los Angeles County were Negroes.

More than 90 per cent of Los Angeles Negroes live in the city's Central District, south of Downtown. Nearly all of these are in nine of the district's thirty named communities, the poorest of the nine being Watts, just north of the city's southern boundary. This part of affluent Los Angeles is a far cry from Beverly Hills, but it is also unlike the congested slums of eastern cities. There were nine swimming pools and thirty other public recreational facilities in the area. A motorist driving along its miles of wide avenues receives an impression of palm trees and colorful flowering plants, of modern homes, tidy gardens, and shiny automobiles. (Ten per cent of Los Angeles Negro families have incomes over $10,000 a year.) In some neighborhoods an observant pedestrian would have noted dilapidated and overcrowded houses, shabby stores, and knots of idle, despondent loiterers on the streets. But even Watts is spacious, and, with its tree-lined avenues and many attractive bungalows on neatly landscaped plots, is not, to the casual view, wholly out of line with the generally pleasing pattern.

Nevertheless Negroes terrified Los Angeles with the most destructive civil disorder thus far in the nation's peacetime history. At its height 10,000 rioters (by the minimum estimate) attacked white motorists, overturned and burned automobiles, exchanged shots with law enforcement officers, looted, set fire to stores, and stoned and obstructed firemen. The destruction was spectacular and appalling—to the cry of: "Burn, baby, burn!" When order was restored, 34 persons had been killed (25 of them Negroes) and 1,032 wounded or hurt; 3,952 had been arrested; 977 buildings had been looted, damaged, or destroyed.

Property damage far exceeded the total of all previous racial disorders of the 1960's. The lurid picture of smoke and flames, and chaos in the streets, lent itself to exaggeration by the most respected news media. Typical were the estimates of property damage in the *New York Times*, first of "over $100 million," then of "near $200 million" and, a week later, of "$46 million." Estimates ultimately settled down to the figures of $35 or $40 million.

As is often the case, the incident that ignited the fuse seemed unimportant. The official investigating body, known as the McCone Commission, in its report four months later gave the following account:

> On August 11, 1965, California Highway Patrolman Lee W. Minikus, a Caucasian, was riding his motorcycle along 122nd Street, just south of the Los Angeles city boundary, when a passing Negro motorist told him he had just seen a car that was being driven recklessly. Minikus gave chase and pulled the car over at 116th and Avalon, in a predominantly Negro neighborhood, near but not in Watts. It was 7:00 p.m.
>
> The driver was Marquette Frye, a 21-year-old Negro, and his older brother, Ronald, 22, was a passenger. Minikus asked Marquette to get out and take the standard Highway Patrol sobriety test. Frye failed the test, and at 7:05 p.m., Minikus told him he was under arrest. He radioed for his motorcycle partner, for a car to take Marquette to jail and a tow truck to take the car away.

They were two blocks from the Frye home, in an area of two-story apartment buildings and numerous small family residences. Because it was a very warm evening, many of the residents were outside.

Ronald Frye, having been told he could not take the car when Marquette was taken to jail, went to get their mother so that she could claim the car. They returned to the scene about 7:15 p.m. as the second motorcycle patrolman, the patrol car, and tow truck arrived. The original group of 25 to 50 curious spectators had grown to 250 to 300 persons.

Mrs. Frye approached Marquette and scolded him for drinking. Marquette, who had been peaceful and cooperative, pushed her away and moved toward the crowd, cursing and shouting at the officers that they would have to kill him to take him to jail. The patrolman pursued Marquette and he resisted.

The watching crowd became hostile, and one of the patrolmen radioed for more help. Within minutes, three more highway patrolmen arrived. Minikus and his partner were now struggling with both Frye brothers. Mrs. Frye, now belligerent, jumped on the back of one of the officers and ripped his shirt. In an attempt to subdue Marquette, one officer swung at his shoulder with a night stick, missed, and struck him on the forehead, inflicting a minor cut. By 7:23 p.m., all three of the Fryes were under arrest, and other California Highway Patrolmen and, for the first time, Los Angeles police officers had arrived in response to the call for help.

Officers on the scene said there were now more than 1,000 persons in the crowd. About 7:25 p.m., the patrol car with the prisoners, and a tow truck pulling the Frye car, left the scene. . . .

Someone spat on one of the officers as they were leaving and they stopped long enough to arrest a young Negro woman and a man said to be inciting the crowd to violence. Exaggerated and false rumors spread fast—that the young woman was pregnant and had been abused by the police, that the Fryes had been maltreated, and more. The crowd began to stone automobiles and attack white motorists. Sporadic rock-throwing and vandalism continued until the early hours of the following morning, when twenty-nine persons had been arrested.

Thursday morning the situation was simmering, but it did not boil over until the evening. Efforts were made by both Negroes and whites during the day to ease tensions. The McCone Commission was to report: "We have heard many vivid and impressive accounts of the work of Negro leaders, social workers, probation officers, churchmen, teachers and businessmen in their attempts to persuade the people to desist from illegal activities, to stay in their homes and off the streets, and to restore order." Some of these attended a meeting of several hundred which the Los Angeles County Commission on Human Relations arranged Thursday afternoon at Athens Park, eleven blocks from the scene of the Frye arrests. Mrs. Frye herself, free on bail, appeared there and urged the crowd to "help me and others calm the situation down so that we will not have a riot tonight." The meeting misfired, however. Firebrands took over, and it ended in confusion.

A smaller group, meeting afterward, proposed that white police should be withdrawn from the area and that Negro officers in civilian clothes and unmarked cars should be substituted for them. Police authorities pointed out, however, that, at the urging of Negro leaders, the 200 Negro members had been integrated at random in the widely dispersed force. They could not be readily identified and rushed to one section of the city. It may be added that the Los Angeles police force was not large—5,000 police for 2.65 million people spread over 452 square miles. (New York had 28,000.) The maximum commitment to the rioting was 934 city police officers, aided by 719 men from the county sheriff's office.

The violence that started again Thursday evening spread rapidly and—reaching its greatest fury at night, tending to subside wearily in the morning hours—continued until Saturday evening. A mob of more than 1,000 gathered around 116th and Avalon about 7 P.M. Thursday. Three automobiles were overturned and set afire. For the first time a fire was set in a commercial building. Police had to hold back rioters while firemen fought the flames. The turmoil moved north on Avalon Boulevard, and east—until Watts erupted. Watts seemed to be waiting for the spark. By midnight 500 police officers, deputy sheriffs, and highway patrolmen were struggling to disperse 8,000 rioters. The time had come when both humanity and public safety demanded a massive, nonbrutal show of force—the National Guard. But that would have to wait another twenty-four hours.

Dick Gregory, the wealthy Negro entertainer and intermittent civil-rights crusader, left a night club twenty-five miles away and drove into the riot area about midnight Thursday. Gregory, who had more than once suffered beating at the hands of frenzied white persecutors of the Negro in the Deep South, now roamed the streets at the risk of his life, imploring frenzied Negroes to go home. He received a flesh wound from a bullet (probably intended for a policeman) but labored on through the night.

Seventy-six buildings had been looted and burned by Friday morning. White store-owners rivaled the police as objects of Negro hatred. They had a reputation—justified in many cases—for overcharging, and cheating ignorant Negroes in installment-payment deals. The smaller Negro-owned shops mounted "Blood Brother" signs and were almost always spared. Thousands of men, women, and children looted though they engaged in no other disorder. Looting was widespread at all times. It seemed natural to grab needed articles before stores went up in flames.

By early Friday afternoon, 3,000 were rioting in Watts and two blocks of buildings were burning. Ambulance drivers and firemen refused to go into the area without armed escort. Violence reached fifty blocks to the north, with looting and burning in commercial centers several miles apart. This was the worst night. Firearms came more and more into play. By dawn Saturday, a sheriff's deputy, a city fireman, and eight looters had been killed.

At 10 P.M., 1,336 members of the California National Guard were at last deployed in the area. Their number increased to 3,356 by Saturday morning and by Saturday midnight to the full commitment of 13,900.

The performance of California officials of the highest responsibility reflected not only the general surprise at the outbreak, but a failure on the part of several to sense the gravity of the situation when it came. Only Police Chief William H. Parker gave the riot his undivided attention. Though tactless and obtuse in the area of psychological and social problems, Parker enjoyed national eminence as a policeman in the narrowest sense, and in a riot-suppression crisis of these dimensions he was at his best.

Governor Edmund G. Brown was on a vacation in Greece. His office reached him in Athens with news of the rioting only Friday afternoon. The governor advised calling the National Guard and suggested a curfew before flying back to California the next day. Parker had alerted the adjutant general of the National Guard Thursday afternoon to the possible need for its help. At 10:50 A.M.

on Friday Parker made a formal request for the Guard. Lieutenant Governor Glenn Anderson, the acting governor, was in Berkeley, attending a meeting of the finance committee of the University of California. Some hours of consultation and indecision passed before Anderson arrived in Los Angeles and at 5 P.M. signed a proclamation calling the National Guard.

Mayor Sam Yorty was in San Diego Thursday and in San Francisco Friday meeting speaking engagements. He conferred with Parker by phone Friday morning—concurring in the desirability of calling the Guard—then took a 10:05 plane to keep his engagement at the Commonwealth Club in San Francisco. To the investigating committee afterward the mayor said preposterously: "I have to decide whether I am going to disappoint the audience in San Francisco and maybe make my city look rather ridiculous if the rioting doesn't start again, and the mayor has disappointed the crowd."

Burning, looting, and bloodshed continued Saturday, but in the afternoon the disorders yielded slowly to the massive sweep tactics of Guardsmen marching shoulder to shoulder down the wide streets. (The mob was notably less hostile to the National Guard than to the police.) Armed Guardsmen riding on fire engines stopped the sniping and rock-throwing at firemen and enabled the 100 engine companies then in the area to work effectively. Road blocks were set up, and a curfew, imposed Saturday evening, made it a crime for any unauthorized person to be on the streets after 8 P.M.

"Watts" has become a national sobriquet for the Negro section of Los Angeles and to a large extent for the upheaval itself. However, the community of that name—an independent town before its incorporation in Los Angeles in 1926—covers only two and a half square miles, with a population of about 40,000. The area of disorder in which it was found necessary to impose a curfew spread over 46.5 square miles. It extended from 20th Street south, to the city's southern boundary and ten blocks beyond, to 139th Street in the county. Its population, which was predominantly Negro, was estimated in 1965 at 575,000.

In the relative quiet of Sunday Governor Brown toured the riot area. Many stores having been destroyed, emergency food distribution was instituted. Martin Luther King also arrived in Los

Angeles Sunday, coming from Puerto Rico, where he had addressed a World Convention of Churches Saturday evening. Monday, escorted by six policemen, King visited Watts (where many Negroes had never heard of him) and talked nonviolence to a meeting of about 300. Scattered instances of looting and arson occurred Monday, but virtually ceased Tuesday, and Tuesday evening the curfew was lifted. National Guardsmen continued to control the area until the following Sunday, August 22, when all but a handful were withdrawn.

(During the same week minor racial disturbances flared in the adjacent city of Long Beach and in San Diego. Farther away, short-lived rioting occurred in Chicago and Springfield, Massachusetts. But these disorders were overshadowed by Watts.)

On August 19 Governor Brown announced the appointment of the commission to investigate "the meaning of the incredible events of last week"—eight highly respected citizens, headed by John A. McCone, who had been director of the Central Intelligence Agency until the previous May and was chairman of the Atomic Energy Commission under President Eisenhower. Two of the eight were Negroes: the Reverend James Edward Jones, a member of the board of education, and Earl S. Broady, a superior court judge.

President Johnson sent Under Secretary of Commerce LeRoy Collins to untangle the snarl between Mayor Yorty and others and the OEO, and $1,770,000 of federal antipoverty funds was released for rehabilitation in the riot area. The President also sent a task force headed by Deputy Attorney General Ramsey Clark to confer with city, county, and state authorities and ordered that $29 million worth of school, job-training, small business, and health programs should be expedited. A variety of other rehabilitation activities were undertaken during the next two years. But all of them together were far from adequate.

It was widely predicted in 1965 that even greater turmoil was yet to come. The McCone Commission itself entitled its report: "Violence in the City—An End or a Beginning?" The city was indeed frightened momentarily by a disturbance in Watts in March, 1966, when over 600 Negroes rioted for four hours over a twelve-block area, resulting in two dead and twenty injured, but this outbreak was quelled with both discretion and dispatch by the police. Watts proved no exception to what seemed to be the rule

of the Negro revolution in Northern cities, that—even though subsequent improvements were insignificant compared to the vast
changes needed—one huge convulsion was a catharsis not likely
to be repeated in the same ghetto.

Not only the McCone Commission, but other investigating
groups and hundreds of individuals from far and near visited Los
Angeles to find the explanation for "the incredible events" of mid-
August. Many others had ready judgments without going to much
trouble.

To millions of whites it seemed all a part of the civil-rights
movement: the thing had just gone too far. But nothing was more
misleading. The only well-known figure in the civil-rights crusade
who appeared on the scene was Dick Gregory, vainly trying to
stop the rioters. Had the area been embraced in the civil-rights
movement—had civil-rights organizations marshaled the Negroes
earlier to let off steam in nonviolent demonstrations—Los Angeles
undoubtedly would have been spared much grief. Martin Luther
King called the riots "absolutely wrong, socially detestable and
self-defeating." Roy Wilkins and Whitney Young urged the maximum use of force to stop "rioting and looting" and to "protect life
and property." Said Wilkins in an article in the *New York Amster-
dam News:* "God help black Americans if this is their revolution
and these their revolutionaries." All three, however, urged a vigorous attack upon the underlying causes of Watts unrest. Governor
Brown asked the public to "bear in mind that what happened in
Los Angeles was a senseless, formless riot—not a civil-rights demonstration." President Johnson saw in it "no resemblance to the
orderly struggle for civil rights that has ennobled the past decade."

A large element, of which members of the John Birch Society
are typical, viewed this, like all other public disturbances, as Communist-inspired. The many public and private investigations produced nothing to support this. The McCone Commission reported:
"After a thorough examination, the Commission has concluded that
there is no reliable evidence of outside leadership or preestablished
plans for the rioting. . . ." It noted that the sudden appearance of
Molotoff cocktails and inflammatory handbills and "the unexplained movement of men in cars" supported "the conclusion that
there was organization and planning after the riots commenced,"

but this appeared "to have been the work of several gangs, with membership of young men ranging in age from 14 to 35 years."

Across the Atlantic the London *Times* and the *Economist* both took the view that the Los Angeles riots were not so much a racial problem as a problem of big cities in the modern world—"an American phenomenon," the *Economist* said, "only in the sense that the United States is half a generation ahead of the rest of the world in the development of an industrial urban society with the special problems that it brings. . . ." The *Times* said the riots were directed "not against specific grievances or direct racial discrimination but against a whole complex of frustrations that involve Negroes largely because it is the Negroes who are concentrated in the urban centers."

Incidentally Los Angeles had another ethnic minority, about equally numerous: at the time of the 1960 census there were 576,716 Mexican-Americans living in Los Angeles County. The Mexican-American fared, statistically, only a little better in average family income, a little worse in education and housing, than the Negroes. The McCone Commission observed: "That the Mexican-American community did not riot is to its credit; it should not be to its disadvantage." Why did it not riot? A comprehensive analysis will not be attempted here, but several reasons suggest themselves. Although a majority were concentrated in sprawling ghettos, more Mexican-Americans than Negroes lived in other sections of the county. Many citizens of Mexican origin were indistinguishable in appearance from "Anglos," and found it easier to enter the mainstream. Family stability was a Mexican characteristic: the divorce rate among Mexican-Americans was lower than that among either Negroes or "Anglo" whites. Perhaps most important of all, the Mexican-Americans in 1960 retained a lively sense of racial pride—which was respected in Los Angeles. Mexican Independence Day brought forth many Mexican flags, and public buildings displayed streamers congratulating citizens of Mexican origin on the glorious anniversary. No flags ever flew for Negro Americans.

The prestigious McCone Commission went to work with a staff of 29, aided by 26 consultants. It heard 59 sworn witnesses and interviewed several hundred more; written surveys were conducted of 10,000 persons. The report, rendered December 2, in eighty-eight pages of text, gave a concise account of the events of August 11-17 and made a number of vigorous, if unimaginative, observations and recommendations.

It dealt gently with all public officials, although in the matter of calling the National Guard it felt that Lieutenant Governor Anderson "hesitated when he should have acted," and it noted that Chief of Police Parker was "distrusted by most Negroes." It recommended "expanded community relations programs" for Los Angeles police. On a question debated in many cities, it felt that a civilian review board "would endanger law enforcement," proposed instead an "inspector general" within the police department to hear citizen complaints. It urged recruitment of more Negro personnel for both the city police force and the county sheriff's force. Only 4 per cent of the former and 6 per cent of the latter were Negroes. (It also recommended recruitment of more Mexican-Americans, of whom the percentages were even smaller.)

The Commission recommended for the "curfew area" improvements in educational and health services and transportation facilities, greater efforts to reduce unemployment, and "a continuing urban rehabilitation and renewal program." Noting that two-thirds of the adults in the area had failed to finish high school and nearly 14 per cent were "functional illiterates," it called for a drastic reorganization of the school system. It found the unemployment problem "difficult to assess," but was sure that "unemployment in the Negro community is two to three times that in the white community." (Others estimated unemployment in Watts as high as 34 per cent.) It said the situation demanded "a form of leadership that we have not found" on the part of government, business, labor, the news media, and Negroes themselves.

It might have been added that family instability contributed to the social disintegration in Watts, as Moynihan did not fail to point out. Only 44 per cent of the children there under eighteen were living with both their parents. Also the news of police brutality and unpunished crimes against Negroes in the Deep South encouraged a feeling that the Law was not a protector but an enemy of Negroes. But all of the factors we have mentioned were present to an equal or greater degree in the Negro ghettos of half a dozen other cities. Why did the greatest cataclysm strike Los Angeles?

The McCone Commission asked in a subtitle: "Why Los Angeles?"—but the few paragraphs on this point in its report were not a serious attempt to answer the question. They noted the rapid growth of the Negro population of Los Angeles County, which had increased from 75,000 in 1940 to almost 650,000 in 1965. The high hopes of Negroes who had come in such large numbers had met with disillusionment and frustration. California Negroes also nourished resentment over the adoption by a two-to-one vote, in a bitterly fought referendum in 1964, of Proposition 14, repealing fair housing legislation. The Commission said also that "the fundamental problems, which are the same here as in the cities which were racked by the 1964 riots, are intensified by what may well be the least adequate network of public transportation in any major city in America."

The two pages devoted elsewhere in the report to this subject were the Commission's most original contribution. It found the bus service both "inadequate and too costly," and noted that only 14 per cent of the families in Watts are car owners as against at least 50 per cent elsewhere in the county. Five miles from Downtown, a Watts resident had to do some walking and transfer from bus to bus at a cost of a dollar or more to even look for a job there. Ghetto dwellers in New York and Chicago were able to move back and forth and maintain a contact with the outer world. Twenty cents or even a good pair of legs could get one out of Harlem at least for the day.

The Commission could have said also that the problem of police-Negro relations was greater in Los Angeles than in any other large city outside of the Deep South. Above all, the personality of Chief Parker was a constant provocation. If indeed no city had a police chief more skilled in the techniques of law enforcement, certainly none had one more tactless and blind to its social and racial implications. Cynical and racist in his philosophy, Parker deplored the "current soft attitude on the part of the public to crime and civil-rights demonstrations" (putting both in the same category). On Saturday of the rioting he was reported by the Los Angeles *Times* as saying it "might not have occurred if police hadn't been handling Negroes with kid gloves." Parker talked far too much. He said at one news conference that it all started when "one person threw a rock and then like monkeys in a zoo others started throwing rocks." When the riots got under control, he said: "We're on top and they are on the bottom"—which in the Parker view seemed to be the situation to be desired at all times.

The lack of organization and leadership also was more marked in Watts than in other big-city ghettos. The peculiar nature of Los Angeles city administration—there was no political "machine" —deprived the area of the ward heelers and political clubs that elsewhere at least provided a link with the Establishment. The NAACP, CORE, and other civil-rights organizations were represented in Los Angeles, but almost not at all in Watts. Negro ministers in Watts exercised no significant leadership outside of the limited range of their various congregations. There were no organizations more effective than a small band of Black Muslims and numerous gangs of hoodlum youths.

The Negro magazine *Ebony*, with superb aplomb, devoted its August, 1965 (before Watts), issue to "The White Problem in America." In a collection of articles by Negro writers of the first rank it set forth the sins, errors, and shortcomings of the "unthinking white man" which had created the racial crisis. The "white problem" was particularly acute in Los Angeles. Complacency and aloofness had characterized the attitude of most Los Angeles whites toward Negro unrest in the nation. They accepted limited participation by Negroes in public affairs as a safeguard against racial agitation in Los Angeles and as a necessary evil. But, busy making and spending more money per capita than the citizens of any other city in the world, they had little time for sociological or racial concerns. Many were unaware before August, 1965, of the existence of a community called Watts. An undoubted majority shared the views of Police Chief Parker, who was a hero to them. Mayor Yorty vigorously defended Parker and attributed the riots largely to "false, unexplained charges against the police department." James Francis Cardinal McIntyre, the Roman Catholic archbishop of Los Angeles, who, differing radically from other Catholic prelates in the United States, had disciplined priests for civil-rights activities, was also typical. The archbishop characterized the riots as "seemingly unjustifiable demonstrations . . . an instigated revolt against the rights of neighbors and the preservation of law and order."

Nevertheless, after weighing all the exceptional factors mentioned, I find the question: "Why Los Angeles?" not completely answered. Visiting Harlem again, I wondered why that vile ghetto was not the scene of the more terrible conflagration. Alexis de Tocqueville, assessing the causes of the Revolution of February, 1848, in France, observed that "chance, or rather that tangle of secondary causes which we call chance, for want of the knowledge how to unravel it, plays a great part in all that happens on the world stage. . . ." And there I leave it.

FIFTEEN

Crime and Punishment
1965-1966

It is time to take up again the story, which we left off in Chapter 9, of the travesties of justice in Southern courts in the matter of crimes of whites against Negroes and Negro sympathizers. The impunity which perpetrators enjoyed, the sham trials, mistrials, and almost routine acquittal of persons accused of murdering civil-rights workers—while Negroes accused of molesting whites were being punished with a heavy hand—continued to deepen the bitterness in Negro hearts. They contributed significantly to the contempt in many quarters for established (white) authority, and to the spirit of desperation which seized an element of the civil-rights movement in 1966. Several trials involving the race issue in which a flickering of conscience began to emerge were still the exceptions that emphasized the ugly rule. The occasional bombing of a Negro home, the burning of a Negro church, the torturing of a Negro individual in a cowardly night visit—even some obscure killings—might receive little attention from the news media (and less from law enforcement authorities). However a series of murder cases in which the victims were white champions of the Negro cause were heavily publicized and were followed with disgust by the American public.

It will be recalled that one Negro, Jimmie Lee Jackson, and two white Negro sympathizers, the Reverend James Reeb and Mrs. Viola Liuzzo, lost their lives during the agitation in the Selma area in the early part of 1965. Another white idealist, Jonathan Daniels, was murdered there in August. The state trooper who shot Jackson was cleared without indictment on the ground that he had acted in self-defense. What the state courts did in the other three cases furnished an illuminating example of the degradation of judicial processes.

Three men, William E. Hoggle, Namon O'Neal Hoggle, and Elmer J. Cook, accused of bludgeoning and mortally wounding the Reverend James Reeb on March 8, were indicted in Selma on April 13. The charge of Circuit Judge James L. Hare to the grand jury at that time foreshadowed their ultimate acquittal. Judge Hare instructed the jurymen briefly to indict "if you have reasonable cause to believe that the crime was committed as charged," but he orated for forty-two minutes on the ordeal that he said the community had suffered at the hands of civil-rights agitators. He said Selma whites had "shown unbelievable restraint," and fumed: "Many of the ministers of the Gospel who came here would do well to stack their picket signs and get back in the pulpit." The three were not tried until December.

The trials of men accused of killing Mrs. Liuzzo and Jonathan Daniels were held in the old, white-washed Hayneville courthouse in Lowndes County, the county in which those murders occurred. Lowndes lies contiguously east of Dallas County, of which Selma is the county seat. Negroes, though representing 81 per cent of Lowndes' population, had never voted or served on juries in that county in the twentieth century. Three Ku Klux Klansmen from the Birmingham area, Collie Leroy Wilkins, Eugene Thomas, and William Orville Eaton, had been indicted on the charge of murder in Mrs. Liuzzo's death. The first to go on trial—and the only one of the three to be tried in 1965—was Wilkins, a self-employed auto mechanic of twenty-one.

When this trial opened on May 3, Imperial Wizard Robert M. Shelton, Jr., of the United Klans of America and Alabama Grand Dragon Robert Creel were smugly conspicuous in the courtroom. The Klan's general counsel, "Imperial Klonsel" Matt H. Murphy, Jr., conducted the defense. Moton, the Negro youth who had been in the car with Mrs. Liuzzo, and Gary Thomas Rowe (for six years a paid FBI informant inside the Klan), who rode in the murder car with the Klansmen, gave lurid details of the tragedy as they saw it. Instead of producing witnesses to refute their testimony, Klonsel Murphy fouled the air with slimy aspersions upon the Negro race and upon the character of Moton, Rowe, and even Mrs. Liuzzo. He was not completely effective in this instance: phenomenally ten white jurors voted to convict the defendant. But two jurymen voted for acquittal and a mistrial was declared. Another trial would have to be held. Nevertheless the Ku Klux Klan was in a triumphant mood. Wilkins rushed off to attend a rally in Anniston, Alabama, and he marched in a Klan parade in Atlanta. Klonsel Murphy addressed a rally in North Carolina. They were hailed as heroes in Klan circles.

In October the farce was replayed, with certain variations. Matt Murphy had been killed in an auto accident in August; Arthur H. Hanes, a former mayor of Birmingham, conducted the defense this time. Richmond Flowers—who had brought an unprecedented concern for equal justice to the office of state attorney general—exercised his right to supersede the county prosecutor. The attorney general told the jurymen if they did not vote for conviction, "the blood of this man's sin will stain your county for eternity." But after one hour and forty-five minutes of deliberation they voted unanimously for acquittal. When the verdict was announced, the crowd of whites in the courthouse broke into noisy applause.

The murder of Jonathan Myrick Daniels on August 20, followed by testimony from many quarters to the lofty motivation of this twenty-six-year-old intellectual, produced a special wave of shock and sadness in the nation. Tribute was paid from many pulpits to a young man who, as the Right Reverend Paul Moore, Suffragan Episcopal Bishop of Washington said, "felt the call of duty and went down to Alabama to help those people only to be the victim of a brutal shotgun slaying."

A native of Keene, New Hampshire, Daniels had graduated as class valedictorian from the Virginia Military Institute, had studied a year at Harvard, and at the time of his death was between his second and last year at the Episcopal Theological Seminary in Cambridge, Massachusetts. He had worked in the Selma area off and on since March. In a typical article for his theological seminary journal Daniels had written: "We are truly in the world, and yet ultimately not of it. For through the bramble bush of doubt and fear and supposed success we are groping our way to the realization that above all else we are called to be saints. . . ."

Daniels and a companion, the Reverend Richard Morrisroe, a Roman Catholic priest from Chicago, had been arrested, along with twenty-seven Negroes, following a demonstration. Shortly after their release on August 20 the two clergymen were shot down by a cursing, shouting white man who emerged from a Hayneville grocery store. Father Morrisroe was critically wounded, but recovered.

(In view of developments to be recorded in the next chapter it is pertinent to note the reaction of one Stokely Carmichael, the local field secretary of the Student Nonviolent Coordinating Committee. At a Negro indignation meeting in Hayneville two days later Carmichael was reported to have voiced his wrath in language of which the seminarian Daniels would not have approved: "We're going to tear this county up! Then we're going to build it back brick by brick until it's a fit place for human beings!")

Identified as the gunman was Thomas L. Coleman, a state highway department engineer and part-time deputy sheriff, fifty-five years of age. Coleman was a man of considerable standing in Lowndes County, a brother of the superintendent of schools and father of a state trooper. He was indicted only on the charge of manslaughter. The refusal of Circuit Solicitor Arthur Gamble to seek a murder indictment "shocked and amazed" Attorney General Flowers, who entered this case also as prosecutor. The prosecution's chief witness, Father Morrisroe, being in a Chicago hospital still too ill to appear, Flowers asked in vain for a postponement of the trial, which was to open September 28. When the trial opened as scheduled, Flowers' assistant, Joe Breck Grant, refused to proceed. Judge L. Werth Thagard's response was to remove the state attorney general from the case. Gamble and the local prosecutor were ordered to proceed with it.

Grand Dragon Creel, Wilkins, and other Klansmen were again present. The proceedings—amid laughter at Negro witnesses and insinuations of immorality in Daniels' relations with a Negro young lady witness—"assumed," according to *Newsweek* magazine, "an oddly surrealistic character. The prosecution blurred with the defense. Sometimes it seemed Jonathan Daniels was on trial." A plea of self-defense was constructed on vague allegations that the seminarian and the priest were advancing with objects that "looked like" an open pocket knife and a pistol—although Father Morrisroe protested from his hospital bed that they were both unarmed. On September 30, after deliberating one hour and twenty-nine minutes, the jury found the defendant "not guilty."

Attorney General Flowers called the performance a "mockery of law and order." "Now," he said, "those who feel they have a license to kill, destroy and cripple have been issued that license...." The *Washington Post* commented: "It is all very well to say that Hayneville has made a spectacle of itself before the civilized world. The tragedy of the situation is that Hayneville doesn't care. Its sense of justice simply does not extend to civil-rights workers and Negroes."

At the end of November two trials were in progress which would prove at last that punishment of racist murderers was not impossible in Alabama. In the city of Anniston in the northeastern part of the state a white man was on trial in a state court for killing a Negro. In a federal court in Montgomery the three Ku Klux Klansmen accused of slaying Mrs. Liuzzo were being tried, not for murder, but, under the old Reconstruction Era law, for conspiracy to violate the rights of an American citizen.

In Anniston in the excitement following a rally of the anti-Negro National States Rights party on July 15, a Negro, Willie Brewster, driving home from his work at the Alabama Pipe Company foundry, had been shot and fatally wounded from a trailing car. But in Anniston, unlike the Black Belt towns, the mayor and several hundred community leaders had taken a public stand against lawlessness. The Anniston *Star* raised $20,000 as a reward for information leading to the arrest and conviction of the murderer. Three white men were arrested and one of them, Hubert Damor Strange, was brought to trial. After hearing the evidence and the arguments —including that of the defense counsel, a vice president of the National States Rights party, who had addressed the Anniston rally —the twelve white men on the jury rendered a verdict December 2 that was unheard-of in recent Alabama history: Strange was found guilty of murder in the second degree. He was sentenced to ten years in prison.

The federal court jury in Montgomery rendered its verdict on Wilkins, Thomas, and Eaton the next day. This had been the first trial under the old federal law since the modern civil-rights movement began. Federal efforts to prosecute persons accused of the 1964 murders, related in Chapter 9, of Colonel Lemuel A. Penn in Georgia and of three civil-rights workers, Chaney, Schwerner, and Goodman in Mississippi, had been blocked by federal district judges on the ground that such cases came under state and not federal law. Those cases were still under challenge before the Supreme Court.

The trial in federal court in Montgomery proceeded with a solemnity which was in marked contrast to the rowdy burlesque in the state court at Hayneville. The decision again rested with a jury of twelve white Alabamians, people of diverse views chosen from a twelve-county area. Judge Frank M. Johnson, Jr., spent an hour impressing upon them their duty to put prejudices, emotions, and sociological issues aside and to reach a verdict in keeping with the evidence and the law. Witnesses went over much of the ground covered in the two previous trials of Wilkins, and Arthur Hanes was again counsel for the defense. United States Assistant Attorney General John Doar headed the prosecution. The jury found all three defendants guilty of conspiring to violate Mrs. Liuzzo's civil rights; each received the maximum sentence of ten years.

The federal court judgment was appealed, and the case had still a long road to travel, but Wilkins found himself in jail a few weeks later nonetheless. A Birmingham judge sentenced him to one year and a day in federal prison for violating probation on an earlier charge of carrying unregistered firearms.

The trial of the three men accused of killing the Reverend James Reeb, which opened in Selma on December 7, saw a depressing return to Black Belt "justice." Circuit Solicitor Blanchard McLeod, who publicly called the state's case "weak," turned the prosecution over to an assistant. Although the population of this county was 58 per cent Negro, the jury as usual was all white. Two Unitarian ministers, companions of Reeb, were unsure of two of the three accused attackers, but positively identified one of them. Four other eyewitnesses did not testify at all: two had left the state; one, himself originally a suspect, refused to testify; and a fourth was ruled mentally incompetent by the judge. The jury, in one hour and thirty-five minutes of deliberation, found each of the three defendants "not guilty."

While these Deep South court proceedings were fresh in the minds of the public, two timely reports appeared: a brochure of October 18, 1965, prepared jointly by the Southern Regional Council and the American Civil Liberties Union, entitled "Southern Justice—An Indictment"; and a 118-page volume issued by the United States Commission on Civil Rights on November 4 under the title, "Law Enforcement—A Report on Equal Protection in the South."

The SRC and ACLU recalled that "from the sit-in demonstrations of 1960 through the spring of 1965 at least 26 Negroes and white civil-rights workers died at the hands of racists in the South," and that "only one of the assailants was sentenced to prison, and he for 10 years." Meanwhile " 'justice' was dispensed in double measure when whites were slain by Negroes."

These organizations said:

> In many areas of the South dual justice is a standing abuse to all Negroes—the maid, the undertaker, the field hand, the school teacher, the minister . . . . It exists in the day to day brushes with "the law": the policeman on his beat, at traffic court, in civil cases. It exists in the more awesome confrontations with judges and juries in rape and murder cases. To the extent that it exists, it provokes desperation among Negroes, shakes their faith in democracy, causes them to shun the policemen and the courts as enemies. . . .
>
> Dual justice survives because Presidents continue to treat federal judgeships as political rewards and pacifiers. It survives because the Justice Department fails to exercise the power that it has to correct abuses. It survives because the judicial network, federal, state and municipal, is still one of the most segregated institutions in America. It survives through a built-in discrimination in the selection of juries, state and federal, and through the ill-concealed contempt of many courts and police officers for the rights of Negro citizens. . . .

The two organizations saw in all this a "monstrous corruption"—with a direct bearing on a trend in the Negro revolution that, as it became more pronounced in 1966, will be discussed in the next chapter:

> Now, with the nation seemingly unable to abolish this particular corruption pragmatically, a new mode of reform is arising. It is a

radical reform whose adherents are uncommitted to liberal democracy and the American tradition of pragmatism. These new reformers, who proudly wear the name of radical, move at the fringes of the civil-rights movement, working frankly at the total destruction of the system that deals unjustly. Occasionally one hears a bitter young civil-rights worker call openly for a riot, on the theory that only through violence can the white majority be made to take its foot off the neck of the oppressed minority.

The Civil Rights Commission described its long report as "a study of the failure of local officials in several Southern states to adhere to their oath of office." The Commission's staff had made extensive investigations in Mississippi, Alabama, Georgia, and Florida of "the failure of local officials to prevent or punish acts of racial violence," and of "interference by the officials with the assertion of constitutional and statutory rights by Negroes, including the right of public protest."

The Commission recognized that in some Southern communities, "where local citizens have insisted upon fair and effective law enforcement, violence has been averted and the integrity of the processes of law maintained." But it found that:

> In some instances, law enforcement officers have stood aside and permitted violence to be inflicted upon persons exercising rights guaranteed under federal law. In others, prosecutors have failed to carry out their duties properly. In the few cases in which persons have been prosecuted for violence against Negroes, grand juries and petit juries—from which Negroes have been systematically excluded and which express deeply rooted community attitudes—have failed to indict or convict.

Correction of the evil by a national government with completely centralized authority might have been a simple matter, but under our federal system it presented a problem of the utmost perplexity. "The lesson which these hearings" drove home to Erwin N. Griswold, Harvard Law School dean and a member of the Commission (later United States Solicitor General), was "the crucial importance of doing what we can to change the atmosphere in southern courts and the approach of southern law enforcement officers." However, the Commission made certain recommendations for federal action. It suggested that the President had not made full use of the statutory powers that he possessed "to use force to protect a class of citizens when local officials fail to protect them from widespread violence." Additionally, the Commission recommended specific federal legislation which would "make criminal any act of violence, threat, intimidation, or punishment against a person engaged in certain protected activities" and would "permit the prosecution in federal court of cases of racial violence that violate state law," where the attitude of local officials and of the community precluded equal protection in the administration of justice.

There was something grimly ludicrous in the spectacle of the great government of the United States attempting to punish foul murder by rounding up suspects and prosecuting them only on the charge of depriving the murdered persons of their civil rights. This was all that the loosely drawn Reconstruction Era statutes permitted, and there was some doubt there. However the Justice Department was still following this circuitous, laborious, and uncertain course. A few weeks later the Department scored its first success, in the conviction on the lesser charge of the three defendants in the Liuzzo murder. It had not abandoned the case of Colonel Penn, the Negro educator killed in Georgia in 1964—nor that of the three civil-rights workers slain in Mississippi in that year, though more years would pass before the defendants in the latter would be brought to trial.

In a decision of March 28, 1966, the Supreme Court strengthened somewhat the hand of the Justice Department under the old statutes —even while expressing dissatisfaction with them. (Six justices went out of their way to say in separate opinions that Congress had ample power under the Fourteenth Amendment to draw a more specific law.) The high tribunal reinstated indictments against seventeen persons accused of killing the three civil-rights workers in Mississippi, and against six Klansmen charged with killing Colonel Penn, which had been dismissed by federal district judges. On July 8, two of the defendants in the Penn case, Joseph Howard Sims and Cecil William Meyers (who had been acquitted when tried for murder in state court), were convicted in federal court of conspiring to violate Penn's civil rights. They were sentenced to the maximum of ten years each in prison. The four other defendants were acquitted.

President Johnson in his State of the Union message on January 12, 1966, asked Congress

> To take additional steps to ensure equal justice to all our people—by effectively enforcing nondiscrimination in federal and state jury selection—by making it a serious federal crime to obstruct public and private efforts to secure civil rights—and by outlawing discrimination in the sale and rental of housing.

On April 28 the President sent to Congress a package under the title, "The Civil Rights Act of 1966." This contained provisions which would prevent the exclusion of Negroes from both state and federal jury service and made it a federal criminal offense—with penalties up to life imprisonment when death occurred—to injure, intimidate, or interfere by force or threat of force with persons in the lawful exercise of their civil rights. However, the bill also contained provisions against discrimination in housing, and it was around these that controversy raged. Congress failed to pass the bill and took no other steps to correct the evils of "dual justice" in 1966.

The systematic exclusion of Negroes from jury service in predominantly Negro counties was the subject of a widespread outcry after the Hayneville and Selma trials. A group of six organizations—the Southern Regional Council, the American Civil Liberties Union, King's SCLC, the Leadership Conference on Civil Rights, the Episcopal Society for Cultural and Racial Unity (ESCRU), and the National Council of Churches' Commission on Religion and Race—pledged themselves to seek reform through new federal legislation and enforcement of existing laws. The American Civil Liberties Union launched an attack upon the evil through local federal court action. The Department of Justice joined ACLU in several of the suits, including one seeking to end the exclusion of Negroes from juries in Lowndes County. On February 6, 1966, the three-judge federal court at Montgomery handed down a decision, ordering the Lowndes County Jury Commission to destroy its existing all-white jury roll and draw up a new one without regard to race.

But the first result of the change was disappointing. The last round in state court in the Liuzzo case proved that, in the atmosphere of intimidation and fear prevailing in Lowndes County, more than the selection of Negro jurors would be needed to secure the punishment of a white man for the murder of a white champion of the Negro cause. Of the three Klansmen charged with Mrs. Liuzzo's murder, Wilkins had been acquitted in state court and Eaton had died of a heart attack when the third, Eugene Thomas, was brought to trial late in September, 1966. Forty-two Negroes were among the seventy-five men called for jury duty. The jury chosen consisted of eight Negroes and four white men. The trial itself was a replay of the Wilkins trial—with an important exception: State Attorney General Flowers, who headed the prosecution, thought it better not to use again two unpopular witnesses—Moton, Mrs. Liuzzo's Negro companion in the car, and Rowe, the FBI informer with the Klan. An hour and a half after the predominantly Negro jury got the case, it returned another verdict of "not guilty."

The federal court at Montgomery had also ordered a revision of the jury list in Macon County, Alabama, where another civil-rights murder had created an exceptional furor. There, in the town of Tuskegee, a young Negro student and civil-rights worker, Samuel L. Younge, Jr., had been shot to death on January 3, 1966, by Marvin L. Segrest, a white filling station operator, 67 years of age. Segrest was arrested and indicted on the charge of second degree murder. Macon County is the home of the famous Tuskegee Institute: its large Negro majority has aggressive and highly articulate spokesmen. Angry Negro demonstrations occurred almost daily for several weeks after the killing. Although the situation had quieted considerably by October, when the case was brought to a pretrial hearing, the defense council was right in saying that the incident had "created intense excitement and resentment." More significant was the fact the Negroes on the Macon County jury list now outnumbered whites two to one. The trial was transferred to adjoining Lee County, where an all-white jury accepted the defendant's plea of self-defense and in short order voted for acquittal.

The long investigation of the House Un-American Activities Committee into the activities of the Ku Klux Klan, and more particularly the hearings of that committee which opened October 19, 1965, and closed February 24, 1966, received a large amount of publicity. The public grew weary of the repetitious performances in the hearings, but many bizarre characters who came into the limelight furnished readable copy and the day-to-day accounts were given prominent newspaper space on days when more sensational news was in short supply. The fact that the investigation was going on prompted a somewhat greater than usual flow of special articles on the Klan and its history. But it is doubtful if HUAC's inquiry will seriously concern historians or that it merits an extensive report here.

Nearly all of the active Klan leaders subpoenaed monotonously declined to break their Klan oath of secrecy, invoking their Fifth Amendment protection. From the fact-finding of its staff and the testimony of 187 witnesses the Committee collected a mass of miscellaneous information regarding the Ku Klux Klan in its dozen varieties. This included little that was essentially new and important. The Committee's report, which was issued on October 24, 1966—unlike some of its colorful hearings—was almost unnoticed by the public. And no legislation resulted.

The widely published accounts of the hearings undoubtedly made Klan villainies better known to a larger number, but that nefarious organization was already almost universally condemned by the American public. Whether the exposure actually hurt the Klan was a matter of debate. Odious as the publicity was to normal sensibilities, it appeared to have reminded some paranoids who favored bombing and murdering Negroes of an organization to which they could rally. Klan recruiting and organizing activities actually increased during and immediately after the investigation. A report of the Anti-Defamation League of B'nai B'rith, one of the most knowledgeable watchdogs on the Klan, reported in October, 1966: "Last May, over-all Klan strength . . . was in the neighborhood of 35,000 to 45,000. Today it has jumped to 51,000." It added that between 55,000 and 75,000 sympathizers in the small towns of the rural South had also been drawn into the Klan orbit during the previous six months.

SIXTEEN

Black Power
1966

The year 1966 saw radical and divisive changes in the civil-rights movement. Most significantly they included the entry of SNCC, CORE, and King's SCLC into the agitation against the United States war effort in Vietnam and a sharp turn by SNCC and CORE—deplored by Dr. King—toward black nationalism, under a new slogan, "Black Power." The other two of the Big Five, the NAACP and the National Urban League, remained opposed to both of these departures. James Farmer of CORE, whose face had become familiar to the American public, retired to the sidelines; and John Lewis of SNCC, another key figure hitherto, virtually disappeared from view. Meanwhile, a fiery new SNCC leader, Stokely Carmichael, seized the spotlight for a time as one of the nation's most controversial personalities.

Ghetto riots, while in no case equaling the magnitude and ferocity of the Watts upheaval, hit many more cities in 1966 than in any previous year. Though the civil-rights agitation had tended to embolden Negroes generally, the ghetto rioting had been, and remained on the whole, a separate phenomenon from the organized civil-rights movement. Significant efforts were made to relate the two in 1966—in very different ways. In the Chicago area Martin Luther King and his associates labored, with some success, to channel the energies of riot-prone elements into nonviolent demonstrations and to focus them on specific objectives, especially open housing. SNCC and CORE, breaking away from the mainstream of the civil-rights movement, adopted language and tactics in tune with the frenzy of rioters. Also, for the first time in this decade, some of the 1966 disorders in the North and West saw substantial participation by anti-Negro whites.

In many respects, including its confinement to a racial minority, comparison of this modern American phenomenon with the French Revolution would of course be overdrawn. Yet certain analogies with that convulsion may be apt. The American Negro Revolution, preached for years by Negro intellectuals and set in motion in the earlier 1960's by elements of the bourgeoisie, witnessed in 1966 a rising, turbulent and misguided, of the sans-culottes.

Dr. King began to express "grave concern" over the situation in Vietnam soon after he was honored with the Nobel Peace Prize for 1964. Before a Negro gathering in Petersburg, Virginia, in July, 1965, he called for a negotiated peace, and said: "The long night of war must be stopped." He criticized the American war effort increasingly during 1966, and in 1967 he was leading demonstrations which were more antiwar than pro-civil-rights.

SNCC and CORE leaders were bitter and vituperative in agitation against the war in Vietnam throughout 1966. CORE's former director James Farmer, although a pacifist of long standing, wanted the movement to concentrate all its efforts on civil rights. When, in July, 1965, CORE's national convention, in Durham, North Carolina, adopted a resolution demanding the withdrawal of United States forces from Vietnam, Farmer succeeded in getting the resolution retracted. In 1966, however, new leaders of CORE were screaming that demand.

On January 6, 1966, SNCC's twenty-three-member executive committee issued a formal statement in which it declared: "Vietnamese are being murdered because the United States is pursuing an aggressive policy in violation of international law" and expressed sympathy with "the men in this country who are unwilling to respond to a military draft." Floyd McKissick, having just succeeded Farmer as executive director of CORE and not yet in his stride, joined the latter in a statement merely opposing "escalation of the war." Dr. King, still observing a degree of restraint, commented that he "would be the last person to condemn one who on the basis of conscience is a conscientious objector." Roy Wilkins was quick to disassociate the NAACP from the SNCC statement, pointing out that SNCC was "only one of the many civil-rights groups, of what is loosely called the civil-rights movement"; and Whitney Young of the National Urban League was careful to avoid involvement of his far-flung organization.

The Negro "doves" related their attitude to the civil-rights movement by pointing out that the United States effort in Vietnam was draining away billions of dollars that were urgently needed to improve the lot of Negroes at home. It was also sometimes represented as a war against a nonwhite race. The Negro "doves," like the white "doves," were noisier and more spectacular than the "hawks." But opposition to the American war effort was by no means general among the Negro public. Nelson Jack Edwards, the ranking Negro in the United Automobile Workers Union, was probably right in his appraisal in 1966 that Negroes were "a bit more—but not substantially more" opposed to the war than whites. James Meredith, an Air Force veteran and, since his stormy admission to the University of Mississippi, one of their public figures most admired among Negroes, said: "As one who has been a soldier most of my adult life, I fully support the war effort." Edward Brooke, the first Negro elected to the United States Senate since Reconstruction, had doubts about Vietnam in 1966, but after a visit to the war area in March, 1967, he took a position in support of President Johnson's policy.

Negroes served their country in Vietnam with efficiency and conspicuous valor. Military service there was more popular among Negroes than among whites. The Negro re-enlistment rate was nearly three times that of white servicemen. The Armed Forces regime of integration and equal opportunity—though grossly violated at the officer level—gave them, many Negroes felt, a "better break" than they had at home, and many relished this opportunity to prove the dignity and worth of Negro manhood. Although Negroes represented only 11 per cent of the nation's population, over 18 per cent of the United States forces in Vietnam were Negroes. Because Negroes often sought duty in the more dangerous units, the Negro percentage of casualties was even higher.

An element of disunity more disruptive to the civil-rights movement was the change of leadership and direction in CORE and SNCC. This manifested itself in a growing spirit of aversion to the collaboration of white sympathizers, which the NAACP, SCLC, and the Urban League warmly welcomed, and of scorn for the rule of nonviolence, to which those three groups remained firmly attached.

Members of CORE and SNCC, as we have seen, had already been distinguished by their impetuous aggressiveness as well as by their courage in the civil-rights battle line. CORE had close ties with a group whose members manifested their abandonment of nonviolence by carrying arms. Bogalusa, a Louisiana town near the Mississippi border, had long been both the center of activities of the Deacons for Defense and Justice and a special concern of CORE. During many months, while Bogalusa had been the scene of incessant struggle against white persecution and Ku Klux Klan intimidation, CORE had given Bogalusa Negroes local leadership and a voice of protest in official quarters in Washington. The Deacons, CORE's allies there, had been befriended, if their methods were not endorsed. Deacons—as well as Black Muslims—had addressed CORE's Durham convention.

SNCC had come a long way since it was organized by idealistic college students in the midst of the remarkably successful lunch counter sit-ins of 1960. Then their restraint and decorous behavior had impressed even white segregationists. In subsequent years SNCC had also been a rallying point for liberal white students as well as Negroes. Responding in part to SNCC's call in Mississippi in 1964, hundreds of whites had endured hardship and made sacrifices—in Neshoba County two had given their lives—for the cause. Amid the rising tide of antinonviolence and antiwhite sentiment, SNCC's chairman John Lewis, though his militancy had shocked many in an earlier context (notably at the March on Washington ceremonies), remained a sturdy anchor to the principles on which the organization was founded.

The change of leadership in CORE came at the turn of the year. James Farmer resigned his position as executive director on December 27, 1965, with a view to launching the "National Center for Community Action Education, Inc.," a project aimed at advancing literacy and job skills among the chronically unemployed. He understood that he had been assured of an allocation of $860,000 by the Office of Economic Opportunity, but because of suspicion of the radical leaders who gathered around the project—and in part to the hostility of Negro Chairman Adam Clayton Powell of the House Labor and Education Committee—the money never came through. After trying unsuccessfully for some months to obtain either government or private funds, Farmer abandoned the undertaking. In September, 1966, he joined the faculty of Lincoln University as a professor of social welfare.

On January 3, 1966, Floyd McKissick, the unpaid chairman of CORE's board of directors, was elected to succeed Farmer as executive director. Long overshadowed by the latter, McKissick had played an inhibited and relatively obscure role. Now, in the bigger job (with a salary of $16,000), he began to reach for newspaper headlines with sensational outbursts and launched upon a career of fire-eating bravado. Farmer's exit was followed by the resignation of three other CORE officers—Dr. George Wiley, associate director; Edward Day, business manager; and Greg Harris, publicity director.

SNCC was moving faster and going farther in the same direction. In traditionally penurious SNCC, where all salaries were uncertain, the chairmanship became the dominant office. The change of command in SNCC was effected in something like a coup d'état. In an all-night secret meeting held outside Nashville on May 14-15, chairman Lewis and executive director James Forman were first re-elected, and then in the early hours of the morning were finally ousted from their posts. Stokely Carmichael, a swashbuckling young herald of the new militancy, was elected chairman; the lesser post now of executive director was given to Mrs. Ruby Doris Robinson, of SNCC's office staff.

Forman, a former schoolteacher nearing forty and a kind of uncle to SNCC's young men, actually had a hand in the changeover, and as a member of the executive committee he would continue to play a powerful behind-the-scenes role. John Lewis, thoughtful and in manner reserved and polite—one of the founders of SNCC—was deeply troubled. He first resolved to stay with the organization, but six weeks later—witnessing the thunder and lightning of Carmichael's "Black Power" eruption—he severed his connection completely, saying: "I'm not prepared to give up my personal commitment to nonviolence." Lewis joined first the staff of the Field Foundation and later that of the Southern Regional Council. Julian Bond, publicity director, also left SCC. (Bond was one of the eight Negroes elected to the Georgia House of Representatives in 1965, but that body refused to seat him because of his extreme statements against the war in Vietnam and the draft. A Supreme Court ruling later caused him to be given his seat.)

The new leader of SNCC was a dashing, highly articulate young man of twenty-four. Stokely Carmichael was a native of Trinidad, who had come to New York with his parents at the age of eleven. He was educated mainly at the Bronx School of Science and Howard University, graduating from the latter in 1964. The term "Black Panther" was linked to his name at this stage rather than "Black Power." The Black Panther was the symbol of an abortive all-Negro political movement which he had been strenuously promoting in Lowndes County, Alabama. Mrs. Liuzzo and other civil-rights workers had been murdered in that area; Negro churches had been bombed and burned; and Carmichael had seen the perpetrators of these outrages go unpunished, even applauded, by many whites. He himself had been insulted and harassed daily. He had become cynical and distrustful of white men generally, and he boiled over with a bitter desperation, which he had a rare talent for putting into words. His oratory resembled at times the antiwhite fulminations of Malcolm X (whom he greatly admired), at times a harangue of Spartacus to the Roman gladiators, at times the senseless bawling of an angry child. As for the civil-rights movement's cherished principle of nonviolence and its objective of racial integration, Carmichael considered the former foolish and the latter "irrelevant."

James H. Meredith has something in common with those heroes, of whom Lindbergh is an illustrious example, who, having accomplished a resounding feat in their early manhood, do not quite know what to do with the rest of their lives. In Meredith a vein of inscrutable mysticism was an added complication. Meredith was the Hero of the Ole Miss Breakthrough. In that flash of rebellion in 1962—already a long time ago in the progress of race-relations change—when United States marshals and soldiers fought an all-night battle against a segregationist mob to secure the admission of the first Negro student to the University of Mississippi, Meredith was the Negro student. And, if he was only a symbol, he was the best symbol that could have been found. Gentlemanly in appearance and manner, he bore himself, through harassment, threats, and cruel ostracism all the way to graduation in 1963, with extraordinary dignity and courage.

He was then twenty-eight years of age. He spent the next three years as a student, first in Nigeria and then at Columbia University Law School. His voice was occasionally heard in the protest movement, but he was rarely in harmony with other Negro spokesmen, or with any organization. He complained that not even Negroes understood him. Lonely and introspective, he nourished an urge somehow to return to the stage of history.

On Sunday afternoon, June 5, 1966, Meredith set out on a pilgrimage from Memphis, Tennessee, to Jackson, Mississippi, 220 miles, through country swarming with hostile whites. He said his undertaking would dramatize "that all-pervasive and overriding fear that dominates the day-to-day life of the Negro in the United States, especially in the South and particularly in Mississippi." He hoped that his example would spark the courage needed by thousands of Mississippi Negroes to exercise their right to vote. At the same time, he wanted to prove something to himself. Like other Mississippi Negroes, Meredith had known fear all his life. "That is one purpose of my march," he said "—to get rid of this fear." About a dozen friends accompanied him as he set out on Highway 51.

The next day, barely ten miles into Meredith's native state, a white man (not a Mississippi racist but a Memphis eccentric, it was later learned) stepped out of the roadside underbrush with a shotgun and fired three rounds that sent the young man sprawling in the dust. An erroneous first Associated Press report, corrected half an hour later, said Meredith had been "shot dead." It later proved that seventy-five pellets had struck Meredith's head, neck, back, and legs only superficially. The news reverberated across the nation.

President Johnson instantly ordered the Attorney General to "spare no efforts" to bring the guilty party to justice. (The gunman, Aubrey James Norvell, was sentenced in due course to two years in prison.) On Capitol Hill, momentary hopes were raised for action on the pending civil-rights bill, which sought to strengthen federal protection for civil-rights crusaders. Negro leaders rushed to Memphis to visit Meredith in hospital there and to take up the

Memphis-Jackson march where he had left off. King, McKissick, and Carmichael were among the first to arrive. These three became the leaders of the new march. The other two of the Big Five, Wilkins and Young, flew to Memphis a day later, when a rally was held, followed by a planning conference, marchers shuttling back for these meetings.

The "Meredith March" developed into something very different from what Meredith had envisioned and something of which he never entirely approved. It lasted three tumultuous weeks and included forays into several towns to the right and left of Highway 51 to push the registration of Negro voters and generally to stimulate resistance to oppression. The number of marchers grew from less than 100 to more than 1,500, and thousands of other Negroes gathered around them along the way. James Farmer and John Lewis were among the throng of idealists, pragmatists, passivists, extremists, and entertainment stars (a few white liberals among them) who got into the act.

The ambush attack had affected Meredith's nerves as well as his body. On leaving the Memphis hospital on June 8 to fly to New York, he attempted a statement to newsmen but broke down in tears and fainted. He continued his convalescence in New York until June 24, then flew back to Mississippi. Once more on Highway 51, he resumed his own march, at first trailing behind the big procession but moving to the vanguard for the entry into Jackson on June 26. By then Meredith had become a relatively inconspicuous figure in the "Meredith March." The Negro name most on the lips of Americans was not Meredith, or even Martin Luther King, but the frightening new luminary, Stokely Carmichael.

A deep division among the Big Five civil-rights organizations showed itself at the meeting in Memphis, when the march was getting under way. What were to be the objectives? In the minds of many Negroes the fact that Mississippi was there was reason enough for a march—and now an attempt had been made upon the life of James Meredith. What the march was *against* was clear, but what should it be *for*? An angry "manifesto" was issued, saying the march would be a "massive public indictment and protest of the failure of American society, the Government of the United States, and the state of Mississippi to 'fulfill these rights' " (quoting from the President's Howard University speech). Demands included federal voting examiners in all the 600 Deep South counties and a sweeping revision of the pending civil-rights bill. Wilkins and Young, believing that such a document would hamper their efforts to secure enactment of the pending bill, refused to sign the manifesto. A few days later Charles Evers, the successor to his murdered brother Medgar as the NAACP's field secretary in Mississippi, in high dudgeon, denied a claim that he had signed the manifesto and scorned the whole project, saying: "I don't want this to turn into another Selma, where everyone goes home with the cameramen and leaves us holding the bag."

King, with his zeal for unity in the movement, signed the manifesto. But he found himself in a running debate with extremists from then on. King and Stokely Carmichael sought an appearance of harmony, marching together and being photographed arm in arm, but their preachments remained poles apart. The former held to his doctrine of nonviolence, cooperation with white sympathizers, and racial integration; the latter, in vague but incendiary language, called Negroes to resist their white oppressors and "seize power." McKissick, who took his turn as march leader, echoed Carmichael with less personal magnetism and in a slightly lower key. The slogan "Black Power" first caught the attention of the news media on June 17. Proclaimed in torrents of menacing invective in tense Mississippi, it had a fiercely provocative ring. "The term 'Black Power' is unfortunate," King insisted. "We must never seek power exclusively for the Negro, but the sharing of power with white people." But Carmichael men shouted, "Black Power! Martin Luther King is the greatest man in the world. Black Power!"

As a theme for the project the controversial manifesto quickly evaporated. Though the style of the new march was far from Meredith's, the objective became essentially that which he had set: it was a march against fear. On the constructive side, several thousand Mississippi Negroes mustered the hardihood to register for voting, and civil-rights activity was started in several more communities that had none before. But victory over fear was also expressed in jeering at policemen, in shouting taunts at white onlookers, in treating the Confederate banner and a Jefferson Davis monument with disrespect—in one town, in a stampede to use courthouse lavatories reserved (no longer legally) for whites only. The objective of exorcising fear united King and Carmichael, but their methods differed: King was content to march with dignity into the lion's den; Carmichael sought to twist the lion's tail.

King, whom no blustering Black Powerist excelled in courage, led 250 marchers on a detour which was the most perilous undertaking of the whole three weeks. It was a memorial pilgrimage to Philadelphia, the county seat of Neshoba County, where Chaney, Schwerner, and Goodman were murdered in 1964. After a prayer service at the jail where the three civil-rights martyrs were held prisoner before their murder, the procession moved to the front of the Neshoba courthouse. A crowd of jeering whites was clustered on the lawn. The officer who stopped King's party at this point was Deputy Sheriff Cecil Price, one of those still under federal charges of complicity in the 1964 crime.

When King said in a speech, "They'll have to learn to kill all of us" a white man drew laughter from the mob by yelling, "We sure as hell will try!"

"They don't understand this movement," King went on—characteristically above the Neshoba intellectual level—"because they haven't love in their hearts. . . . Anybody who is prejudiced is a slave, anybody who hates is a slave. . . ."

The pilgrims had been stoned as they marched into town, and cherry bombs exploded under their feet as they stood in front of the courthouse. As they moved away, angry whites drove autos toward them, squealing to a stop just a few feet from the column. A dozen whites surged into the procession, flailing with clubs, hoes, and ax handles. At this point, nonviolence broke down. A half-dozen Negroes started slugging back, and local police (who had been passive onlookers hitherto) wedged in to stop the melee.

In line with his policy never to let white hoodlums feel that violence could keep him away, King led a smaller party back to Philadelphia three days later. This time state troopers were on hand in force and relative order prevailed.

The State Highway Patrol, under wavering orders from Governor Paul B. Johnson, Jr., had given the marchers irregular and grudging protection most of the way. But in the town of Canton on June 23 state troopers turned on them with something more than zeal for law and order. When the marchers started to pitch their two big tents in the yard of a Negro school, they were informed that the local school board had denied them use of the property. Workers went on pitching the tent amid cries from their comrades: "Pitch the tent!" After a final warning from the city attorney, state troopers put on masks and began firing tear-gas canisters into the crowd. The tent collapsed. Some marchers scattered, others fell to the ground. The latter were kicked and rifle-butted until the area was cleared. This episode, graphically reported by the news media, prompted demands in many quarters for federal military intervention.

When the march was over at last, what had it done to fear? Carmichael bade the tent-pitchers in Canton, "Tell the white folks most all the scared Negroes in Mississippi are dead." The scared Negroes were still there, but they were not as scared as before—and more whites were scared. Evers and the local organizations would have to pick up the pieces and go on with the hard day-to-day struggle. The tumult and the shouting over, and the visiting celebrities gone, most Mississippi Negroes dropped back into the rut of submission to white supremacy. But the rut was not so deep as before. Sparks had been lit that would not go out. Another long stride had been made in the awakening of the Mississippi Negro.

And Mississippi whites had not slept well at night. Fear of what Negroes might sometime do, in part a vestige of the ancient terror of a slave uprising, was never entirely absent among the whites. In the context of the 1960's, not a few had shuddered during these tense weeks at the thought that "their own" Negroes—a majority in many sections—might be seized with the fury of Watts. That catastrophe they had been spared, but their relief was sobered by a further change in the image of the Negro. Even the non-nonviolence of Stokely Carmichael had a certain value—"If a man steps on you and you let him, you deserve to be stepped on!" The prosecuting attorney of a county through which the march had passed observed correctly that "militant whites and the militant colored are more militant than before." But there was a difference. The bullies, who are essentially cowards, had made the disconcerting discovery that the Negro was no longer safe and submissive game. Carmichael lieutenants shouting—"If anybody touches one of our workers, we're going to tear this place up!", or even "White blood will flow!"—was something new in Mississippi. If white fear rose as Negro fear diminished, it was not an unhealthy phenomenon. It might not make for immediate brotherhood or peace, but it had brought the two races a little closer to a viable point of mutual respect.

Floyd McKissick's June schedule was characteristically hectic: leaving a huge White House Conference on Negro problems on June 2, he was at the bedside of James Meredith four days later, and the conclusion of the Memphis-Jackson march on June 26 left him less than a week in which to look into an antidiscrimination campaign launched by CORE in Baltimore in May, and to prepare for the annual convention of CORE in that city over the Fourth of July weekend. That organization was at a low ebb, declining in membership and heavily in debt. The 1966 convention confirmed and accentuated CORE's change of direction. Some felt that it marked the abdication of CORE's earlier rational and responsible role in the movement.

The meetings drew hardly more than 100, with rent-strike leader Jesse Gray from Harlem, Deacon Vice President Ernest Thomas, Muslim leader Lonnie Shabazz, and wearers of Malcolm X buttons conspicuous among them. Both James Farmer and Stokely Carmichael addressed the convention before it got down to business. Then in a closed session on July 4 it adopted resolutions calling for withdrawal of United States forces from Vietnam, rejection of nonviolence as a technique, and setting up of Black Power instead of integration as its goal.

One white lady, a CORE veteran, stalked out of the meeting in tears. Some absent members later terminated their affiliation. One of these was Lillian Smith, then in her sixty-eighth year and dying of cancer. The author of *Strange Fruit* repudiated the "adventurers and nihilists, black nationalists, and plain old-fashioned haters who have finally taken over," and she commented sadly that "the stubbornness and dishonest methods of segregationists, the violence of the Klan and the blind complacency of many white church people have made it easy for the haters to take over from the more wise and patient leadership."

It should be said, however, that CORE's approach to Black Power in practice was somewhat more constructive than that of Stokely Carmichael's SNCC. Its choice of Baltimore as the "target city" had aroused much dismay and anxiety, even shared by many Baltimore Negroes. But by the year's end, the project had registered a few positive gains—in the desegregation of apartment buildings and taverns, and in the establishment, with the help of government and industry, of a job training program for school drop-outs. CORE received some praise, even from the commissioner of police.

Beginning July 5, the National Association for the Advancement of Colored People held its annual convention, its fifty-seventh, in Los Angeles. Here 1,800 delegates heard the familiar calls for racial integration and cheered attacks on Black Power. Speakers included Vice President Humphrey; Mrs. Esther Peterson, special assistant to the President; Roger Wilkins, director of the Community Relations Service; Harry Golden; and John H. Johnson, publisher of *Ebony*. In his keynote address Roy Wilkins reviewed the controversy over the "Meredith March." He had wanted the march to be used to win support for the pending civil-rights bill, which he was pushing in Washington at the same time. (SNCC was actually lobbying *against* the bill. A SNCC statement declared: "Any civil-rights organization or Congressman who works for the passage of this bill . . . is sharing in the hypocrisy of President Johnson and his Administration.") Wilkins said that, though the NAACP had supplied much of the money, food, housing, and transportation for the march, its field secretary had been barred from participation in its final rally in Jackson. The breach between the NAACP and the Black Powerists of SNCC and CORE was complete.

Representative Adam Clayton Powell hailed Black Power with enthusiasm, although he disavowed such "sterile ends" as black supremacy or black nationalism, and in a sermon on October 9 he criticized Carmichael for using the slogan "as a fuse to set off rebellion in the streets of America." Powell recalled that he himself had used the expression "audacious power" in several speeches early in the year. He called Black Power "a working philosophy for a new breed of cats—tough, proud young Negroes who categorically refuse to compromise or negotiate any longer for their rights . . . who reject the old-line established white-financed, white-controlled, whitewashed Negro leadership." He said the phrase, which meant only a "dynamic process of continuous change toward a society of true equals," had been "deliberately distorted" by "self-righteous, old-fashioned leaders," out of touch with the Negro masses.

The flamboyant Negro Congressman was not popular among civil-rights leaders, though he had a large following among the Negro masses in Harlem and elsewhere. He announced plans for a "National Black Power Conference" to be held in Washington, October 15-16, which he estimated that from 500 to 600 delegates would attend. But this project got no further than a preliminary meeting on September 3, which drew about 100 representatives of miscellaneous, mostly radical, groups. Wilkins and King had other engagements—though, Powell said, they sent friendly messages. No one came, of course, from the Urban League. McKissick, according to Powell, was "out passing the hat." Carmichael himself was detained by a SNCC meeting in Atlanta. (Muslim leader Elijah Muhammed also declined an invitation.)

A group of forty-eight leading Negro clergymen issued a statement published as an advertisement covering nearly a page in the *New York Times* of July 31, warning against "expending our energies in spastic or ill-tempered explosion without meaningful goals." "What we see, shining through the variety of rhetoric," they said, "is not anything new but the same old problem of power and race which has faced our beloved country since 1619." The Negro needed to exert more power, of course— individually and through group action in cooperation with other groups. But power was "not a thing lying in the streets to be fought over." Getting power involved twofold "reconciliation." Negroes needed to be reconciled to themselves—"to find our way to a new self-image in which we can feel a normal sense of pride in self, including our variety of skin color and the manifold textures of our hair." They needed also "reconciliation with our white brothers . . . on the firm ground that we and all Americans are one." The Reverend J. H. Jackson, head of the five-million-member National Baptist Convention, presided over a meeting of 100 Negro clergymen in Chicago which condemned Black Power in a manifesto.

Nearly all the old-line civil-rights leaders frowned upon Black Power. John Lewis was impelled finally to terminate his connection with SNCC. James Farmer approved of emphasis on Negro "dignity" and "self-esteem," but at this stage he wished "the term 'Black Power' had never been devised." Roy Wilkins had strong language for Black Power: "separatism . . . wicked fanaticism . . . ranging race against race . . . in the end only black death." Whitney Young said: "The greatest power is to be right, and if you're right and believe in that right you can get power." Bayard Rustin wrote in September's *Commentary:* "'Black Power' not only lacks any real value for the civil-rights movement, but its propagation is positively harmful. It diverts the movement from any meaningful debate over strategy and tactics, it isolates the Negro community, and it encourages the growth of anti-Negro forces."

An impressive group of civil-rights leaders united in sponsoring a three-quarter-page advertisement in the *New York Times* which reaffirmed the traditional goals of integration and interracial co-operation, and declared: "We repudiate any strategies of violence, reprisal or vigilantism, and we condemn both rioting and the demagoguery that feeds it." Wilkins, Young, A. Philip Randolph, and Bayard Rustin were among the signers. Martin Luther King endorsed the statement, but refused to sign it, saying he was concerned about "furthering division" in the movement and he hoped "to continue to meet with SNCC and CORE."

(An opportunity for an appropriate white response to this pledge of interracial cooperation in the orderly pursuit of the movement's goals was missed. A group of white friends of the movement prepared a statement for publication in the *Times* accepting the hand of continued cooperation extended by the Negro leaders, but a week's canvass met with so many refusals to sign, especially on the part of businessmen, that the plan was abandoned.)

Carmichael, who spoke now on television panels and many platforms as well as in the street, varied his language according to the audience and occasion. He might say to newsmen: "I have never said anything antiwhite in my life." Sometimes he made sense: "Black Power means that in Lowndes County . . . if a Negro is elected tax assessor, he will be able to tax equitably and channel funds for the building of better roads and schools serving Negroes. If elected sheriff, he can end police brutality. . . ." But the following was more typical: "When you talk of Black Power, you talk of building a movement that will smash everything Western civilization has created. When you talk of Black Power, you talk of picking up where Malcolm X left off . . . ," or: "You've got to say: 'To hell with the laws of the United States.'" His contribution to the revolution was a cry of anger. In the wrongs that Negroes had suffered in the long past and those they still suffered, there was cause indeed for great anger. But what could anger accomplish?

For a few weeks Black Power outdid miniskirts, draft card burners, and LSD as a thing to talk and write about in the nation. Editors, columnists, and television pundits delved into the subject. Sociologists and psychologists brought their learning to bear. Every civil-rights personality and nearly every politician either volunteered an opinion or responded to the question: "What about Black Power?" The phrase was scrutinized, analyzed, turned over, and squeezed to extract the last particle of imputed meaning from it. But there was not much meaning there. The idea of an impoverished 11 per cent of the population seizing control of the most powerful nation on earth was a palpable absurdity. Short of that Black Power said nothing new. That the Negro should be given the opportunity to increase his economic power, that he should use the ballot to increase his political power—these had been urged by civil-rights leaders all along. If Black Powerists advocated violence only in self-defense, as they were likely to claim when pinned down, that right was also recognized in the most respectable civil-rights circles.

The phrase, "Black Power," survived, however, and came to have greater relevance to the Negro revolution than its author. On the positive side, the concept tended to promote Negro self-respect and self-reliance. It helped increasingly to stimulate interest in Negro history and culture, and a healthy pride in *négritude*. To the general public the label served to identify the growing number of activists who followed the antiwhite-man, anti-integration, and antinonviolence line. It came to be applied vaguely to the whole trend toward Negro violence. Whatever it might mean—and however little it might mean—"Black Power" had a grandiose and warlike ring that emboldened many Negroes and intoxicated some. It would reverberate for many months to come.

SNCC and CORE, seceding from the Big Five of the civil-rights movement, drew nearer to a variety of extremist groups, including the black nationalist organizations—although they did not embrace the fading dream of a separate Negro nation. Besides the Black Muslims, there were about a dozen more or less obscure old nationalist groups few, if any, of which had as many as 1,000 members. New organizations were springing up, like the Organization for Black Power, headed by Jesse Gray of Harlem.

The epidemic of ghetto rioting that began in Omaha, Nebraska, over the Fourth of July weekend gave more impetus to the Black Power movement than the rioting received from it. Neither Carmichael nor the new slogan had any large part in those 1966 disorders. The cry "Black Power!" was heard here and there in the late summer, but "Burn, baby, burn" and "Get Whitey" were already more incendiary—and, in the opinion of some rioters, more to the point. Actually no stereotyped slogan was used by many rioters. Carmichael visited Chicago during the turbulence there, but he made no significant dent in a situation in which Martin Luther King was unmistakably the dominant Negro figure. He was more effective in Atlanta, SNCC's home base, where some rioting was set off directly by him.

Carmichael's popularity with SNCC itself was waning—not on account of his extremism, but because of his prima donna role and his total neglect of the organization—and it was accurately predicted at the year's end that he would not be re-elected to its chairmanship when his term expired in May, 1967. SNCC, now only a rump of less than fifty aggressive fanatics, continued on its nihilistic course, its voice growing shriller as its membership and financial resources declined.

In July and August of 1966 hardly a day passed without Negro rioting in some American city. Chicago sputtered for six weeks during this period. The rioting season, or the "long, hot summer," closed with an upheaval in San Francisco at the end of September. The cities hit by serious disturbances or full-scale riots included: Omaha, Des Moines, Philadelphia, Chicago, New York, Cleveland, Atlanta, Dayton, Providence, Oakland, Minneapolis, Milwaukee, St. Louis, Troy (New York), South Bend (Indiana), Jacksonville (Florida), Perth Amboy (New Jersey), Waukegan (Illinois), Amityville (Long Island), Lansing, Benton Harbor, and Jackson (Michigan). In the worst single outbreak, Cleveland saw five nights of burning, looting, and sniping, with four Negroes killed, 46 persons injured, and 187 arrested. In that city and in Chicago, Dayton, Milwaukee, and San Francisco, National Guard troops were called to aid police in restoring order.

The mid-1960's were a period of restlessness on the part of American youth generally. University students mounted unruly demonstrations for a variety of causes, ranging from free speech and withdrawal from Vietnam to changes in dormitory rules and better dining room fare. Rioting at the University of California at Berkeley in 1964 had resulted in over 800 arrests. On Easter, Fourth of July, and Labor Day holidays thousands of white students of both sexes gathered at half a dozen beach resorts for wild sprees, which ended in rock-throwing, window-breaking, and battles with police. Units of the National Guard had been needed to quell some of these completely senseless rampages.

Negro rioting had, of course, a deeper meaning, but the excitement of it had a certain similar appeal to Negro youths. Also, as it has everywhere from time immemorial, the opportunity for looting made public turmoil attractive to criminal elements. A desire for revenge—a desire to repay "Whitey" for countless rebuffs and insults and larger wrongs—was also there, though this was more likely to be directed impersonally against the white man's stores and buildings than (except in the case of police) against his person.

In the larger cities, rioting was incited to some extent by professional or visiting agitators—Black Power advocates, Deacons for Defense, Black Muslims, members of the half a dozen old black nationalist groups—and Communists. But the influence of these "outside agitators" was widely exaggerated. Local Negroes resented the presence of some of these, and nobody seemed to pay any attention to the Communists. The *New York Times* of July 31, 1966, observed in its "Review of the Week": "One of the most remarkable things about the riots and the unrest is that those organizations that would normally try to exploit such developments for their revolutionary and ideological aims have failed miserably." The Negro riots were the products each of its own city. Spearheaded though they often were by young Negro hoodlums, the causes were to be found in the poverty, frustration, hopelessness, and bitterness of the ghetto.

The cry of "police brutality" rose in every riot, and in spite of more and more courses in community relations for policemen, Negro-police relations worsened with increasing turmoil. Negroes were at war with the police, and the police, often prejudiced to begin with and now called to long hours of dangerous duty by Negro rioting, taunted and cursed and obliged to grapple with frenzied rioters, were not without a feeling of being at war with Negroes.

Police incidents lit the riot fuse in many cases, but not all. In Cleveland it was the refusal of a white bartender to give a Negro a pitcher of water. The triggering incident was generally the least important detail. In Chicago, however, it contained a mildly helpful suggestion, which should have occurred to authorities before. The Chicago rioting started with an argument over the illegal opening of a fire hydrant. In the summer heat the opportunity to splash in cold water from a hydrant could both refresh sweltering Negro youths and help cool ghetto tempers. When the riot subsided, the Mayor, prompted by Martin Luther King, ordered fire hydrants to be equipped with sprinklers for this purpose without delay.

A feeling of isolation, a feeling that City Hall was indifferent to conditions in the ghetto, contributed to the desperation of Negroes. Mayor John V. Lindsay of New York and Mayor Ivan Allen, Jr., of Atlanta made valiant efforts to combat this, displaying their genuine concern in frequent personal visits to ghetto areas. It did not entirely eliminate rioting in their cities, but it helped.

None of these gestures got at the roots of the matter. The most important single immediate need as a riot preventive was jobs, especially summer jobs for Negro youths. These remained in shamefully short supply. A quarter of a million Negroes were out of work, and the national unemployment rate for Negro teenagers in June, 1966, was two and a half times the rate for white teenagers. For quick results more recreation facilities could be a significant palliative; and over the months and years graver problems of health and education cried for attention. But what the turmoil emphasized above all was the fact that the ghetto itself was a monstrous evil. Until Negroes should be able to find homes elsewhere, until whites should be ready to accept Negroes as neighbors, there could be no lasting peace.

In most respects the rioting resembled that of 1964 and 1965 described earlier. The 1966 turbulence, however, saw one ominous new element: clashes between Negroes and whites (other than police). To be feared above all things was the dark possibility that the revolution might one day take the form of a massive, bloody struggle between white man and black man. In 1966 for the first time some of the rioting seemed to approach the brink of that catastrophe.

White civilian casualties in the rioting hitherto had been few. Not many whites had ventured into the riot area and Negro rioters had never emerged from the ghetto to defy whites elsewhere. Moreover, in the 1960's, outside of the South, white attacks upon Negroes had been rare; in the earlier rioting Negroes had been opposed only by the forces of law enforcement. Now in a number of situations whites harassed or attacked Negroes, and Negroes, in a posture of nonviolence, marched from the ghetto into white neighborhoods.

In Baltimore a mob of 1,200 whites, incited by a rally of the racist "National States Rights party," began chasing Negroes in the streets with cries of "kill niggers," but they were stopped by police an hour and eight arrests later. Elsewhere white hostility developed on the fringes of the ghetto. It stemmed precisely from the threat to neighborhood segregation. When Negro demonstrators marched into a white residential district of Milwaukee, white youths shouted insults and hurled bricks and stones over the heads of police until National Guardsmen got them under control. In Cleveland armed vigilantes patrolled an Italian-American neighborhood bordering the Negro ghetto, and two Negroes, a motorist and a pedestrian, were shot dead in their vicinity. Carloads of white hoodlums and a band of white motorcyclists also rode through and around the Cleveland ghetto during the rioting. In the East New York section of Brooklyn, Negroes were harassed by members of "SPONGE"—the Society for the Prevention of Negroes Getting Everything—and 1,500 policemen were required to suppress a Negro-white melee. The greatest interracial tension developed in Chicago and the adjoining city of Cicero.

Chicago's 1966 experience merits closer examination for several reasons. In that city the militant nonviolence of Martin Luther King and the violence of rioters converged, and to a certain extent blended. Many charged that the former was responsible in part for the latter. Certainly King's campaign did not prevent the city from being plagued with two months of intermittent violence. But who can say what would have happened if King had not come into the situation? Had he not directed Negro militancy toward specific objectives and drawn many who might have been rioters into nonviolent marches, had he not been able to report certain gains, it is possible that in the 1966 riot contagion, Chicago might have been hit by a cataclysm of the dimensions of Watts.

King had long contemplated a thoroughgoing drive against racial discrimination in Chicago. A score of SCLC missionaries under his young assistant, the Reverend James Bevel, had been working quietly there since the summer of 1965. Many, including such old friends as Bayard Rustin, advised Dr. King against this undertaking, saying that his methods should be reserved for the South and pointing to the impossibility of imbuing Chicago's teeming Negro population with the doctrine of nonviolent action before action of the other sort might erupt. Nearly a third of Chicago's three and one-half million people were Negroes—with incomes generally near the poverty level. Negroes, streaming into the city from the South for a quarter of a century, had been crammed mainly into the deteriorating slums of the West and South Sides, creating a vast ghetto, where most of them spent their lives.

In January, 1966, the Nobel Prize winner installed himself in a shabby third-floor, walk-up Chicago tenement and announced that the drive was on. It was to be SCLC's "first sustained Northern movement." With his manifold activities elsewhere, King could be in Chicago only now and then, but his assistants carried on the work of organizing and indoctrinating Negro groups for the next six months. A local civil-rights alliance, the Coordinating Council of Community Organizations, merged its efforts with King's to form the Chicago Freedom Movement.

A climax was reached in a rally in Soldier's Field on Sunday, July 10. Though the attendance, estimated by police at 30,000, fell below the 100,000 predicted, it was not wholly discouraging. Incidentally, among the speakers on the platform were James Meredith and Floyd McKissick, the latter averring cooperatively: "Black Power does not mean violence." Dr. King listed a series of objectives, including school desegregation, jobs, and the correction of police abuses, but the primary target was housing— "the task of wiping out racism, slums and ghettos in order to make Chicago an open city. . . ." "Our power," Dr. King said, "does not reside in Molotoff cocktails, knives and bricks. . . ."

But, alas, two days later Molotoff cocktails, knives, and bricks took over—and gunfire was exchanged—in widespread rioting of the familiar sort. Tuesday afternoon, when the temperature was close to 100 degrees, some Negro children had been playing in the cold water from a fire hydrant, illegally opened. Policemen turned off the water and arrested a man who turned it on again. Onlookers shouted "Police brutality!" and the riot began. The next day police allowed hydrants to gush until 5 P.M., but it was too late. Violence was spreading over the ghetto, and it continued through nearly four days. More than 1,000 heavily-armed police were unable to quell it. When 4,000 National Guardsmen arrived Friday evening to restore order, two Negroes had been killed, 57 people (including six policemen) had been injured, and 282 had been arrested—in addition to uncalculated property damage.

King and his associates still worked to draw Negroes into a non-violent but aggressive drive for open housing. Beginning near the end of July, the Chicago Freedom Movement began a series of marches into all-white, largely East European neighborhoods to dramatize the barriers which made it impossible for Negroes to escape from the ghetto. Leaders charged that real estate firms in those areas told potential Negro customers that they had no listings, while white prospects were given long lists of homes and apartments; and reports of white and Negro testers bore this out. The "invading" Negroes were met with curses, harassment, and violence from hostile whites. A sprinkling of white ministers, priests, and nuns marched with the Negroes; one of the nuns, Sister Mary Angelica, was hit by a brick thrown by a jeering white youth and blood soaked her veil and white collar.

The danger of open interracial strife led many, including Roman Catholic Archbishop (now Cardinal) John Patrick Cody, to urge an end to this initiative. The archbishop, considered a friend of the Negro movement, made his plea "with a heavy heart" because of "the shameful reaction of some to a basic freedom of the land." But Bevel, replying for the movement, found it necessary "regretfully to reject this appeal to cease our nonviolent protests against the immorality and injustice of racial segregation in Chicago housing."

Chicago Police Superintendent O. W. Wilson said of Dr. King: "Inadvertently, he has created hatreds which are to the disadvantage of the Negro population." Mayor Richard J. Daley secured a court injunction limiting marches to one a day and participants to 500 persons. But the marches went right on, heavily guarded by police. Sometimes 600 policemen guarded 500 marchers. Where policemen were few, whites hurled bricks, stones, and bottles at the marchers. Crowds of up to 1,000 whites waved Confederate flags and shouted: "Nigger, nigger, nigger!"

It was a congenial atmosphere for professional anti-Negro hate-mongers, who hastened to Chicago. "Führer" George Lincoln Rockwell found himself in the (for him) unusual situation of being surrounded by crowds of admirers. Over 500 whites attended a rally where they were harangued by representatives of the American Nazi party, the National States Rights party, and the Ku Klux Klan. Police had to fire into the air to halt the violence that followed.

Meanwhile King and Al Raby, head of the Coordinating Council of Community Organizations, negotiated for two weeks with Mayor Daley and seventy-nine of Chicago's foremost political, economic, and religious leaders. On August 26—"an historic day," the mayor called it—they concluded a formal agreement. Dr. King hailed it as "a significant victory in justice, freedom and democracy." Marches and demonstrations in Chicago were suspended.

In the ten-point agreement, the Chicago Commission on Human Relations undertook to take various specified steps to strengthen enforcement of existing open housing regulations: the Chicago Housing Authority, the Department of Urban Renewal, and the Cook County Department of Public Aid would direct their housing activities toward a dispersal of Negro families across the city; mortgage bankers would lend mortgage money to home-buyers without regard to race; the Real Estate Board withdrew opposition to the "philosophy of open housing"; the labor unions would try to place Negro members in white neighborhoods; and the representatives of Chicago's major religious faiths undertook a continuing seven-point program of education and action to combat discrimination.

A victory it was indeed. To have forced the Chicago powers-that-be to sit down at the table and talk was itself a moral victory of the first order. There was a victory also in concrete accomplishment—as accomplishments go in the baffling area of residential segregation. Some progress was made in the months that followed. The church groups carried on an unflagging campaign against the immorality of excluding Negroes from white neighborhoods. But in this baffling area the prejudices and fears of the public tend to thwart the best intentions and bravest undertakings of leadership. The ghetto continued to grow at a faster rate than residential integration in Chicago.

Dr. King had scheduled a march into Cicero, a city of 70,000 people bordering Chicago on the west. He was now ready to give this up, but an impetuous faction of the movement—including members of CORE, SNCC, the Deacons for Defense, and the far-left W.E.B. DuBois Clubs—was determined to go on with it. Cicero offered an intriguing challenge. This lily-white community was notorious for its hostility to Negroes. The attempt of one to move into Cicero in 1951, and the massive violence which ensued, were still remembered.

Led by Robert Lucas of CORE, about 200 Negroes (with a few white comrades) advanced into Cicero on September 4 and marched almost the length of the city. Lines of scowling whites were held back by police until finally a mob of about 3,000 attacked the marchers. National Guardsmen, firing into the air and wielding bayonets—half a dozen whites were slashed—rescued the marchers in time to prevent a massacre. A hail of rocks, curses, and obscenities followed the Negroes as they marched back to their Chicago ghetto.

Events of 1966 resulted in a change in the attitude of many whites in the North and West toward the Negro revolution. Earlier the intermittent anti-Negro atrocities and the dignity and restraint of the Negro protest in the South had enabled Northerners to indulge in moral indignation and had created an image of persecuted Negroes opposing Christian nonviolence to intolerance and brutality. That image was shattered in the riot-torn cities of the North and West. But it was momentarily revived by an incident which occurred in Grenada, Mississippi, on September 12.

Some fifty Negro children had been lawfully admitted to two of the town's previously all-white public schools. A crowd estimated at 400 white men and women gathered. As the children were leaving school, white men attacked them, some with fists, some with ax handles, pipes, and chains. At least thirty-three children were beaten. One boy's leg was broken and three others required hospital treatment. Meanwhile, white women cursed the children, and local police stood around doing nothing.

The reports of such inhumanity to children were more sickening than news of the murder of an adult might have been. "There is no excuse . . . for the black mobsters in Atlanta, Chicago and other cities," said the Washington *News*. "But at least they haven't deliberately mistreated children." Nevertheless the "black mobsters" quickly returned to the national spotlight and sympathy for Negro children in Mississippi faded in the thought of Molotoff cocktails nearer home. The 1966 balance sheet of white good will showed a heavy loss.

SEVENTEEN

White Backlash
1966

A graph of the fluctuations of public sympathy with the Negro and with his efforts to throw off the disabilities of inferior status would register a high point at the March on Washington of August 28, 1963. School boycotts and the increasing militancy of Northern Negroes during the subsequent winter and the riots in Harlem and other eastern cities in the late summer of 1964 pulled the line down, but it rose with the exhilaration attending the enactment of the Civil Rights Act of 1964, the shock of the murder of three civil-rights crusaders in Mississippi, and Johnson's resounding victory over Goldwater in November. The cause of interracial justice gained many recruits, and sympathy with the Negro continued strong through 1964. It tended to increase with racial crises in the South and to decline when demonstrations and disturbances brought the revolution home to the North and West. Pro-Negro sentiment probably reached its highest emotional peak with the Selma-Montgomery march in the spring of 1965. Then came Watts in August, 1965, and the beginning of a steady depletion of the reservoir of white tolerance and good will. In the language of Dow Jones calculations, a civil-rights bull market topped out at Selma and a long bear market began.

It was on June 4, 1965—between Selma and Watts—that President Johnson delivered his Howard University speech and promised "this fall . . . to call a White House Conference of scholars and experts and outstanding leaders of both races and officials of government at every level" to develop a program "to fulfill these rights" of equal citizenship for all. The project assumed mammoth proportions; the fall meeting became only a planning session for the full conference, which was held on June 1 and 2, 1966. Rarely has a meeting been held in such grandiose atmosphere, with such elaborate preparation and such large and representative participation; never have the talents of so many able and knowledgeable students of the race problem been brought to bear at one time—with so little visible accomplishment—as in this "White House Conference 'To Fulfill These Rights.' "

When the President spoke to the Howard University students in June, 1965, new civil-rights legislation was moving easily toward enactment, and the American commitment of troops in Vietnam had barely reached 46,500. In June, 1966, the Administration's latest civil-rights bill was running into difficulty and more than 260,000 American fighting men were in Vietnam. A certain malaise had begun to settle over both the civil-rights movement and the national impulse for social reform. The White House Conference addressed itself to costly and far-reaching proposals at a time when Negroes were divided among themselves and a large element of the public, turning now to other concerns, was asking: "What more do they want?"

In the one-year interval also the Moynihan Report on the broken Negro families in urban ghettos, which had largely inspired the Howard University speech, had aroused such ire among Negroes that this whole theme had been cast aside. That a diagnosis of Negro distress which contained so much truth and wisdom should have proven so disruptive may need some explanation. Part of the trouble lay in the language of the Moynihan Report. The expression, "the Negro family," seemed to imply that the instability which caused concern was a general characteristic of Negro families—when he was writing about less than half of them. A majority of the Negro families in the United States—including the families of participants in great meetings like the White House Conference—were quite as stable on the average as white families. The point of the deterioration of the Negro family structure in the slums would have to be made with caution, precision, and the utmost delicacy, if it were possible to make it at all in the midst of a nationwide struggle for Negro rights. The implication of the Moynihan Report—or rather the exaggerated interpretation given it in many quarters—was that there were evils which Negroes themselves needed to correct before they could claim equal status with the white man. The image given of a race demoralized by its disintegrating family structure was not likely to encourage industrialists to employ Negroes or white families to welcome them as neighbors. The need for Negro self-improvement was recognized by Negro leaders, but it was not to be talked about in a loud voice at this stage. The thrust of the civil-rights movement now was to place the blame for the Negro's afflictions, and the obligation to relieve them, upon the shoulders of the white man—where indeed they ultimately belonged. So the problem was eliminated from the Conference's agenda.

The planning session for the conference, which was held in Washington on November 1 and 2, with some 200 key persons in attendance, had itself been torn with dissension. Its chief result was a realization that it was hopeless to expect the 2,400 delegates to be invited to the full conference to reach agreement on any concrete program. It was decided, as the only practicable procedure, that a council, consisting of a small group of civil-rights leaders, industrialists, educators, lawyers, and others, should prepare a comprehensive report to be submitted to the larger gathering for discussion. The report would not be voted upon, but "all reactions, comments and suggestions" would be recorded verbatim and presented in due course to the President.

A White House announcement of February 23, 1966, fixed the date for the conference and named twenty-eight members appointed to the President's Council. A. Philip Randolph, the elder statesman of the civil-rights movement, was honorary chairman and King, Wilkins, Young, McKissick, and Lewis represented the Big Five organizations; Miss Dorothy Height, president of the National Council of Negro Women, and Vernon E. Jordan, Jr., of the Southern Regional Council were also members. The chairman of the Council was Ben W. Heineman, chairman of the Chicago and North Western Railway Company. Half a dozen prestigious business executives were members, including President James A. Linen III of Time, Inc., and Courtland S. Gross, chairman of the board of the Lockheed Aircraft Corporation. There were also the late Stephen R. Currier, president of the Taconic Foundation, George Meany, president of the AFL-CIO, former Assistant Attorney General Burke Marshall, a state governor, a former governor, a university president, and other notables. Additionally, forty-four consultants were engaged. These also included persons distinguished in many fields; some of them had a large hand in shaping the council's report—notably five who were listed as "Special Consultants": Harold C. Fleming, of the Potomac Institute, Philip Hauser, of the University of Chicago, Vivian Henderson, president of Clark College, M. Carl Holman, of the Commission on Civil Rights, and George Schermer, of George Schermer Associates.

This impressive aggregation labored for three months and produced an elaborate 104-page "Council's Report and Recommendations to the Conference." Each prospective participant in the conference received a handsome vinyl portfolio, containing this report, a heavier volume of statistical data on the "Economic and Social Situation" of the Negro, prepared for the occasion by the Department of Labor, a copy of the Howard University speech, a summary of the Civil Rights Act of 1964, an OEO report, and a program—together with "White House Conference" note paper and a "White House Conference" ball point pen.

Events from then on were less felicitous. A group of civil-rights leaders, meeting in New York on the eve of the conference, warned that it would be mostly "a frivolous exercise." One of their number —Dr. Benjamin F. Payton, a Negro minister, then serving as executive director of the Commission on Religion and Race of the National Council of Churches—said: "The more conferences you hold that speak in general terms, that fail to come to terms with commitments . . . the more you raise expectations . . . and raise the danger of violence" when these expectations are not fulfilled.

The conference was held in Washington's resplendent Sheraton-Park Hotel, overflowing into the Shoreham, a block away. As delegates arrived on May 31 and June 1 they passed, though they were not deterred by, a handful of pickets—self-styled "wild men of the movement," led by Julius Hobson, of the Washington ACT group, and Jesse Gray, of the Harlem rent strike—who shouted, "Uncle Toms!"

Inside, before and between scheduled meetings, the multitude milled around in the spacious lobbies and facilities of the Sheraton-Park, greeting old friends, making new acquaintances, and meeting celebrities. Among speakers at the evening banquets were Vice President Humphrey, Thurgood Marshall, Roy Wilkins, and, briefly and unexpectedly, the President himself. Martin Luther King, the movement's greatest orator, but now campaigning against the Administration's Vietnam policy, was present but not asked to speak. Stokely Carmichael, disdainful of white collaboration, had announced that SNCC would boycott the conference. Floyd McKissick, now racing to overtake Carmichael's extremism, derided the conference as being "rigged," but participated by way of pressing his demand for United States withdrawal from Vietnam.

The conference's twelve committees (200 members each), six meeting in each hotel, were like public hearings, where participants argued, orated, and fulminated, not only on items in the Council's report, but over an incredible variety of subjects related to Negro grievances and Negro aspirations. The only conceivable topic omitted seemed to be the problem of broken families. (The Vietnam issue was kept safely under control; McKissick's obstreperous efforts were handily rebuffed.)

The 2,400 participants in the White House Conference dispersed afterward, many with the satisfaction of having let off steam, but most of them with an uncomfortable feeling of emptiness. The American public took passing note of the fact that a large gathering of civil-rights people had been held, and resumed its anxiety over Premier Ky's efforts to cope with Buddhist unrest in Vietnam. The President's Council had said in its report: "The major emphasis of this Conference should be on immediate, practical steps to enlist in this cause the great mass of uncommitted, uninvolved Americans." Alas, the great mass of Americans was moving in the opposite direction.

The "Council's Report and Recommendations" was the project's most substantial product. That document analyzed briefly the major problems in the areas of economic security, education, housing, and the administration of justice, and called for sterner enforcement of civil-rights statutes, "guaranteed employment" for everybody able to work, legislation to protect civil-rights workers and to provide compensatory damages for the victims of civil-rights crimes, public school integration across boundaries between city and suburb, the creation and enforcement of federal welfare standards, mandatory desegregation in urban renewal projects, equalization throughout the country of per-pupil spending on education—while nearly doubling the figure to $1,000 a year—free junior college for anyone and "acceptance of the government's responsibility for guaranteeing a minimum income to all Americans."

In the light of the waning enthusiasm for reform in the nation and the loss of momentum in the civil-rights movement, the President's Council's report to the White House Conference suggested Browning's lines:

> That low man seeks a little thing to do,
>   Sees it and does it;
> This high man, with a great thing to pursue,
>   Dies ere he knows it.
> That low man goes on adding one to one,
>   His hundred's soon hit:
> This high man, aiming at a million
>   Misses an unit.

It was a compendium of goals for the exertions and hopes of men of good will—undertakings for which the nation might be ready, not in the forseeable future, yet long before the millennium.

The Administration's proposed Civil Rights Act of 1966 was sent to Congress on April 28. It had two major purposes. One was to protect civil-rights workers from violence in the South and end all-white juries in communities of substantial Negro population; the other was to strike a blow at residential segregation. The latter evil was somewhat more prevalent in the North and West than in the South, where most of the other civil-rights legislation had had its greatest impact—a circumstance which led Senator Sam J. Ervin of North Carolina to observe: "For the first time, we have a bill which proposes that other than Southern oxen are to be gored."

The bill did not contain all that civil-rights leaders wanted: it omitted provision for indemnification of civil-rights workers killed or injured and for removal of certain cases from state to federal courts. But it prohibited threat or injury to persons engaged in the exercise of their constitutional rights, including voting, education, housing, employment, jury service, and the use of public facilities —or in urging or aiding others, by speech or peaceful public assembly, to exercise such rights. Violators were punishable up to a $10,000 fine and ten years in jail, or, if death resulted, by any term up to life imprisonment. The bill contained strong provisions to assure the selection of state and federal juries without regard to race. One section also broadened the authority of the Attorney General to bring suits to end remaining segregation in schools and other public facilities. In a separate bill these provisions in some form would probably have been enacted into law.

But the bill also attacked the dragon of neighborhood segregation. It would ban racial and religious discrimination in the sale, rental, and financing of all housing. Millions of whites, including many who had considered themselves liberal on the race issue, bristled at this. Senator Ervin, who was chairman of a subcommittee conducting hearings on the bill, said in May that he had received 2,000 letters opposing the open-housing section and only half a dozen in favor of it. Other members of Congress said their letters were running 100 to one against the bill. The letter-writing was stimulated in large part by propaganda of the National Association of Real Estate Boards, but such a one-sided deluge was unexpected. Most ominous of all in view of his role in the passage of the Civil Rights Act of 1964, Senate Minority Leader Everett Dirksen declared that the open-housing section was "absolutely unconstitutional."

When debate began in the House on July 25, Black Power was in the air, and eight cities had been hit by rioting. Disorders continued as the Senate considered the bill in September. Members of Congress sensed a rising "white backlash," and the November election was not far off. In contrast to the atmosphere of urgency that had surrounded debate on civil-rights legislation in 1964 and 1965, the mood even among liberal members was one of apprehension and timidity and Administration pressure was relatively feeble.

The House adopted a compromise amendment, which some liberals supported in the belief that it was necessary in order to save the bill: it made the open housing provisions inapplicable to owner-occupied properties of four units or less or to brokers acting on written instructions from owners of such property. This exempted all but about 23 million units (only 6 million of them in the suburbs)—an estimated 40 per cent—of the housing market. Reacting to the wave of rioting, the House also added a provision making it a federal criminal offense to cross state lines with intent to incite a riot or to commit any act of violence during the riot. The House passed the amended bill on August 9 by a vote of 259 to 157.

Votes on cloture suggested that the Senate also, which debated the House bill the second week in September, favored it, by a bare majority. But here the inevitable filibuster made the vote of two-thirds of the senators present necessary to bring it to a vote. Senator Dirksen dashed any hopes of a relenting on his part with the remark: "For all practical purposes the civil-rights bill is dead."

After some desultory debate on the question of taking up the bill—with adjournment on three days for lack of a quorum—a cloture resolution was rejected by a vote of 54 for to 42 against. On a second try on September 19 the vote for rejection was 52 to 41. Then efforts to take up the bill were abandoned. It was the first time since 1957, when the first modern civil-rights legislation was enacted, that an Administration civil-rights bill had been lost.

Another important civil-rights bill that had the blessing of the Administration died in the Senate. The House had approved on April 27, by a vote of 300 to 93, an Equal Employment Opportunity Act of 1966, which would have broadened and strengthened Title VII of the Civil Rights Act of 1964. The Commission on Equal Employment Opportunity had been severely handicapped in administering this title by its lack of enforcement powers. The House bill would have authorized the EEOC to initiate charges of discrimination, to issue cease and desist orders, and to order hiring and reinstatement, with or without back pay. It also would have extended coverage to employers of fifty or more persons after July 2, 1966, and of 8 or more after July 2, 1967. However, the Civil Rights Act of 1966 having received all the attention the Senate was prepared to give to civil rights in the fall of 1966, no action was taken on this measure.

The retreat from civil rights was indicated in other ways. A Senate Appropriations Committee report sharply criticized the Department of Health, Education and Welfare for the guidelines by which it had been trying to enforce desegregation of hospitals and schools. Majority Leader Mike Mansfield, long a supporter of civil-rights measures, said he thought HEW had "gone too fast" in this area, though he later limited his criticism to hospital desegregation. A rider was attached to the appropriations bill permitting hospital segregation when physicians deemed it necessary for the well-being of the patient—a loophole which might have more or less perpetuated hospital segregation in some sections of the South. This was removed in the conference committee, but a sharp cut was made in HEW's enforcement budget. Pressing the desegregation of thousands of hospitals and school districts was a cumbersome undertaking, which required more personnel than HEW had available. When the Senate refused to restore a House cut of $927,-000 in the funds requested for this work, David Seeley, director of HEW's Office of Equal Educational Opportunity lamented: "This may be the turning point similar to that after the Civil War, when the nation turned its back on the Negro."

The *Washington Post* of September 30, looking both at Congress and at the results of recent Democratic primaries, in which moderate candidates for governor in Georgia and Maryland had been defeated by blatant racists, said: "An ominous and dangerous reaction has gripped this country."

At a time when the unrest in urban slums cried out for expansion of the War on Poverty an unexpectedly small Administration request for the Office of Economic Opportunity, of $1.75 billion, was reduced to $1.66 billion. The appropriation was also earmarked for specific programs, severely restricting the controversial community action program. OEO Director Sargent Shriver said the War on Poverty "has been dealt severe and crippling blows and will have to retreat on several fronts. . . . There will be no money for summer programs; teen-age programs will have to be curtailed. . . ."

A better grasp of the magnitude of the poverty crisis was shown by 140 representatives of civil-rights, religious, and labor groups who signed a so-called "Freedom Budget," issued by the A. Philip Randolph Institute, on October 26, 1966—after the passage of the bill on October 21 and before its signing by the President on November 8. This document advocated "maximum government effort to provide full employment and guaranteed income for all who cannot or should not work," and called for a federal expenditure of $185 billion in the next ten years.

The much advertised "white backlash," which failed to materialize in 1964, was very real in the elections of 1966. Some candidates who tried to exploit the backlash were defeated by moderates, and a Negro was elected to the United States Senate for the first time since 1881. The South saw a healthy abandonment of racist demagoguery together with an impressive demonstration of the power of the Negro vote. But across the nation the elections reflected a hardening of white attitudes toward the Negro and a loss of interest in, or growing opposition to, the civil-rights movement. In Congress the rising tide of conservative sentiment resulted in a resounding victory for the Republican party, which severely handicapped an Administration that had secured more legislation in the interest of the Negro than any other since Reconstruction.

Early backlash signals came in the gubernatorial primaries. The smashing victory of the wife of Governor George Wallace in the Democratic primary in Alabama in May, the heavy vote for Ronald Reagan and the poor showing of liberal Governor Pat Brown in California's Republican and Democratic primaries in June, the capture of Democratic nominations by segregationist candidates in Arkansas in August and in Georgia and Maryland in September gave successive shocks to liberals and civil-rights advocates. It was not quite as bad as it looked at first: Democratic nominees for governor in Arkansas and Maryland were both defeated in November by moderate Republicans. But the liberal reverses in the primaries did much to alert Congress and the nation to a change in public sentiment. White supporters of the Negro cause became less outspoken, and, with the summer rioting, all politicians stressed the need for bringing violence to an end. In the fall campaigns law and order was clearly a more popular theme than civil rights.

The term "white backlash" was largely a misnomer when applied to what was happening in the South. Southern whites did not "lash back" at Negro rioting; they had seen very little Negro rioting. The violence in the South had been mainly that of whites, directed against Negroes and friends of the Negroes. Of late there had been Negro outbreaks in several cities, but these were relatively minor, not to be compared with the convulsions that hit cities in the North and West. Although Southern cities had more or less segregated Negro neighborhoods, the bulk of the Negro population was still widely dispersed. There were few whites who were not personally acquainted with some Negroes, and vice versa. Even limited communication or a master-servant relationship was less pregnant with explosive violence than the ostracism of Negroes in Northern cities. The problem of social adjustment in the old home of the Negro in the United States was basically different from that elsewhere, and progress in that region continued to be made. It had been accelerated by the new participation of the Negro in political decisions.

The tone of political campaigns in the South in 1966 showed a revolutionary improvement over previous years. Crass appeals to racial prejudice were almost entirely absent from the public debate. The Alabama Democratic Executive Committee, in April, struck the ancient slogan "White Supremacy" from the official Democratic party emblem in that state. Many white candidates for office shook Negro hands, some addressed Negro meetings, and few had unkind words for the Negro race. However, this did not prevent the Negro question from being an issue—the records and views of candidates were well known—and the heavy support for segregationists in several conspicuous contests was a jarring reminder that racial prejudice was still deeply entrenched.

Governor George C. Wallace of Alabama, segregation's knight in shining armor, building on the more pronounced white backlash in the nation, was plainly headed for another venture as a candidate for President. Barred from succeeding himself as governor, he launched his wife, Mrs. Lurleen Wallace, as a candidate for that office. Billboards urged frankly: VOTE FOR LURLEEN AND LET GEORGE DO IT. In the May 3 primary Mrs. Wallace won a majority in a field of ten candidates, which included Attorney General Flowers (in second place with 20 per cent of the vote) and relatively moderate former Congressman Carl Elliott (in third place). In the November election she easily defeated her Republican opponent, Representative James D. Martin.

The Republican party saved one Southern state from a segregationist candidate for governor, but gave a segregationist governor to another. In Arkansas, where the now somewhat mellowed Orval Faubus was retiring, hard-core segregationist James Douglas Johnson won the Democratic nomination to succeed him, but he was defeated by moderate Republican Winthrop Rockefeller in November. On the other hand, in Florida, Republican Claude Kirk, Jr., favored by the segregationists, won the governorship over the liberal Democratic nominee, Mayor Robert King High of Miami.

In Georgia Lester G. Maddox—who in his last-stand resistance to desegregation had handed out ax-handles to white customers for use against any Negro who dared to enter his Atlanta restaurant—won the Democratic nomination to succeed moderate Governor Carl Sanders. Ellis Arnall, a moderate former governor, led in the first round of the September primary, with a 45,000-vote margin in a field of six, but segregationist voters, uniting behind Maddox in the runoff, gave the nomination to the latter. In the November election an equally segregationist Republican candidate, Howard Calloway, received a narrow margin of votes over Maddox, but a write-in vote for Arnall prevented him from getting the necessary majority. In the midst of heated controversy and litigation the election would be thrown into the Democrat-controlled Georgia legislature, where Maddox was elected governor in early 1967.

In the border state of Maryland the state house was saved for moderate policy only by the election in November of Republican Governor Spiro T. Agnew. George P. Mahoney had won the Democratic nomination in a campaign against open housing with incessant repetition of the refrain: "Your home is your castle."

Nationally the Republicans gained eight state houses, bringing the number of states under Republican governors to twenty-five, including five of the seven most populous states. The most sensational setback both for the Democratic party and for liberal racial policy came in California. In that state the reaction to Watts was reflected, not in a demand for correction of the conditions that caused that holocaust, but in a surge of apprehension and anti-Negro feeling. The result, aided by other factors, was a wholesale desertion of voters from veteran liberal Governor Pat Brown to the anti-Negro mayor of Los Angeles in the Democratic primary and to his ultraconservative opponent in the general election. Ronald Reagan, a rising new figure in the Republican party, won in November by nearly a million votes.

Observing the trend in the most populous state in the Union, columnist Joseph Alsop said even in late July: "So we have drifted onward towards trouble that hardly bears thinking about." In December Governor Brown in his final days in office concluded sadly that the nation was "a generation away" from understanding between the races. "Whether we like it or not," he said, "the white desire for separation is a potent force, and I don't know what we're going to do about it."

The principle of civilian boards to review police action, persistently urged by Negroes, received a crushing blow in New York City, where the Civilian Complaint Review Board, created by Mayor Lindsay, was submitted to the voters for approval in a referendum. The board was smothered under an avalanche of votes In another referendum, Los Angeles failed to give the necessary two-thirds vote for the construction of a hospital in Watts.

In Congress the Republicans gained 47 seats in the House of Representatives and three in the Senate. The Democratic party would still have impressive majorities—248 to 187 in the House and 64 to 36 in the Senate—but traditionally conservative Southern Democrats could be expected to vote with Republicans in many situations. The party line, of course, did not necessarily separate liberals from conservatives, but surveys indicated that in the House from 30 to 35 identifiable liberals had been replaced by conservatives and self-styled middle-of-the-roaders. The Eighty-ninth Congress having balked at civil-rights legislation, the prospects for it in the Ninetieth were dim indeed.

There was evidence not only of the traditional off-year swing to the opposition party, but of a broader swing of the pendulum in a historic sense: the country had grown weary of innovation and reform.

In another respect the 1966 elections were favorable for the Negro. The number of Negroes elected to office and the impact of the Negro vote upon results in the South showed a marked advance toward integration of the Negro in the body politic. An exceptional triumph over racial bias was registered in the election of Republican Edward William Brooke III as senator from Massachusetts. This able and attractive Negro, a former state attorney general, running against both white backlash and Black Power, defeated former Governor Endicott Peabody with 61 per cent of the vote—in a state where Negroes were less than 3 per cent of the total population. In the nation, 154 Negroes were elected to 27 state legislatures, representing a gain of more than 50 per cent over 1964. Of these, 123 were state representatives, 31 state senators.

In the South, for the first time, the Negro vote proved a major factor in the 1966 elections. The Voter Education Project of the Southern Regional Council, which had reactivated its program of promoting Negro registration in the South, had added 100,000 Negroes to the voter lists during the year. The VEP also made careful studies of progress made, and its reports were considered authoritative in this field. A VEP press release of December 14, 1966, reported: "Negro voter registration in 11 Southern states now stands at 2.7 million. In 1962 it was 1.5 million; in 1964, 2.2 million." About one half of the Negroes of voting age were now registered, compared with 70 per cent of the white adults.

In Alabama, despite meager gains at the county officer level, the 1966 experience was mainly one of frustration. In this state Negro voter registration had more than doubled since the passage of the Voting Rights Act of 1965, rising from 112,000 to nearly 250,000. But the newly enfranchised Negroes lacked organization or concerted strategy—and luck. Martin Luther King urged Negroes to vote for the most acceptable white candidate where no qualified Negro had a chance of winning; Stokely Carmichael urged Negroes to stay away from the primaries and vote only for Negro candidates in the general election. Carmichael's Black Panther "Freedom Party" venture proved a fiasco, electing no candidate and weakening the Negro impact upon white contests. Of 82 Negro candidates for minor offices only 5 were elected. Three of these were from Macon County, where Negroes had held a voting majority for several years; one of them, Lucius D. Amerson, became Alabama's first Negro sheriff in this century. Negro votes also enabled the more nearly moderate Wilson Baker to end the career of the much-hated Jim Clark, of Selma fame, as sheriff of Dallas County.

A Negro was elected to the Jefferson County school board in Mississippi, becoming the first of his race to be elected to a county office in that state since Reconstruction; and several Negroes were elected to parish school boards in Louisiana. Less than 55,000 Negroes were estimated to have voted in Mississippi, out of approximately 170,000 registered. In Louisiana there were no statewide contests.

A further account of the effects of the Negro vote in the November elections in the South is given in the following extracts from the Voter Education Project's December 14 survey:

> Election results gathered by VEP in 11 Southern states show that Negroes supplied the winning margin for a U. S. Senator, one and probably two governors, and at least two U. S. House members. . . .
> Twenty Negroes were elected to state legislatures in the South—an increase of nine. And Negroes were elected to county-level posts

—in one case, to the office of sheriff—and in such Deep South states as Georgia, Louisiana, Alabama and Mississippi.

The Negro vote clearly provided the margin for Winthrop Rockefeller's election as governor of Arkansas. The Republican candidate received approximately 300,000 votes. The Democratic candidate, ardent segregationist Jim Johnson, got about 255,000 votes.

An estimated 80,000 to 90,000 Negroes voted, more than 90 per cent of them for Rockefeller. Thus Negroes supplied Rockefeller's margin of 45,000, with plenty to spare. . . .

Negro voters in South Carolina plainly provided the margin for a U. S. Senator and probably for a governor.

Ernest F. (Fritz) Hollings was elected to the Senate over Republican candidate Marshall J. Parker by a mere 12,000 votes. Gov. Robert E. McNair defeated Republican challenger Joseph O. Rogers, Jr. by a more comfortable 72,000 votes.

The Negro turnout was estimated at 100,000—just over half the Negro registration of 191,000. The Negro vote went almost totally Democratic. . . .

In North Carolina's Fifth Congressional District, Negroes provided the victory margin for Democrat Nick Galifianakis over Republican G. Fred Steele, Jr. Returns from eight predominantly Negro precincts in Forsyth County gave Galifianakis 5,156 votes to Steele's 284. Four predominantly Negro precincts in Durham County gave Galifianakis 2,400 and Steele 163. Galifianakis won by 5,300 votes. . . .

Negroes provided the margin for Democrat Ray Blanton over Republican Julius Hurst in West Tennessee's Seventh Congressional District. Blanton won by about 2,700 votes, despite the fact that the district went for Republican Howard Baker in the U. S. Senate race by 3,000 votes. Nine predominantly Negro precincts in Memphis gave Blanton 7,824 votes to Hurst's 353. . . .

Six Negroes were elected to the Tennessee Legislature—an increase of five. Three are from Memphis, two from Nashville, and one from Knoxville. The latter was the only Democrat elected to Knox County's eight-man legislative delegation. . . .

Negroes won 11 seats in the Georgia Legislature—an increase of one. The new legislator is from Augusta. The total includes Julian Bond of Atlanta, who again was elected to the seat that had been denied him by the Georgia House. . . .

Three Negroes were elected to the Legislature in Texas—two in Houston and one in Dallas. One, Miss Barbara Jordan, a Houston attorney, was elected to the Senate. They are the first Negroes to be elected to the Texas Legislature in this century. . . .

State Senator William B. Spong coasted to an easy victory in one of two Virginia contests for the U. S. Senate. Spong amassed about 425,000 votes, against some 243,000 for his Republican challenger and 58,000 for the Conservative candidate.

In Virginia's other U. S. Senate race Harry F. Byrd, Jr. won. However, Byrd ran considerably behind Spong with 383,000 votes. Spong had more than 58 per cent of the vote in his race, whereas Byrd had 54 per cent in his.

At least part of the difference is explained by the Negro support Spong received. Many Negroes who supported Spong voted for Byrd's Republican opponent, Lawrence M. Traylor.

With Negro support, Spong narrowly defeated Sen. Willis Robertson during the summer for the Democratic nomination.

EIGHTEEN

Calm Before the Storm
1967

The winter of 1966-67 found champions of the Negro cause in a mood of deepest pessimism. The organized civil-rights movement was in a state of disarray and near-paralysis; there was a feeling of uncertainty as to what direction to take and of inability to advance in any direction. President Johnson's State of the Union message on January 10 devoted only forty-five words to civil rights. The War on Poverty was under heavy attack, and the battered Office of Economic Opportunity seemed threatened with dismemberment. Martin Luther King saw "desolate days" ahead. "The civil-rights movement is dead," was heard in many quarters.

Historian C. Vann Woodward, in an article in the January, 1967, issue of *Harper's Magazine*, looked at the situation against the background of the history of the Negro in the United States, viewing the movement of the 1950's and 1960's as "the Second Reconstruction." "Veterans of the Second Reconstruction and planners of the Third," Woodward said, "would do well to face up to the fact that the one is now over and the other is still struggling to be born."

The President renewed his commitment to "equal justice for all Americans" in a message sent to Congress on February 15 and offered another civil-rights bill, but few expected the Ninetieth Congress to pass any new legislation in this field. The OEO survived and carried on, though it was unable to expand to the dimensions that the stage in its development and the need demanded; Congress gave it a supplementary appropriation in May of $75 million. Slow progress in its programs continued to be made through the first half of 1967, but little improvement was visible to Negroes in the simmering ghettos.

References to "perseverance" and the need for "years of trial and error," such as the President made in his February 15 message, gave little comfort to those who saw the need for immediate steps on a massive scale. Many civil-rights leaders who abhorred violence, despairing of accomplishing any more by peaceful exhortation and demonstrations, said that a violent upheaval was inevitable, and added privately that nothing short of one would arouse the nation. Martin Luther King was "convinced that, if the intolerable conditions of Negroes in the ghettos are not dealt with and removed with haste, we are faced with many dark nights of hate." Among whites, while predictions of calamity in some quarters became more and more dire, fewer and fewer worried about the matter at all. The revolution drifted in an ominous calm. The wind that would blow come July would be of hurricane proportions.

The Adam Clayton Powell affair—which for a few weeks in January, 1967, made that Negro Congressman one of the most photographed, quoted, and talked about men in the country—added to both white backlash and Negro unrest. The revelations of Powell's free and easy behavior as chairman of the House Education and Labor Committee tended to exacerbate the increasing anti-Negro feeling, and the refusal of the House to seat the most powerful Negro representative in that body angered nearly all Negroes.

Powell was at the same time pastor of Harlem's huge Abyssinian Baptist Church, a Congressman of more than average ability (when in the right mood), and the playboy of the Negro revolution. His glamorous way of life gave vicarious pleasure to humbler Negroes, and his personality nourished Negro pride. For he was as far from the old racist stereotype of the shuffling, cringing "darkie" as could well be imagined. Handsome, clever, sophisticated, arrogant, his attitude toward the white man was often one of condescension or scathing sarcasm, never one of subservience. Even his financial irregularities and his luxurious European jaunts in company with pretty white and Negro secretaries gave a certain satisfaction to Negroes. They were a refutation of the old assumption that, while white leaders might do those things with impunity, Negroes could arrive at an equal level of distinction only by the path of diligence and rectitude. So Powell was popular among most Negroes; under fire he became a hero. Many Negro intellectuals and civil-rights leaders found him hard to get along with, but these also for the most part resented the action taken against him by his colleagues in the House.

Powell was elected in November, 1966, to his twelfth consecutive term as the representative of the Harlem district in the House of Representatives. He had been on the whole an effective, if erratic, chairman of the Education and Labor Committee, through which a mass of important legislation had passed; but his capricious and highhanded methods had exhausted the patience of the other members of that committee. Already in September they had taken steps to strip him of most of his powers. Adding to his embarrassment during most of 1966, Powell had been obliged to stay away from his New York district to avoid arrest for failure to pay a judgment in a defamation suit—except on Sundays, when he was immune from arrest in a civil case. In December New York's highest court issued an order for Powell's arrest for criminal contempt whenever he should set foot in New York, even on a Sunday.

Then a subcommittee of the House Administration Committee, investigating the financial affairs of the Education and Labor Committee, made a series of shocking disclosures. It appeared that Chairman Powell and Corinne Huff, a Negro beauty-contest winner, whom he had put on the committee's payroll at $19,200 a year, had taken "many airline flights" at taxpayers' expense under assumed names; that other flights were charged on the credit cards of committee employees who did not in fact make them; that Powell had put on the committee payroll a Negro girl who testified that she worked as a cook and maid in his retreat on Bimini Island; and that Powell kept his third wife—estranged and living in Puerto Rico—on his Washington payroll at $20,578 a year, depositing most of her pay checks in his own account.

The question of racial bias in what happened when the Ninetieth Congress met is blurred. Powell and his friends claimed that other members of Congress engaged in practices similar to those with which he was charged. This was no doubt true, but probably no other member was entangled in such a web of flagrant mischief; and a number of erring white Congressmen had been censured, excluded, or otherwise disciplined in the past. Negroes pointed to a white lawmaker, Senator Thomas Dodd of Connecticut, who was the subject then of an investigation for unethical practices (which led to a formal censure later in the year). Meanwhile the Senate was welcoming with extraordinary cordiality and respect the first Negro senator in this century. Senator Brooke, however, was little identified with the Negro protest movement; Powell was one of the most vociferous of Negro protesters. The latter would undoubtedly have been administered a rebuke regardless of his race, but the stern treatment that he received, the surprisingly overwhelming vote by which the House acted, and the flood of angry letters from constituents were not unrelated to the white backlash. One veteran Congressman described the vote to the *New York Times* as representing "a small amount of conviction, a large amount of fear, a touch of puritanism and a little racism."

On January 9 a Democratic caucus stripped Powell of his chairmanship of the Education and Labor Committee. The next day— with 1,000 Negroes protesting on the Capitol steps—the House first rejected a motion to seat him pending a report of a Select Committee appointed to weigh the problem, then voted a thundering 364 to 64 not to seat him for the present.

The Select Committee reported five weeks later. It recommended that Powell should be censured and fined $40,000, but that he should be seated. Nevertheless the House on March 1 voted 307 to 116 to deny him his seat.

A week later Powell, joined by thirteen Negroes of his district, filed a suit in federal court challenging the constitutionality of the House action in denying him the seat to which he had been duly elected, and charging that it "was based at least in substantial part on reasons of race."

Since mid-January Powell had been following events from the pleasant distance of South Bimini—"Adam's Eden," he called it— the little island in the Bahamas that he began visiting in 1963. He was comforted there by the comely Miss Huff, and visited by a stream of admirers and newsmen and cameramen. He made friends with the natives and occasionally preached a sermon. There were bathing, fishing, and dominoes, and afternoons usually found him at his favorite bistro, the End of the World, where he entertained friends and newsmen with quips and comment on the "conspiracy" that had brought about his "lynching." In March he was a candidate *in absentia* in a special election to fill the seat from which he had been ousted. The politically naive James Meredith was induced by Republican leaders to enter the contest, but upon better advice from friends he withdrew six days later from a race against the Harlem idol. Another Republican candidate and a conservative opposed him in a lackadaisical contest. Powell received 80 per cent of the vote. But he had no desire to risk another rebuff from his colleagues. After all, he had said: "Anyone who would leave Bimini would be a fool."

The National Association for the Advancement of Colored People continued to flourish in 1967. It busied itself with protesting racial discrimination of every type, pressing for stronger enforcement of civil-rights laws, lobbying for the cause in Washington, and defending the interests of Negroes in hundreds of local situations through negotiation or legal action. It was significant that so large an element of the Negro minority was identified with this organization, which, despite some Black Power sputtering within its ranks, kept the even tenor of its way. However, the 441,000 members of the NAACP were drawn largely from the Negro middle class. It was frequently charged that the Association was out of touch with the urban slums. Its membership also was between 10 and 15 per cent white, and the friendly relations of its leaders with whites in positions of authority raised a suspicion of collusion with "the enemy" and aroused bitter hatred in extremist circles. In June, 1967, police foiled an alleged plot of sixteen members of a secret organization of fanatics, calling itself the Revolutionary Action Movement, to assassinate both the NAACP's Roy Wilkins and Whitney Young of the National Urban League.

The NAACP, the NAACP Legal Defense Fund, and the Urban League were the three civil-rights organizations most conservative, most integrated, most cooperative with liberal whites, and most affluent. The NAACP was making a special effort in 1967 to increase its white membership. While the glare of publicity was generally directed toward the other end of the civil-rights spectrum, each of these in its field was rendering indispensable service to the Negro cause. The NAACP and the Urban League constantly urged steps to improve the lot of Negroes and warned of upheavals to come unless the problems were met boldly and soon. It was the Urban League's Whitney Young who in 1963 first proposed a program of rehabilitation of Marshall Plan dimensions. Together in 1967 the three organizations disposed of over $7 million. The NAACP's projected spending for the year was $1.9 million, about a quarter million more than in 1966. The National Urban League, which had an income of $2.37 million in 1966, was operating on a budget, including special projects, of about $3.5 million.

The NAACP Legal Defense Fund was promised help from an interesting new source. In March a group of wealthy Negroes meeting at the Harvard Club in New York formed the National Business and Professional Committee for the Legal Defense Fund. Dr. Percy L. Julian, a research chemist of suburban Oak Park, Illinois, and Asa T. Spaulding, an insurance executive of Durham, North Carolina—both millionaires—were co-chairmen of the committee, which undertook to raise a million dollars a year for the Fund. This move was of particular interest in view of the frequent criticism that Negro millionaires ignored the civil-rights movement. Actually, some like Dr. Julian had contributed generously to civil-rights organizations.

"The time has come," Dr. Julian said in a *New York Times* interview, "to make an all-out effort to assure the less advantaged that we who by the grace of God are more advantaged really do have a deep concern for their welfare." He denounced Stokely Carmichael, "who slaps in the face the millions of whites who have suffered, bled and died for us, for our larger freedom"; but he realized "painfully" that "there is a bit of Stokely Carmichael in nearly every American Negro, even in me."

Martin Luther King was taking a leading part now in the campaign against American involvement in Vietnam; the Reverend James Bevel, his chief lieutenant in Chicago in 1966, was giving all his time to the peace movement. That circumstance was depriving his Southern Christian Leadership Conference of some financial support. SCLC's budget of $1.5 million in 1965 had been trimmed to $1 million in 1966, and SCLC officials said it was "running at about $1 million" in 1967. The staff had been reduced from 150 to 85.

Outside of either of the above organizations and largely beyond their reach was a large element of impatient, sullen Negroes, in big cities across the land, who were united only by a common infection with the thing called Black Power. These met here and there with miscellaneous extremist groups or merely on the ghetto street and were mostly unorganized; they had many would-be leaders but remained leaderless. SCLC had contact with them and Martin Luther King never ceased in his efforts to bring more of them into his nonviolent fold. But CORE and SNCC moved in the midst of this element. The disproportionate attention given by the news media to those relatively small and penurious organizations was due no doubt in the first instance to their extravagant and colorful behavior. But there was a sounder reason for it: those two groups reflected the mood of a multitude of Negroes who were beginning to pose the nation's gravest problem.

CORE, unlike SNCC, sought to retain a certain dignity, but it continued to agitate for Black Power, with its anti-white-man connotations. Some of the views expressed at its annual meeting in Oakland, California, in July were as shocking to old line Negro civil-rights workers as to whites. Speakers deprecated racial integration, the cherished goal of so many, and urged concentrated Negro voting power to achieve "a black folks' government on black folks' terms" in each Negro area. James Farmer, CORE's former national director, was reported to have warned against "efforts of racists in the North to move you out of the ghetto into the suburbs"—the dispersal which was the prime objective of thousands of Negroes and Negro well-wishers.

The Student Nonviolent Coordinating Committee (which never bothered to expunge either "Student" or "Nonviolent" from its name) continued on its nihilistic course. Its small "staff" was the organization itself, but it was a cadre, whose members were all chiefs and no Indians. A few mysterious "angels" and some collections at rallies kept it financially above water.

At SNCC's annual meeting in May, Stokely Carmichael was replaced as chairman by a native of Baton Rouge, Louisiana, named Hubert G. Brown, who had adopted the name of H. Rapp Brown. A young man of twenty-three, Brown had been identified with SNCC inconspicuously for about four years. He lacked Carmichael's dash and personal magnetism, but his manner and language were somewhat closer to those of the Negroes of the ghetto and no less violent than Carmichael's. A few weeks after his election

Brown said to reporters: "The white man won't get off our backs, so we're going to knock him off. . . . If it comes to the point that black people must have guns, we will have means and ways to obtain those arms."

Stokely Carmichael visited London for ten days in July. He was an object there of lively curiosity on the part of the public and of uneasy concern to Scotland Yard. He spoke to two large, mostly white audiences, and some were impressed as, according to the London *Sunday Telegraph,* he drew "heavily on such well-known philosophers as Sartre, Camus, Machiavelli, and Lewis Carroll." But to West Indian, Asian, and African groups Carmichael reportedly said: "It is time to let the whites know we are going to take over. If they don't like it, we will stamp them out"—and more of the like. He journeyed next to Havana, Cuba, where he was received with open arms; he had a place of honor on the platform with Fidel Castro, while the Cuban dictator proclaimed his country's solidarity with embattled American Negroes. Carmichael's next destination was North Vietnam.

President Johnson sent a strong civil-rights message to the Congress on February 15. To emphasize his unwavering commitment to the cause, he quoted from his Howard University speech of June 4, 1965—first the goals: "jobs," "decent homes in decent surroundings," "an equal chance to learn," "welfare and social programs better designed to hold families together," "care of the sick," and "an understanding heart by all Americans"; then the promise: "To all these fronts—and a dozen more—I will dedicate the expanding efforts of the Johnson administration."

The new Administration civil-rights bill, which was introduced in the House and Senate on February 20, combined substantially the provisions of the civil-rights bill of 1966 and of the bill giving enforcement powers to the Equal Employment Opportunity Commission. The new bill also extended the life of the Civil Rights Commission, due to expire on January 31, 1968, another five years. The provisions against discrimination in housing were made applicable in three stages: they would apply immediately only to housing already covered by the executive order of 1962 and the Civil Rights Act of 1964 (about 4 per cent of the market); in 1968 the coverage would be about the same as in the bill passed by the House in 1966 (40 per cent); and all housing would be covered in 1969.

The Administration's poverty bill for fiscal 1968, introduced in the House and Senate on April 10, called for an appropriation of $2.06 billion for the Office of Economic Opportunity. President Johnson also requested a supplementary appropriation for fiscal 1967 of $75 million "to provide urgently needed funds for ... supervised playgrounds and swimming pools, and for training, employment and education programs to take care of our idle youth in our teeming cities." This looked like an item of insurance against summer rioting, and Congress on May 26 granted the President's request.

In the hope that some part of the Administration civil-rights bill might escape the rejection expected for the package as a whole, six separate bills were introduced in Congress each embodying the provisions of one of its sections. The bill extending the life of the Civil Rights Commission passed the House July 10 by a vote of 326 to 93. Confirmation of a sensational appointment announced by the President June 12, in the opinion of many observers, was as far as the Senate was likely to go in 1967 in the area of interracial amity.

The President nominated Thurgood Marshall, the great-grand-son of a Maryland slave, to be an associate justice of the Supreme Court. Succeeding retiring Justice Tom C. Clark, Marshall would be the first Negro ever to sit in that august body. Although, since his appointment by President Kennedy as a federal circuit judge, followed by his appointment by President Johnson in July, 1965, to the office of Solicitor General, Marshall had been detached from the civil-rights movement, he was an authentic Negro hero. Previously he had served for twenty-three years as counsel for the NAACP and its Legal Defense Fund. He had won many legal battles for equal rights, including his fight for the Supreme Court's momentous decision of 1954, declaring public school segregation unconstitutional. Even the captious Floyd McKissick said of his appointment to the high tribunal: "This has stirred pride in the breast of every black American."

In June, 1967, the Department of Defense began to use an effective weapon of its own to bring about open housing for servicemen at bases in the United States. The President's Committee on Equal

Opportunity in the Armed Forces had recommended in 1963 that the off-limits sanction should be applied where necessary to end discrimination against Negro servicemen and their families in the communities surrounding military bases. A Defense Department survey in 1967 found that of 8,495 servicemen (about 10 per cent of them Negroes) at Andrews Air Force Base, 52 per cent of the white families lived within three and a half miles of the center of the base, but only one per cent of the Negro families had been accommodated in that area. The Pentagon placed all segregated apartments and trailer courts off limits for all incoming military families beginning July 1. At three other Maryland bases the same procedure was followed during the next few weeks. In all four communities race barriers promptly began to fall. A survey of the situation at other military bases in the country was under way, and Secretary of Defense Robert McNamara said the "program to assure fair treatment for all Armed Forces members" would be "pursued as a matter of high priority."

The Supreme Court, beginning with its great decision against public school segregation in 1954, had been a consistent bulwark of the Negro's struggle for "the equal protection of the laws" and equal citizenship. It continued to destroy surviving legal relics of a more bigoted era. In a decision of March 24, 1966, it had outlawed the poll tax as a prerequisite to voting in any election. The poll tax, long used to keep Negroes from the polls in the South, had all but disappeared already. The Twenty-fourth Amendment proscribed it in federal elections and, when knocked down by the court, it was in force in state and local elections in only four states, Alabama, Texas, Mississippi, and Virginia.

In a decision in a Virginia case, handed down on June 12, 1967, the Supreme Court upset the antimiscegenation laws that made it a crime in sixteen states for white and Negro persons to intermarry.

In a decision of May 29, the Supreme Court also upheld an opinion of California's highest court striking down the famous Proposition 14, the adoption of which in 1964 had angered many Negroes. Proposition 14 not only had repealed two open-housing laws, but had amended the state constitution in a manner to bar the state or any of its subdivisions from adopting open-housing laws or policies in the future. California's open-housing laws were reinstated by the court's decision.

Impatient with delay and evasion in ending public school segregation nearly thirteen years after the Supreme Court had declared it unconstitutional, the Fifth Circuit Court of Appeals at New Orleans on March 29 ordered seven school districts in Louisiana and Alabama to complete desegregation of all classes by the beginning of the next school term in the fall. Indirectly the order applied to all cases arising in the territory of that court—Alabama, Florida, Georgia, Louisiana, Mississippi, and Texas. The Supreme Court refused to stay the circuit court's order.

Many concerned individuals in government and industry as well as among race-relations specialists were making a reappraisal of the Negro problem. They sensed increasingly that the crux of it now lay not in overt discrimination—though that evil was still present—but in the area of economics, and in the development of a new pattern of urban life. The basic afflictions that oppressed the Negro masses were poverty and the confinement of millions to intolerable urban ghettos.

The president said in February:

> The struggle against today's discrimination is only a part of the Nation's commitment to equal justice for all Americans. The bigotry of the past has its effects in broken families, children without learning, poor housing and neighborhoods dominated by the fear of crime.
>
> Because these effects are encrusted by generations of inferior opportunities and shattered hopes, they will not yield to laws against discrimination alone. . . .

A tide of migration was segregating American life faster than all the efforts of government and private agencies were desegregating it. The Census Bureau estimated that in six years the Negro population of central cities had increased 24.4 per cent, while the white population had decreased 2.5 per cent. In the suburbs, while the small Negro population had increased only slightly, the white population, twenty times as large to begin with, had increased more than twice as fast. As low-income families crowded the inner city and more prosperous residents left, tax resources lagged further and further behind the skyrocketing costs of expanding school systems, swelling welfare rolls, slum clearance, and dealing with delinquency, crime—and the recently exploding riots. The problem of separate jurisdictions also arose in any project that might cross the city-suburb line.

Remedies proposed involved bold innovations and vast expenditures. The principle of a "guaranteed annual income" was seriously discussed, and the "negative income tax"—by which persons with incomes below a specified minimum would receive not a tax bill but a check from the Internal Revenue Service—was no longer regarded merely as an amusing fantasy. Whitney Young's 1963 proposal of a $145-billion "domestic Marshall Plan" and the $185 billion "Freedom Budget" put forward by   Philip Randolph and company in October, 1966, were given s. ious consideration. In city-rebuilding projections, figures up to a trillion were mentioned. Mayor Lindsay estimated New York's need alone at $100 billion. But apart from all the other difficulties in the way of bold and costly domestic projects, the nation was engaged in a major war against a foreign foe.

When Harry Golden urged a $100-billion Marshall Plan before a Senate Committee on November 30, 1966, Senator Robert Kennedy said: "We're not going to appropriate the kind of sums you're talking about in the immediate future. If the Vietnam war is over, five years from now perhaps we might be doing that." The United States in mid-1967 had 453,000 men in Vietnam; 10,253 Americans had been killed, 61,425 wounded; and the war was costing over $2 billion a month. With that preoccupation, it was not to be expected that a domestic problem of this magnitude would receive an adequate share of the nation's attention or of its resources.

Two related proposals of modest proportions were before the Congress. The Housing Act of 1965 had created a rent-supplement program under which the Federal government was authorized to pay part of the rent of a poor tenant in either new or rehabilitated low-cost housing, the tenant paying at least 25 per cent of his income and the government making up the rest. Twelve million dollars was appropriated for rent supplements in fiscal 1967, and President Johnson requested $40 million for fiscal 1968. The House, which acted in May, refused to appropriate any more money for this program.

In the Demonstration Cities and Metropolitan Development Act, passed in October, 1966, Congress had authorized what had become the Model Cities Program. (The name was changed because of contemporary connotations of "demonstration.") However, only $11 million for planning expenses had been appropriated. The Model Cities Program contemplated the tying together of a wide array of existing programs in a coordinated attack upon both human and physical deterioration. Model Cities would deal with land use, slum clearance and rehabilitation, housing, health, welfare, employment, and public order, and would seek to create an entirely new environment in blighted areas. Participating cities—from 60 to 70 were expected to participate under the original act—were to receive up to 80 percent of the required local share of the costs. As a beginning, President Johnson requested $662 million for Model Cities in fiscal 1968. The House slashed the figure to $237 million.

A growing work of planning in the field of urban rehabilitation and of awakening the nation to the urgency of the problem was being done now by an institution, based in Washington, D. C., called "Urban America Inc." The late philanthropist Stephen R. Currier, long a generous supporter of the movement for interracial justice, aroused over the broader problem of the cities, had been instrumental in launching Urban America in 1965. It incorporated the American Planning and Civic Association and later merged with the Action Council for Better Cities. By mid-1966 Urban America's program had begun to take shape. William L. Slayton, former commissioner of the Urban Renewal Administration, was appointed executive vice president and began to build its professional staff. In 1967 it operated on a budget of $1,498,250.

In two years Urban America had assembled an impressive group of several hundred corporation executives, mayors, labor union leaders, city planners, architects, professors, and others deeply interested in the problem of rebuilding American cities. James W. Rouse, a former member of President Eisenhower's Advisory Commission on Housing Programs, long active in urban improvement movements, was president. The honorary chairman of the board was Harland Bartholomew, former president of the American City Planning Institute; Andrew Heiskell, board chairman of Time, Inc., was chairman of the board. From the civil-rights movement, the Urban League's Whitney M. Young, Jr., was a member of the board of trustees.

Urban America's headquarters publication *City* said in its first issue, which appeared in April, 1967:

> In January, Urban America invited the mayors of a cross-section of major cities to a series of Washington meetings from which emerged two plans for action. One was for the formation of an urban

coalition, composed of groups that share a major stake in cities. The other was for the creation of an Urban Economic Council which would examine and evaluate the impact of economic policies on urban areas.

Urban America is now working with a steering committee of mayors to bring together spokesmen for components of the coalition—business, education, civil rights groups, labor unions, and religious organizations. . . .

The Council will appraise the allocation of economic resources and priorities for federal expenditures, assigning the relative importance of urban programs to other national needs. It also will appraise the economic importance of the programs and expenditures of local governments to the national economy, and the potential impact of business fluctuations on cities.

The Council's first report, to be prepared by an established private, non-profit agency, will provide quantitative estimates to 1975 of urban expenditures and urban requirements under a variety of possible situations. . . .

A phase of the Negro revolution—the phase of sit-ins and non-violent demonstrations that spread across the nation in the summer of 1963 and staged its dress parade in the majestic March on Washington—the movement led by King, Wilkins, Young, Farmer, Lewis, Randolph, and Rustin, dominated spiritually by Dr. King —was indeed coming to a close. The fuse was burning toward an explosion that would give the revolution a new character, new dimensions, and new elements of crisis. What the new phase would accomplish must be left to future historians to appraise. The first phase had accomplished much; it had also failed in important respects.

The Reverend Theodore M. Hesburgh, president of the University of Notre Dame, said the first phase of the movement "had accomplished and written into federal law" what he would call "a national conscience on civil rights." Discrimination in public education and in employment were still widespread, but in both it was now unlawful. The whole apparatus of legal segregation in the South had been dismantled. Qualified Negroes were able to vote freely in almost all sections. Actions of the courts, of the executive, and of Congress had established a charter of equal citizenship, which, whatever the waves of racist reaction, was unlikely ever to be revoked. Millions of whites to the contrary notwithstanding, the nation had set itself against racial discrimination.

With the high expectations, the many disappointments, and the current rebuffs, civil-rights leaders were inclined to emphasize the distance still to be covered rather than the progress already made. But a transformation had taken place in American life. A visitor to the United States after an absence of more than four years might have felt for the first time that he was not in a land with an ostracized Negro minority, but in a biracial country. He would be struck with the absence of the "Colored" and "White Only" signs, once omnipresent in Southern and border states, and at the number of well-dressed Negroes mingling with whites in hotels, restaurants, theaters, churches, and public meetings. He would see Negroes on television programs every day, and would be impressed with the growing popularity of Negro stars in movies and theater. If he visited government offices, especially in Washington, he would be surprised to find many Negroes in important positions; a few were in the highest echelons of government.

A survey completed by the American Civil Liberties Union in March, 1966, showed that, although given only about one per cent of the roles in commercials, Negroes had 3.36 per cent of the speaking roles and 8.49 per cent of the nonspeaking roles in regular television programs. With the steadily growing popularity of Negro actors and commentators, the percentages in 1967 were probably higher. Nine Negroes were each a co-star on a continuing television series.

After ten years of hardly visible progress in this area, desegregation of Southern public schools had made a spurt under the financial pressure of the Civil Rights Act of 1964. In the 1963-64 school year only 1.17 per cent of the Negro students in the eleven former Confederate states were in schools attended also by whites. In the 1966-1967 term, 15.9 per cent of the Negro school children were in desegregated schools. Of the 2,877 school districts in the region, 236 were not yet in compliance with HEW guidelines; federal funds had been terminated in 38 cases, deferred in 34.*

---

* *Statistical Summary 1966-1967*, Southern Education Reporting Service, P. O. Box 6156, Acklen Station, Nashville, Tenn. 37212.

On the other hand, de facto school segregation in big-city ghettos throughout the country had actually increased, as the number of nearly all-Negro school districts had grown. That was a part of the problem of residential segregation, and of what was coming to be seen as a cancerous kind of urban malformation, which in itself was assuming increasingly critical proportions. The unwillingness of millions of whites to accept Negroes as neighbors and friends still resisted all the preaching of brotherhood.

The President in his message to Congress of February 15 noted other advances under the Civil Rights Act of 1964:

> This year, Negroes are being admitted to hospitals which barred them in the past. By January 7,130 hospitals—more than 95 per cent of the hospitals in the Nation—had agreed to provide services without discrimination. More than 1,500 of those hospitals have had to change past policies to make that commitment. . . .
>
> Thousands of restaurants, motels and hotels have been opened to Americans of all races and colors. . . .
>
> Now Negro families traveling through most parts of the country do not need to suffer the inconveniences of searching for a place to rest or eat where they will be accepted, or the humiliating indignity of being turned away.

As for the War on Poverty, the President noted that the Head Start program had prepared many deprived children to learn in later years. "Through this and other preschool programs," he said, "two million children have been offered better education and health care." The Neighborhood Youth Corps, the Job Corps, and programs of the Manpower Development Act had enabled many youths to pursue their education and had provided jobs and opportunities for job training for many. "During the last three years," he said, "our training programs have provided the means of self-sufficiency to almost a million men and women."

But the War on Poverty had raised expectations faster than it had solved problems. The President also said:

> The unemployment rate for Negroes is more than double that for whites. About 650,000, more than 20 per cent of all unemployed, are nonwhite. About 213,000 of these are between 14 and 19 years of age. . . .

The best that can be said of the Negro unemployment picture in 1967 is that, if the age of automation had come ten years earlier, it might have been much worse. Thousands of Negroes were denied employment because of lack of training. But racial discrimination was still practiced. Outside of the area of government and government-contract employment, the Administration's attack on job discrimination had been feeble in comparison, say, with its attack on school segregation and voting discrimination. The prohibition of discrimination in Title VII of the Civil Rights Act of 1964 was clear, and that had proved a certain deterrent, but enforcement machinery had not been provided. Cases of violation could only be taken to the courts, and only a tiny fraction of them had been dealt with through this cumbersome process. The Equal Employment Opportunity Commission, however, was making some slow progress through investigation and negotiation. From July 2, 1965, when it began work, to January 1, 1967, it had received 13,628 complaints of discrimination. A little less than half of these, 6,009, had been certified for investigation, and investigation had been completed in about half of them. The commission had found "reasonable cause" to believe that Title VII had been violated in 1,550 cases. Most of the latter were still awaiting conciliation efforts. More or less successful conciliation had been achieved in only 487 cases.

The change that four years had wrought was most striking in the South, which had farther to go in the area of civil rights in the first place than the rest of the country. It is not suggested that the South had been purged of its age-old racial prejudice—far from it. Ku Klux Klansmen and other apostles of fanaticism and hate still did their ugly work. The Wallace gubernatorial family in Alabama and some other Deep South leaders still practiced their brinkmanship defiance of federally-ordered reform. But over the South as a whole a gentler wind was blowing. There were indications, in fact, that this region might yet arrive at a Negro-white relationship of equality and friendship sooner than any other.

At the University of Mississippi, where whites had battled so fiercely in 1962 to bar the first Negro student, nine Negro students now attracted little notice. Another Southern university where initial integration had caused turmoil and tension, the University of Alabama, now had 150 Negro students. In 1958, the city of Norfolk, Virginia, had closed its six white high schools to prevent the admission of the first Negro students to any of them. In May, 1967—with thousands of white and Negro pupils intermingled in the Norfolk school system—a Negro boy, Philip Bond, was elected president of the Maury High School Student Cooperating Association. Seventy-six per cent of Maury's 2,200 students were white, and a white young lady had managed Philip's campaign.

In June, 1967, James Meredith undertook another march, this time almost alone. He drove to the scene of the ambush shooting a year earlier, then walked in eleven days the 150 miles to Canton, Mississippi, where he had resumed his march in 1966. He was un-molested—and little publicized. "I wanted to show," he said (with perhaps excessive optimism), "that the Negro need no longer fear."

Negroes of stature had risen to honored positions on the national stage. In some of the highest governmental bodies the Negro minority was actually represented in 1967 more or less in proportion to its 11 per cent of the nation's population. Thurgood Marshall sat with eight other justices on the Supreme Court; another Negro, Robert C. Weaver, was one of twelve members of the President's cabinet. Weaver, in January, 1966, had been appointed Secretary of the newly created Department of Housing and Urban Affairs. The seven-member Board of Governors of the Federal Reserve System, the five-member board of directors of the Export-Import Bank, and the five-member Atomic Energy Commission had each a Negro member. The Negro incumbents were respectively: Andrew F. Brimmer, Hobart Taylor, Jr., and Samuel M. Nabrit.

Among other Negroes achieving distinction, Clifford L. Alexander was appointed, effective July 1, 1967, to succeed Stephen L. Shulman as chairman of the Equal Employment Opportunity Commission. Emmett J. Rice had been appointed in October, 1966, United States alternate director at the World Bank. Major Robert H. Lawrence, Jr., was chosen in June, 1967, to be the first Negro astronaut. Negroes held the office of postmaster in the nation's three largest cities: John R. Strachan in New York, Henry W. McGee in Chicago, and Leslie N. Shaw in Los Angeles. A Negro, Walter Washington, was appointed in September to the newly created office of executive commissioner of the District of Columbia—or "mayor"—of the nation's capital city.

Among distinguished Negroes outside of government, the Bank of America, in June, 1967, promoted E. Frederick Morrow, a former administrative assistant to President Eisenhower, to vice president of its New York-based international subsidiary; and the University of Chicago chose Dr. John Hope Franklin to be chairman of its history department. In 1966 Leontyne Price sang the star role of Cleopatra in *Antony and Cleopatra* at the brilliant opening of the new Metropolitan Opera House in New York; and Bill Cosby received the Emmy, television's highest award, for the best continued performance by an actor in a dramatic series.

A still greater burst of Negro achievement could be expected from the quarter of a million Negroes enrolled in 1967 in American institutions of higher learning—more than double the number of Negro college graduates in the next four-year age bracket.

"But"—said *Ebony* magazine in a review of Negro achievements in 1966—"as important as were these individual achievements, they meant little to the Negro masses, for whom 1966 was perhaps a year of retrogression." The average family income of Negroes remained a little more than half that of whites, and the income gap had not narrowed but widened. More Negroes than ever were crowded into the urban ghettos. The stimulus of the many recognitions of Negro excellence to the morale of the educated Negro community, and to ambition on the part of Negro youth, is not to be underestimated. But they had not impressed the Negroes of the slums or alleviated their misery. Those millions were finding the conditions of their existence not less but more unbearable.

NINETEEN

The Violent Revolution
1967

The summer of 1967 brought more widespread and destructive civil disorder than had ever been seen before in the nation's peacetime history. Outbreaks occurred in a hundred cities, a score of them full-scale riots, and in each of two great cities anarchy reigned for three days, in what was variously termed "rebellion," "insurrection," and "civil war."

Racial disturbances started early. There were minor outbreaks in April in Omaha, Cleveland, and Louisville, and in May in San Francisco, Chicago, Wichita (Kansas), and Jackson (Mississippi). Rioting erupted also in the spring among Negro students of Fisk and the Tennessee Agricultural and Industrial Universities and at Texas Southern University, following visits of Stokely Carmichael to Nashville and Houston.

Another "long, hot summer," as summers of racial violence had come to be called, was plainly in the offing. The public was becoming more or less resigned now to summer rioting. It had come to be regarded as a seasonal phenomenon, like hurricanes. But municipal authorities, who would have to cope with the violence, were anxiously developing a variety of projects which they hoped would have a deterrent effect. Limited by lack of funds and programmed often for the summer only, some of these were what Roy Wilkins called "lollipop programs."

More fire hydrants were fitted with sprinkler caps to enable sweltering ghetto youths to splash in cold water. Vice President Humphrey, who was chairman of the President's Council on Youth Opportunity, urged cities to turn on fire hydrants, hold block parties, and sponsor basketball tournaments. Fifteen new swimming pools were projected for Washington, D.C. New York's Mayor Lindsay expanded his program of block playgrounds. Addressing a national conference of mayors in Honolulu June 17, Lindsay said: "By July 4 all 100 play streets we have laid out will be ready and we'll pay youngsters to be block supervisors."

Attempts were being made in many cities—most of all in New York—to change the image of the police and improve police-Negro relations. Plain-clothes officers had been assigned for months to New York's 79 precincts to talk with groups on the streets and listen to their complaints. New York police took Negro and Puerto Rican boys to baseball games and to week-end camps, where boys and police played checkers, cards, and ball games together. In Chicago the post of Community Service Sergeant had been created in each residential precinct, and policemen were giving talks to high school students under an "Officer Friendly" program. In Baltimore a police community relations unit of 18 plain-clothes officers was meeting regularly with groups of Negro youths. Detroit had recruited 40 more Negro policemen during the year (although this brought the total number to only 200 in a force of 4,300). Six hundred Detroit policemen were receiving 20-hour courses in human relations under a $100,000 federal grant.

It was recognized, however, that the most urgent need was jobs, especially jobs for Negro youths. Mayor Lindsay set up a Summer Task Force, headed by Thomas P. F. Hoving, director of the Metropolitan Museum of Art, and Andrew Heiskell, chairman of Time, Inc., with the job of providing jobs and recreation. Mayor Yorty of Los Angeles set up a Summer Council of businessmen and officials for a similar purpose, and other cities tackled the problem in various ways. The Office of Economic Opportunity began to bring its $75-million summer emergency fund to bear. But finding jobs was a vastly different matter from turning on fire hydrants and providing playgrounds. It was evident that nothing short of a massive emergency program of public employment could put an appreciable percentage of the idle to work in short order.

Violence erupted in the Roxbury district of Boston on June 2. From then until Newark exploded on July 12, rioting across the nation was comparable to that in July and August, 1966. Tampa,

Cincinnati, and Buffalo suffered convulsions lasting several days in each case. Lesser outbreaks occurred in Dayton, Des Moines, Kansas City, Philadelphia, Atlanta, Waterloo (Iowa), and Lansing (Michigan).

The Tampa upheaval is of special interest because of a riot-quelling technique which it produced. Jim Hammond, the administrator of that city's human relations commission, went into the riot area and persuaded 120 Negro youths, some of whom had been rioting, to go to work as peacemakers. Organized in a City Youth Patrol, they were given white plastic helmets, from which they quickly got the name of "White Hats." Uniformed law enforcement officers tentatively withdrew and turned the job over to these amateurs. Talking in their own way and with only occasional rough handling, the White Hats restored peace to Tampa's Negro community in one night. Their five leaders were retained on the city's payroll at $76 a week for special liaison work. Florida's Governor Claude Kirk paid a visit to Tampa a week later to publicly commend the White Hats.

The riots up to July 12 could all be matched by upheavals of the previous three years, and no one of them was to be compared with the holocaust of Watts. Then all records were broken by the magnitude and fury of Newark and Detroit. Newark for its size was more sanguinary than Watts; Detroit was more terrible on all counts.

Newark was the first city with as much as half of its population Negro to explode in violence. Of its 405,000 inhabitants the Negro portion was estimated at from a little over 200,000 to 260,000. As late as 1950 the Negro proportion of the population had been a scant 17 per cent. The rapid influx of Negroes, accompanied by the usual flight of white residents, had multiplied the problems for Mayor Hugh J. Addonizio and his mainly white city administration. Although the ferocity of this upheaval was appalling, it was no surprise to knowledgeable observers that a riot should have erupted in Newark. The unemployment rate in that city was 10.5 per cent for nonwhites though only 3.2 per cent for whites. Newark's slums were among the most dismal. The city's application for Model Cities funds, submitted to Washington the previous April, said:

> Among major American cities, Newark and its citizens face the
> highest percentage of substandard housing, the most crime per 100,-

ooo of the population and the highest rate of venereal disease, new cases of tuberculosis and maternal mortality.

The triggering incident came at a time when whites and Negroes were already bitterly divided over two issues. One was the city's plan to clear 50 acres in a shabby Negro neighborhood as a site for a new State College of Medicine and Dentistry. The other was an attempt by the mayor to fill a vacant board of education post with a white city councilman rather than with an apparently well-qualified Negro who was serving as the city's budget director.

The incident was the alleged beating of a Negro taxi driver by police. A crowd of Negroes, which gathered at the Fourth Precinct station on Wednesday night, July 12, to protest, broke into violence, and the violence spread. Rioting continued for three days. The more deadly battle with snipers—with Newark virtually under military occupation—continued through two more days. The local police force of 1,400 was augmented by 375 state troopers; the National Guard force numbered 3,000. Twenty-five persons (23 of them Negroes) were reported killed and 1,200 injured. Over 1,300 were arrested. The property damage was estimated by the Newark Office of Economic Development at $10,251,000.

While Newark was blazing, rioting erupted in Hartford (Connecticut), Erie (Pennsylvania), and Newark's adjoining city of Plainfield; in the days following, in Cairo (Illinois), Minneapolis, Durham (North Carolina), Nyack (New York), and Englewood (New Jersey).

Then came the Detroit riot, bigger and worse by far than any of the rest. With a population of 1,600,000 (600,000 of them Negroes), this is the nation's fifth largest city. That Negroes should have rioted in Detroit was a surprise to most observers. Detroit's Mayor Jerome P. Cavanagh was regarded as having an unusual grasp of urban problems, and Detroit was widely considered a model city. It had received $47 million in federal poverty funds, $25 million in the current year. The auto industry, centered in Detroit, paid among the highest industrial wages in the country, and the United Auto Workers were freer than most unions from race discrimination. There was probably more widespread affluence among Negroes in Detroit than in any other American city. In 1960, 57 per cent of Detroit's Negroes owned automobiles, 41 per cent owned their own homes. Less apparent to the casual observer was the extent of Negro unemployment. The Department of Labor made public on December 13 the results of a survey of unemployment in the nation's fifteen largest metropolitan areas. Detroit had the second highest nonwhite unemployment rate—10.7 per cent. The rate for whites was only 3.2 per cent.

After the usual minor incident—in this instance a police raid on a Negro speakeasy—shortly before 4 A.M. on Sunday, July 23, violence began to sputter in Detroit. Looting and burning spread rapidly. By Sunday afternoon more than a dozen stores in a fifteen-block area were in flames and some 3,000 looters were out of control. Michigan's Governor George Romney ordered 1,100 National Guardsmen into the area to augment 370 state police already called in to aid the 4,300-man city police force. As the turbulence continued and spread, more Guardsmen poured in—8,000 were alerted—and on Tuesday the President sent in 4,700 regular Army paratroopers. It was not until Wednesday night that calm was restored. Forty-three persons were reported killed, over 2,000 injured, and over 3,800 arrested. The General Adjustment Bureau, Inc., later estimated the property damage at $85 million.

The rioting had spread on Monday to Flint, Pontiac, and Grand Rapids, Michigan, and across the state border to Toledo and Lima, Ohio. A dozen other cities were hit by the end of the week, including Milwaukee, Youngstown (Ohio), Cambridge (Maryland), Rochester, Mount Vernon, and East Harlem (New York), and Phoenix (Arizona). A brief disturbance occurred in the northeast section of Washington, D. C., on August 1. A more serious one in Syracuse (New York), on August 17-18 resulted in 34 arrests. Violence raged for three days in East St. Louis, Illinois, in mid-September, following a visit of Rap Brown to that city.

Rioting plagued New Haven for four nights from August 19 to 22. The New Haven outbreak was particularly dismaying because this was also regarded as a model city and its mayor, Richard C. Lee, had striven valiantly to solve his city's problems of housing, poverty, and race discrimination. But no one was more aware of the "things we've failed at" than Mayor Lee. "If New Haven is a model city," he said "then God help urban America."

Much turbulence also attended the campaign in Milwaukee of a white Roman Catholic priest and local NAACP leader, the Reverend James E. Groppi, for an open housing ordinance. Starting in

August, Father Groppi led almost nightly demonstrations for several months. They included marches of Negroes out of the ghetto into adjoining white neighborhoods, which resembled the forays of Martin Luther King's followers in Chicago the previous year and met with a similar response from angry whites. (These were among the few instances of white retaliation in the 1967 riots.)

The return of cool weather and a reduction in the number of idle adolescents due to the opening of schools militated against disorder in the streets; ghetto riots in the winter were as yet unknown. Nevertheless, as late as November 2-4, Winston-Salem, North Carolina's second largest city, suffered an upheaval in which 50 persons were injured and more than 100 arrested, and in which 800 National Guardsmen were needed to restore calm.

The Senate Permanent Committee on Investigations released on November 1 a report on civil disorder during the three-year period, compiled by its staff after a canvass of 129 mayors. It showed the following:

Year	Major Riots	Number Killed	Number Injured	Number Arrested	Estimated Cost
1965	5	36	1,206	10,245	$40.1 million
1966	21	11	520	2,298	10.2 million
1967	75	83	1,897	16,389	664.5 million
	101	130	3,623	28,932	714.8 million

The sheer number of riot casualties in three years was not impressive—less than the death and injury toll in automobile accidents on United States highways in a single average day. Of the estimated economic cost, actual property damage came to only $210.6 million—less than the annual profits after taxes of any one of a dozen American corporations.

But this, as far as it went, was civil war, elements of the population in open rebellion. In two great convulsions, it was for a time in wide urban areas an eclipse of government, anarchy and violence beyond control. And always the question loomed: Can this be the beginning of something more terrible? The anxiety of the public outside of the riot-torn cities would subside all too soon, but at the climax in July 1967 the public was thoroughly alarmed. Millions of whites who habitually passed over news of racial troubles could not escape headlines that spread across the front pages of newspapers such as:

NEWARK RIOTERS BATTLE POLICE AND NATIONAL GUARD
FEDERAL TROOPS SENT TO DETROIT
GUN BATTLE RAGES, SIRENS SCREAM, BULLETS BLAZE
INTO THE NIGHT
THE GHETTO EXPLODES IN ANOTHER CITY
SEGMENT OF AMERICA IN OPEN INSURRECTION

The *United States News and World Report* of July 31, announcing a special article, headlined on its cover: IS THE U.S. ABLE TO GOVERN ITSELF?

Absorbed in news of the riots and the utterances of Black Power extremists, many who did not read all the news asked: Why don't the moderate Negroes speak out? Among the vast majority of Negro Americans who abhorred violence a spirit of frustration and confusion prevailed. The men who best represented this element, the leaders of the great civil-rights organizations which had led the substantial Negro advance of the earlier 1960's, no longer held the initiative. They seemed unable either to move the white establishment further or to hold the mobs of desperate Negroes in check. Nonetheless it should be recorded that these leaders did promptly, boldly, and clearly condemn the rioting.

The National Association for the Advancement of Colored People was holding its annual convention in Boston at the time of the Newark upheaval. On July 15 it adopted unanimously a resolution, prepared by Executive Secretary Roy Wilkins, which read in part as follows:

This convention of the N.A.A.C.P. can understand, but not condone, quick violence which occurs to express mass resentment over a particular outrage.

We cannot understand nor do we in any way condone prolonged and seemingly stimulated riotous destruction of life and property extending over days and nights and spreading, apparently under plan, to persons and places not involved in any specific occurrence.

We condemn such violence. However, much of the blame for this unfortunate eruption must be placed on the city administration for its failure to take corrective action to meet any of the grave social ills of the Negro community.

Slum housing conditions in Newark are among the worst of any urban community in the United States. The recent effort of the Mayor to appoint an unqualified white man over an exceptionally qualified Negro to a post on the Board of Education in the face of a unified demand from the Negro community is certainly a contributing cause of the riot.

We call upon all law-abiding citizens of both races to act promptly and sternly to put down such violence. Any indulgence of this destruction of life and property . . . will be but an encouragement to an anarchy in which the whole society loses.

On July 26, at the height of the Detroit rioting, the New York office of the NAACP released a statement signed by Roy Wilkins, Martin Luther King, Whitney M. Young, and A. Philip Randolph. This read in part as follows:

Developments in Newark, Detroit and other strife-torn cities make it crystal clear that the primary victims of the riots are the Negro citizens. That they have grave grievances of long standing cannot be denied or minimized. That the riots have not contributed in any substantial measure to the eradication of these just complaints is by now obvious to all.

We are confident that the overwhelming majority of the Negro community joins us in opposition to violence in the streets. Who is without the necessities of life when the neighborhood stores are destroyed and looted? Whose children are without milk because deliveries cannot be made? Who loses wages because of a breakdown in transportation or destruction of the place of employment? Who are the dead, the injured and the imprisoned? It is the Negroes who pay and pay and pay, whether or not they are individually involved in the rioting. And for what?

Killing, arson, looting are criminal acts and should be dealt with as such. Equally guilty are those who incite, provoke and call specifically for such action. There is no injustice which justifies the present destruction of the Negro community and its people.

We who have fought so long and so hard to achieve justice for all Americans have consistently opposed violence as a means of redress. Riots have proved ineffective, disruptive and highly damaging to the Negro population, to the civil rights cause, and to the entire Nation.

We call upon Negro citizens throughout the Nation to forego the temptation to disregard the law. This does not mean that we should submit tamely to joblessness, inadequate housing, poor schooling, insult, humiliation and attack. It does require a redoubling of efforts through legitimate means to end these wrongs and disabilities.

The public took more notice of another element of the Negro community which was represented in a National Conference on Black Power which assembled in Newark on July 20-23. That a Black Power conference should be called in battered Newark only four days after the sniping ceased seemed to many an act of effrontery and a possible incitement to further violence. Both New Jersey's Governor Richard J. Hughes and Mayor Addonizio had urged the sponsors to find a meeting place elsewhere. Outside of the conference rooms in two hotels, however, no bloodshed or violence occurred. CORE's Floyd McKissick, one of the speakers at the opening of the conference, asked what better place to consider means to "unify and empower black men than in Newark, the most recent symbol of the oppression of the black man?"

The organizers had expected 400 participants; more than twice that number appeared. Rap Brown, Dick Gregory, James Farmer, and the actors Ossie Davis and Ruby Dee were among the well-known figures there. Representative Adam Clayton Powell had been expected, but, to the resentful disappointment of many, he refused to leave his Bimini sanctuary. The wide range of Negro organizations represented included the Black Muslims, Harlem's Mau Mau, and the Organization for Afro-American Unity (which Malcolm X had founded). Not all participants were extremists. Roy Wilkins, Whitney Young, and Martin Luther King stayed away, but members of their organizations attended. However, as is often the case, the most radical and bellicose element came noisily to the top.

The chief organizer was the Reverend Dr. Nathan Wright, Jr., an Episcopal minister, of Newark. "The nation will witness a racial conflagration greater than the Civil War unless racial oppression is stopped," Dr. Wright said in his opening address. "Without black unity we shall all perish." The prevailing spirit was bitterly and menacingly anti-white-man. No whites, except reporters who "behaved," were allowed in the conference rooms. White newsmen, admitted to one press conference a day, were subjected to insults and some manhandling.

On Sunday, July 23, the conference adopted a long series of resolutions, which included a threat of "massive efforts . . . to disrupt the economy" unless a guaranteed minimum wage were instituted immediately, and a call for a "dialog among Americans" on the partitioning of the nation into "a homeland for black Americans and a homeland for white Americans." Then the conference adjourned. The rioting in Detroit had started that morning.

Rap Brown had been only one among scores of firebrands at the Black Power Conference, but he leaped into the spotlight immediately afterward and was in the headlines intermittently for several months. Leaving Newark, the SNCC leader drove south to the town of Cambridge (population 9,000 whites and 4,000 Negroes) on Maryland's Eastern Shore. Cambridge—which resembled in racial attitudes a piece of the Deep South in a border state—had been torn with intermittent racial strife since 1963. Addressing a Cambridge rally on July 24, Brown urged some 300 cheering Negro listeners to "get your guns. You gotta take over these stores," he said, "gotta take your freedom. . . . We are rebelling. Don't you see what your brothers in Detroit are doing?" Later he threatened: "If America don't come around, we're going to burn America down, brother." At one point he said the dilapidated Negro school should have been burned down long ago (as demolished it should have been). Hours later the heart of the Negro section of the town —the school, a church, shops, and homes—was in ruins.

Brown disappeared after his speech. He was arrested in Alexandria, Virginia, the next day on a fugitive warrant, charged by Maryland with inciting to riot. But he was far from silenced. Released on $10,000 bond, he and his lawyers began a game with the courts and the law which left him free for many weeks—interrupted by but a few days in jail—to carry his incendiary talk to a dozen cities. In scheduled speeches or on the most convenient street corner he urged Negroes to arm against a "honky [white] conspiracy." He said the recent riots were just "dress rehearsals for rebellion." Rap Brown's pyrotechnics were lavishly publicized. Through television and radio his vitriol reached the ears of thousands of Negroes in the simmering ghettos.

In the years when Southern white atrocities made most of the sensational news in the racial struggle, the news media had been a boon to the nonviolent Negro movement; now they were in effect an ally of the fanatics of Black Power. The temperate statements of thousands of clergymen and other leaders of the Negro community were not in demand on the news market. The men who insulted, threatened, and incited to violence were constantly surrounded by reporters and cameramen. Inordinate publicity and the riots themselves had done much to make the Black Power movement what it now had become—an ominously powerful force.

That part of the Black Power doctrine which fostered pride in being a Negro was addressed to a crying need. Negro morale and initiative were too often stifled by the feeling of inferiority engendered by centuries of oppression and degradation. The Black Power movement was clearly helping many to throw this off. This —together with the aim of securing political power through the ballot and economic power through Negro enterprise—was applauded by moderate Negroes and understanding whites. Many of these sought to gain a rapport with the movement on this basis and to steer it into constructive channels. A successful work project in the Washington, D. C., Negro ghetto was given the name of "Pride, Inc."

Black Power enthusiasts delighted in using the formerly offensive term "black" instead of Negro. (The once popular polite evasion, "colored," had long since been discarded.) They scorned the old practice of imitating whites in personal appearance and emphasized their Negroid characteristics. The slogan "Black Is Beautiful" was appearing on placards in Negro ghettos, sometimes on auto bumper signs. Martin Luther King joined in promoting the Black-Is-Beautiful theme.

What set Black Power apart ideologically was its advocacy of racial separation. Separatism—without violence and without the extreme aims of black nationalists—appealed to a few intellectuals. Some Negro strategists held that Negroes could exert most political power in segregated enclaves. A number of white liberals, disappointed at the slow progress of integration, began to say that integration would not work and that the nation should concentrate instead on providing better Negro institutions. Though regarded as a retreat and strongly opposed by most civil-rights crusaders, separatism was gaining ground at the year's end. Meanwhile, Negroes in the ghettos were finding an outlet for long-smoldering resentments in the malevolent phase of Black Power. The spectacle of Negroes hurling insults at the white man gave a certain satisfaction to thousands who had been insulted by the white man all their lives.

A distinguished Negro scholar, Dr. Kenneth B. Clark, president of the Metropolitan Applied Research Center of the City College of New York, said in an address to the Southern Regional Council at its annual meeting on November 2:

> "Black Power," in spite of its ambiguity, its "no-win" premise, its programmatic emptiness and its pragmatic futility, does have tremendous psychological appeal for the masses of Negroes who have "nothing to lose" and some middle class Negroes who are revolted by the empty promises and the moral dry-rot of affluent America. . . .
>
> Nonetheless, today "Black Power" is a reality in the Negro ghettos of America—increasing in emotional intensity, if not in rational clarity. And we, if we are to be realistic, cannot afford to pretend that it does not exist. Even in its most irrational and illusory formulations —and particularly when it is presented as a vague and incoherent basis upon which the deprived Negro can project his own pathetic wishes for a pride and an assertiveness which white America continues mockingly or piously to deny him—"Black Power" is a powerful political reality which cannot be ignored by realistic Negro or white political officials.

Incidentally, Dr. Clark noted that civil-rights advances thus far had "benefited primarily only a small percentage of middle class Negroes"—which, he said, had resulted in "increased and more openly expressed hostility" toward them on the part of the Negro masses. "There are some clues," he said, "which suggest that the recent ghetto implosions were not only anti-white, but also involved vague stirrings of anti-Negro middle class sentiment among the rioters."

The crisis struck the nation at a time when leadership in this field was particularly lacking. Obsession with the war in Vietnam, itself a divisive issue, limited both the resources and the attention considered available for racial problems at home. Early maneuvering in anticipation of the 1968 presidential election was another distraction, and it colored some pronouncements on the riots.

During that nightmarish mid-July fortnight of 1967 President Johnson addressed the nation twice. In a midnight broadcast on

July 24, at the peak of the upheaval in Detroit, the President devoted seven minutes to a dull, legalistic explanation of his action in sending federal troops to that city. Incidentally, he made five references to the fact that this action had been requested by Michigan's Governor George Romney, who at the time stood high in public opinion polls as a possible Republican opponent in 1968. "I take this action with the greatest regret," the President said, "—and only because of the clear, unmistakable and undisputed evidence that Governor Romney and the local officials have been unable to bring the situation under control."

In his broadcast of July 27, when calm had returned to Detroit, the President discussed the whole situation of urban unrest, issuing at the same time a proclamation calling for prayers the following Sunday "for order and reconciliation among men." "We have endured a week," he said, "such as no nation should live through, a time of violence and tragedy." He announced the appointment of a special advisory commission to investigate the riots and recommend measures to "prevent or contain such disasters in the future." He said also that the FBI would "continue to investigate these riots in accordance with my standing instructions and continue to search for evidence of conspiracy." He stressed the maintenance of law and order as the first necessity:

> First, let there be no mistake about it: the looting and arson and plunder and pillage are not a part of a civil-rights protest. There is no American right to loot stores or to burn buildings or to fire rifles from rooftops. That is crime. And crime must be dealt with forcefully and swiftly, and certainly under law. . . .
>
> The criminals who committed these acts of violence against the people deserve to be punished—and they will be punished. Explanations may be offered, but nothing can excuse what they have done. There will be attempts to interpret the events of the past few days, but when violence strikes, then those in public responsibility have an immediate and very different job: not to analyze but to end disorder.
>
> That they must seek to do with every means at our command—through local, through police and state officials, and, in extraordinary circumstances, where local authorities have stated that they cannot maintain order with their own resources—then through federal authority that we have limited authority to use.

The National Guard, which had been called out in a score of riot situations, was under heavy criticism. Lacking training and skill in dealing with civil disorder, these part-time soldiers had tended to invade and occupy riot-torn ghettos like a hostile army, particularly in Newark and Detroit. Haphazard use of firearms and shooting into buildings believed to contain snipers were reported to have caused the death of some persons in no way involved in the rioting. The President said:

> I have tonight directed the Secretary of Defense to issue new train-ing standards for riot control procedures immediately to National Guard units across the country. Through the Continental Army Command this expanded training will begin immediately.
>
> The National Guard must have the ability to respond effectively and quickly and appropriately in conditions of disorder and violence. And those charged with the responsibility of law enforcement should, and must, be respected by all of our people.

"It would only compound the tragedy, however," the President said, "if we should settle for order that's imposed by the muzzle of a gun." "The only genuine, long-range solution" lay "in an attack —mounted at every level—upon the conditions that breed des-pair and breed violence." Those conditions, he said, were "ignor-ance, discrimination, slums, poverty, disease, not enough jobs." He cited the salient accomplishments of his Administration in at-tacking these "ancient enemies"—"the greatest governmental effort in all of our American history": "the Model Cities Act, the Voting Rights Act, the Civil Rights Act, the Rent Supplements Act, Medi-care and Medicaid, the 24 educational bills, Head Start, the Job Corps, man power development and training." He scolded the House of Representatives for turning down an Administration re-quest for $20 million "to fight the pestilence of rats" and for re-ducing his request for Model Cities funds by two-thirds.

The President promised to "continue to press for laws that will protect our citizens from violence like the Safe Streets and Crime Control Act . . . and the Gun Control Act." He said this was "a time for action, starting with legislative action to improve the life in our cities," but he had no new suggestion in this area. He avoided advancing any of the costly proposals for a full-scale attack on the evils of the ghetto. And his support of the minimal measures before Congress had lacked the fighting spirit that he had shown in the area of civil rights in 1964 and 1965. A move to add $2.8 billion to the antipoverty appropriation, which had substantial support in the Senate, was opposed by his Administration.

"The strength and promise of laws," the President said, "are the surest remedies for tragedy in the streets." But laws were "not the only answer."

> Another answer lies in the way our people respond to these disturbances. There is a danger that the worst toll of this tragedy will be counted in the hearts of Americans—in hatred, in insecurity, in fear, in heated words which will not end the conflict, but will rather prolong it.

Governor Otto Kerner of Illinois, a Democrat, was named chairman of the new Advisory Commission on Civil Disorders, Republican Mayor John V. Lindsay of New York vice chairman. Other members appointed were: Senator Fred R. Harris, Democrat, of Oklahoma; Senator Edward W. Brooke, Republican, of Massachusetts; Representative James C. Corman, Democrat, of California; Representative William M. McCullock, Republican, of Ohio; I. W. Abel, president of the United Steelworkers; Charles B. Thornton, president and board chairman, Litton Industries, Inc.; Roy Wilkins, executive director of the NAACP; Katherine Graham Peden, Commissioner of Commerce of Kentucky; and Herbert Jenkins, Atlanta chief of police.

The commission gathered at the White House three days later to receive the President's instructions. The basic questions to which he wanted answers boiled down to three:

"What happened?"

"Why did it happen?"

"What can be done to prevent it from happening again?"

The executive order setting up the commission called for an interim report by March 1 and a final report by July 29, 1968. This schedule, which might delay the final report until another summer was half over, was criticized in some quarters, and commission members themselves expressed a desire to get the job done sooner. Governor Kerner indicated to newsmen that the group felt free to make other interim reports to the President on matters of special urgency. The commission, which went to work at once, found such a matter quickly with respect to the National Guard.

In a letter addressed to the President on August 10, it recommended an immediate and substantial increase in the number of Negroes in the National Guard and the Air National Guard. The commisison also urged accelerated riot-control training and a review of procedure for appointing and promoting Guard officers. It pointed out that at the end of 1966 Negroes made up only 1.15 per cent of the officers and men in the National Guard—4,638 out of 404,996. In the Air National Guard the percentage was only 0.6—461 Negroes out of 77,078. "The commission believes strongly that this deficiency must be corrected as soon as possible," its letter said.

The matter was a delicate one in that the Defense Department had no control over the rate at which Negroes volunteered for the National Guard or the efforts of states to recruit them. Some discrimination still existed, and Negroes had shown little eagerness to serve in the Guard. The commission said "the combined efforts of the Department of Defense, state officials and the Negro community" would be required.

It was soon evident that the National Advisory Commission on Civil Disorders, as the commission came to be called, would conduct an investigation of unprecedented range and thoroughness into the nation's critical problem. One million dollars, drawn from various appropriations, was made available for its expenses. It assembled a professional staff of 98 and a clerical staff of 71, under David Ginsburg, who was appointed executive director. Apart from visits of members to many riot-torn cities, by mid-November the commission had sent field investigators to 23 cities where disorders had occurred and had heard over 100 witnesses in closed hearings. It had also awarded a number of contracts to private research institutions, among them: the George Peabody College Center for Community Studies ($31,000) for a study of disturbances in three university communities; the Systemetrics Corporation ($94,000) for reports on urban conditions in 20 cities; and the Brookings Institution ($8,900) for a study of government and private riot-control programs.

On December 13 the commission announced that, since it felt that its findings could not wait until next summer, its final report would be issued by March 1, 1968—to be followed later by certain studies in specialized fields.

The House of Representatives of the Ninetieth Congress, which had shown small interest in measures related to poverty or urban rehabilitation, produced a sorry bit of burlesque at a moment when Negro unrest demanded the gravest attention. A constant torture for slum-dwellers and a major source of Negro complaint were the rats which infested the ghettos. The Administration proposed a $40-million federal grant program—$20 million for 1968 and $20 million for 1969—to aid localities in exterminating rats. The question of taking up the bill came before the House on July 20 (between the Newark and Detroit riots).

Several members pleaded for consideration of "one of the most humane and compassionate bills." New York Republican Representative Theodore Kupferman said to its opponents: "If you were a hard-working father coming home from work to find one of your children bitten by a rat, you might very well start a riot yourself." But the dominant spirit was one of incredible levity. Critics of the bill exchanged banter that passed for wit, with punning references to the "anti-riot (pronounced 'anti-rat') bill" and the "civil rats bill." Republican Representative Joel Broyhill of Virginia thought "the rat smart thing" would be "to vote down this rat bill rat now." By a vote of 207 to 176 the House refused to consider the bill.

The performance gave Negroes one more sting, and the public was not amused. The House of Representatives two months later by a vote of 227 to 173 adopted an amendment to an omnibus health bill that made $40 million available for rat control.

Congressional reaction to the rioting was expressed preponderantly in concern over its criminal aspects and the need for more effective measures of repression, rather than over the underlying causes of unrest. Many members held the belief that the violence had been instigated by some organized conspiracy. The Senate in a resolution adopted on August 11 directed its permanent Subcommittee on Investigations to look for the riots' immediate and "long-standing" causes. A group of liberal senators, led by Senator John Sherman Cooper of Kentucky, urged that the resolution should call specifically for the inclusion of "economic and social causes" in the inquiry, but this request was rejected by a vote of 36 to 26. Senator John L. McClellan of Arkansas, who headed the subcommittee, said repeatedly during the debate that *all* the causes would be investigated. However, culprits rather than conditions were the subcommittee's first, and apparently main, concern. When hearings opened on November 1, Senator McClellan announced: "We will undertake to determine whether the outbreaks were spontaneous or if they were instigated and precipitated by the calculated design of agitators, militant activists or lawless elements."

Some 2,000 miscellaneous radicals and opponents of American involvement in Vietnam met in Chicago the first week in September in what was called the National Conference for the New Politics. The participants were predominantly white, but the stormy meeting was more or less dominated by a caucus of some 400 militant Negroes mainly of the Black Power element. After an investigation of this affair by the Senate Internal Security Subcommittee, the latter's chairman, Senator James Eastland of Mississippi, said: "This material shows that the agitation and the riots in the country are Communist-inspired. The disorder, agitation and riots are highly organized and are directed by the Communist Party."

The House passed a bill which would make it a federal crime to cross state lines to incite violence. It was called the "anti-riot" bill, but its value was questioned in view of the difficulty of proving the intentions of persons when crossing state lines and the fact that most states had statutes covering all manner of riot activity. The Senate Judiciary Committee, conducting hearings on the bill, heard a witness of unusual qualifications in John A. McCone, who, it will be recalled, headed the commission investigating the riots and subsequent developments in Watts. McCone had appeared earlier before the National Advisory Commission on Civil Disorders in executive session. He thought the "anti-riot" bill might be helpful in some situations, but he warned against considering it the answer to the larger problem. (The bill was not acted upon by the Senate.)

McCone reported an improvement in police-Negro relations in Los Angeles and said the business community had found jobs for some 17,900 Negroes since the riots. Attempts to improve vocational training had met with "partial success." However, he did not "want to leave the committee with the feeling that there are no grievances or tensions in the community."

Looking at the national situation, McCone said: "I feel very deeply that unless we answer this problem it is going to split our society irretrievably and destroy our country. It leaves me with a deep worry about how this problem can be solved. The temptation is to say this is hopeless, but I think we have to stay at the job until we find the answer."

All concurred in the imperative necessity of maintaining public order, but a minority of liberals in Congress of both parties were anxious to deal with the conditions which led to the rioting. A variety of proposals were offered, some of them off-hand, others well-studied projects, for action in the fields of housing, employment, and education. Some 40 bills of urban legislation were before Congress in mid-August. They represented thinking out of which remedial legislation might in time develop, but had little chance of early enactment.

For one shining moment the possibility loomed that Congress might address itself to the social problem on a level more or less commensurate with the magnitude of the crisis. The existing programs of the Office of Economic Opportunity as well as the modest attacks which had been made upon the problems of ghetto housing were expected to bring large-scale results only in a period of years. To keep peace in the meantime the crying necessity was jobs. On August 29 the Senate Labor and Public Welfare Committee approved by a vote of 10 to 6 a $2.8-billion emergency program to provide them.

The proposal, which was added to the antipoverty bill, was advanced by Democratic Senator Joseph S. Clark of Pennsylvania, Republican Senator Jacob Javits of New York, and others. It would have made $300 million available for loans to re-establish small businesses damaged in the riots and authorized $2.5 billion to provide emergency jobs during the next two years. The $1 billion authorized for the current fiscal year would have generated an estimated 200,000 jobs, and $1.5 billion was authorized for the following year. The plan would have provided jobs at once where they were most needed, among the largely unskilled unemployed —cleaning and beautifying streets and parks, helping in the maintenance of schools, hospitals, day-care centers, libraries, and recreation areas, and doing other useful work for the public service.

However, this proposal was too bold for either the White House or the Ninetieth Congress. It was opposed by the Administration, and on October 4 the Senate by a vote of 54 to 28 stripped it from the antipoverty bill. A compromise proposal, authorizing $925 million for a one-year work program, received a stronger vote—42 to 47—but this also failed.

For the regular antipoverty program, the Senate raised the authorization requested by the Administration to $2.25 billion, but the House, after strenuous efforts to effect an even larger reduction, cut this to $1.6 billion. The appropriation finally emerged at the compromise figure of $1.773 billion.

The House the previous May had killed the Administration's request for $40 million rent supplements and granted only $237 million of its request for the Model Cities program. The Senate in September approved $40 million for the former and $537 million for the latter. The bills as finally sent to the President on October 26 authorized only $10 million for rent supplements and $312 million for Model Cities.

The Administration's civil-rights bill, introduced the previous February, had been divided into six separate bills in the hope of securing enactment of at least part of the package. However, excepting an extension of the life of the Civil Rights Commission, no civil-rights bill had been enacted into law when Congress adjourned in December.

Most of the officials, reporters, and others who had been closest to the rioting rejected the theory of planned instigation. In the larger convulsions they had seen little evidence of organization or of "outside agitators." For the most part the riots had flared spontaneously, with only miscellaneous local daredevils urging the mob on. FBI Director J. Edgar Hoover reported to the National Advisory Commission on Civil Disorders at the beginning of its labors that he had "no intelligence on which to base a conclusion of conspiracy." Nevertheless the suspicion was widely held both in and out of Congress. Even the NAACP in its first reaction to the Newark upheaval had used the expressions "seemingly stimulated" and "apparently under plan." A Louis Harris Survey released on August 14 indicated that 45 per cent of whites attributed the riots to "outside agitation," "minority radicals," or "Communist backing"; only 40 per cent placed the blame on the treatment that Negroes had received.

The Republican Coordinating Committee appeared to share the suspicion of conspiracy. That body of party leaders issued a statement on the riots on July 24 (while Detroit was in turmoil and hours before the President's first broadcast). It was drafted by a subcommittee composed of former Governor Thomas E. Dewey, Representative William C. Cramer of Florida, and Governor John A. Love of Colorado. Former President Eisenhower attended the conference in Washington that gave its approval. Governor George Romney of Michigan, Governor Nelson Rockefeller of New York, former Vice President Richard M. Nixon, and former Senator Barry Goldwater were among those absent.

The statement urged investigation of "the planning, organization, method of operation and means to bring an end to rioting and civil disorder." It referred in one sentence to the "root causes of discontent," which it said were "of immediate and continuing concern to all of us." Otherwise the statement was entirely devoted to criticism of the Democratic Administration and to calls for effective law enforcement. Various observations were presented in support of the conspiracy theory:

> The principal victims to date have been the Negroes of America whose cause is betrayed by a few false leaders.
>
> Riots have occurred progressively in one city after another in widely separated areas. Factories for the manufacture of Molotov cocktails have been uncovered by the police. Weapons have been placed in the hands of rioters to murder police and firemen in the performance of their duty to protect the community. Simultaneous fires have been started in widely separated areas upon the occasion of the outbreak of rioting.
>
> Leaders of violence are publicly proclaiming and advocating future riots and the total defiance of all government. Hate mongers are traveling from community to community inciting insurrection. Public and private meetings of riot organizers from many sections of the country have been repeatedly reported in the press.

Continuing, the statement said:

> While the duty to protect its citizens devolves primarily upon the local community, when city after city across the nation is overwhelmed by riots, looting, arson and murder which mounting evidence indicates may be the result of organized planning and execu-

tion on a national scale, the Federal Government must accept its national responsibility....

We are rapidly approaching a state of anarchy and the President has totally failed to recognize the problem....

More concern over the conditions that produced riots was expressed by eight Republican governors who met in New York on August 10. This meeting was called by Governor Nelson Rockefeller, who was chairman of the policy committee of the Republican Governors Association. The governors attending were Romney of Michigan, Raymond P. Shafer of Pennsylvania, John A. Love of Colorado, Spiro T. Agnew of Maryland, John H. Chaffee of Rhode Island, John A. Volpe of Massachusetts, and Nils A. Boe of South Dakota. All members of the committee were invited, including Governor Ronald Reagan of California, who, however, "could not be reached" and did not attend. Three other absent members, Governors David Cargo of New Mexico, Tom McCall of Oregon, and Daniel Evans of Washington, telephoned their approval of the report that was drawn up.

That fifteen-page document made a number of recommendations for the strengthening of law enforcement, stressing the need for prompt, firm action in the early stages of civil disorder. It urged acceleration of the riot-control training ordered by the President for the National Guard and urged better organization and equipment of the Guard for dealing with riots. But the governors warned against reliance solely on security measures. This, they said, would lead to the "unacceptable ultimate result of a society based on repression." Misery and frustration were the root causes of riots and to eliminate them would require "a new kind and degree of effort between the various levels of government and the private sector." They offered a number of proposals for improving life in the slums, and called for the immediate establishment of an Urban Action Center to advise all state administrations on urban problems.

Governor Rockefeller went ahead with the Urban Action Center idea and on October 7 he announced the formation of a 50-state organization. It was nonpartisan: Robert F. Wagner, former Democratic mayor of New York, was appointed chairman. The trustees included governors and mayors from both parties, also

Andrew Heiskell, chairman of the board of Urban America, Inc., and civil-rights leaders Whitney M. Young and A. Philip Randolph.

The clearest note of leadership in the crisis was not sounded from the White House or the Congress or any party conference. It came from an "emergency convocation" of some 1,000 representatives of business, labor, religion, civil rights, and local government. They were called the "Urban Coalition."

The idea was conceived the previous winter, when the mayors of a dozen big cities, meeting in Washington, urged Urban America, Inc., together with the United States Conference of Mayors and the National League of Cities, to act as catalysts in forming a coalition to alert the nation to the critical urgency of urban needs. On July 31, on the call of Mayor Lindsay and Mayor Joseph Barr of Pittsburgh, 34 leaders met to form a steering committee, which went to work planning arrangements and drafting a program. The full Emergency Convocation of the Urban Coalition met in Washington on August 24.

The meeting was remarkable in many ways. Its participants were leaders of the highest prestige in their respective fields. The mayors of New York, Chicago, Philadelphia, Detroit, Boston, Atlanta, Pittsburgh, Minneapolis, and Phoenix (Arizona), were members of the steering committee; also a Roman Catholic archbishop, the president of the National Council of Churches, and the president of the Synagogue Council of America; and five representatives of organized labor, including its two most potent figures, AFL-CIO president George Meany and UAW president Walter Reuther. The civil-rights movement was represented by Martin Luther King, Arnold Aronson (of the Leadership Conference on Civil Rights), John Wheeler (Southern Regional Council president), Roy Wilkins, Whitney Young, and A. Philip Randolph. Randolph shared with Andrew Heiskell the role of cochairman of the coalition.

The representation of business was particularly impressive. Rarely if ever have so many captains of industry united in addressing themselves to a social problem; rarely have the directors of so large a segment of the economy gathered in one place for any purpose. Henry Ford II and David Rockefeller, president of the Chase Manhattan Bank, were two famous names among steering committee members. Also in the coalition were the presidents or board chairmen of Litton Industries, Time, Inc., the Aluminum Company of America, the Metropolitan Life Insurance Company, General Electric, Standard Oil, Du Point, Sears Roebuck, Morgan Guaranty Trust, American Airlines, and other great corporations. Whitney Young said of the assemblage at the Shoreham Hotel: "The people gathered in this room have the power, the resources, to turn this country around...."

Mayor Lindsay received the day's biggest applause when he said, with obvious reference to the Vietnam involvement, that the American commitment abroad "should not be allowed to weaken our resolve at home." Later he said: "If our defense commitment, our commitment to space, or any other commitment made before our urban areas were beset by agony is blocking a vigorous effort to end those agonies, those commitments should be reassessed."

Henry Ford II declared: "Our country today faces its greatest internal crisis since the Civil War— a crisis which demands no less than a massive national response." Walter Reuther, referring to United Auto Workers contract negotiations then under way, observed that he and Ford were sitting on "opposite sides of the table in Detroit. But on the great issues that face us and the crisis that challenges us all," he said, "I am privileged to sit on the same side of the table with Mr. Ford and to work together to find the answers." David Rockefeller said: "The task of breaking the bonds of poverty is one that must fall very heavily upon the shoulders of all of us here today." Half a dozen other speakers stressed the need for prompt and far-reaching measures of relief.

Whitney Young said in behalf of civil-rights leaders:

> There has been much discussion in the past few weeks and months that established Negro leadership has failed and has lost its influence. Historians will point out differently. They will point out that it is a miracle that established leadership has for so long a time enjoyed the support of Negro citizens—living as they are in squalor, poverty and unemployment while still retaining their hope and faith in the society....

Young added that the time had come for "responsible, intelligent, sensitive, humane, decent human beings to say to the American Negro 'I believe in you' and demonstrate it tangibly."

A statement, prepared earlier by the steering committee, and adopted by the coalition by a rousing voice vote, said: "We believe the American people in the Congress must reorder national priorities, with a commitment of resources equal to the magnitude of the problems we face." Calling upon the nation "to end once and for all the shame of poverty amid general affluence," it urged the Congress to "move without delay" on "additional civil-rights legislation, adequately funded model cities, anti-poverty, housing, education, and job-training programs. . . ." It called for an emergency work program with the goal of "putting at least one million of the presently unemployed into productive work as soon as possible" and immediate steps toward providing "a million housing units for lower-income families annually." The complete text of the coalition's Statement of Principles, Goals and Commitments is given in the appendix.

Some events of the fall of 1967 need to be recorded here which, though not directly related to the violence in the streets, were nonetheless a part of the Negro revolution.

On October 20 a white federal court jury in Meridian, Mississippi, returned a verdict that made an appreciable stride toward redemption of the honor of Mississippi and the restoration of confidence in Southern justice. In Chapter 9 we told of the murder in Neshoba County, Mississippi, of three young civil-rights workers, Michael Schwerner, Andrew Goodman, and James Chaney. We have referred repeatedly to the seemingly hopeless efforts of the Department of Justice to secure a conviction of the perpetrators of this, the most famous in the series of rarely punished murders of Negroes and white champions of their cause. Now at long last a jury of white Mississipians found seven white men guilty under federal law of conspiracy to commit this murder. Sentences were pronounced by Judge Harold Cox on December 29: Samuel H. Bowers, the Imperial Wizard of the White Knights of the Ku Klux Klan, and one other received the maximum penalty of ten years in a federal prison; two, including Cecil Price, the county's chief deputy sheriff, were sentenced to six years each; and the other three were given three-year sentences.

The November elections marked a historic milestone in the advance of Negro Americans. In addition to a substantial number of Negroes who were elected to minor public office, two major cities, one of them the nation's eighth largest, elected Negro mayors. The Negroes of Cleveland, Ohio, and Gary, Indiana, proved that genuine power could be achieved more surely with votes than with Molotoff cocktails.

Springfield, Ohio, and half a dozen smaller cities already had Negro mayors, but in their form of government the mayor had little authority and was chosen by the city council from among its members. The District of Columbia had just inaugurated a Negro chief executive appointed by the President. But never before in a major American city had a Negro won the office of mayor by popular vote.

Carl B. Stokes was elected mayor of Cleveland. Negroes represented less than 40 per cent of that city's population of 800,000, but, in addition to the virtually solid Negro vote, an estimated 20 per cent of the whites voted for him. Something like normal election decorum and good will prevailed in Cleveland, but in Gary, where Negroes were a majority (approximately 55 per cent) of the population of 180,000, the contest was fought bitterly along racial lines. The successful candidate, Richard G. Hatcher, who had won the Democratic nomination, had been repudiated by the Democratic county chairman and received little white support. In both cities the elections were won by narrow margins.

Though no Negro candidate was involved in the mayoralty election in Boston, the outcome there was also favorable from the Negro point of view. Mrs. Louise Day Hicks, whose long campaign for "the neighborhood school" had a strongly anti-Negro flavor, was defeated by moderate Kevin White, who was supported by Negro voters.

In elections to minor offices from justice of the peace to state legislators Negroes registered significant gains. Mississippi and Virginia each elected a Negro to its legislature for the first time in the century. The number of Negro office-holders in the nation increased by more than 50 to over 650.

As the year drew to an end, steps were being taken to strengthen police and the National Guard and increase their effectiveness in suppressing riots. A presidential commission was conducting a massive study of the problem, with earnest attention to the underlying causes of Negro unrest. Business leaders were displaying unprecedented concern. The "white backlash" had not approached anything like a vendetta. It had not prevented Negroes from making striking gains in the political spectrum. Negro mayors presided over two of the nation's nine largest cities.

On the other hand, the stubborn aversion of a majority of whites to personal association with Negroes remained a grave obstacle to the equalization of opportunity in education and employment and, most of all, in housing. Congress had adjourned after a year of virtual standstill in the areas of urban rehabilitation and relief for the oppressed Negro minority. More and more Negroes were listening to extremists who preached violence; more and more whites demanded sterner law enforcement. Public interest focused, however, on the war in Vietnam and the 1968 presidential contest, already getting under way.

The winter respite from violence had set in—until the next "long, hot summer."

Dr. Raymond M. Wheeler, chairman of the executive committee of the Southern Regional Council, said at its annual meeting in November:

> The summer of 1967 has been a time of bewildering and disturbing events, which seem to dramatize an increasing separation of the black and white races, with positions hardening and communications and understanding dwindling....
>
> There has been much investigation, considerably less self-examination and hopefully some reassessment of goals and priorities by our nation's leaders. A torpid Congress, sometimes appearing spiteful and irresponsible, has not only failed to provide leadership but has seemed to mirror to a frightening degree the dullness of spirit, the apathy and the hardness of white America. In that mirror we see plainly prejudice, ignorance and near total inability to understand what the black man is saying.
>
> .... Brave, eloquent, responsible Negro leadership has been saying that the black man, and the poor white as well, wants in—loves this land, wants to be a part of it. . . . And now there are new leaders, challenging their predecessors, determined to give us no choice but to hear a different message. They are saying that they no longer have any faith in the expressed good intentions of white America, that the existence of the black people today is intolerable, and they are ready to give up their lives if that kind of confrontation is necessary.

And if America should choose the course of violent reaction, if it should be so foolish as to attempt to seal the ghettos with guns and soldiers—hoping the problem will go away—then these young men are saying that they will make it as hard on us as possible. And the wreckage will be the wreckage and ashes, not just of our cities but of the American dream.

August 28, 1963, when 170,000 Negroes "marched on Washington," was a day of peace in the nation's capital. Only three persons were arrested all day long—a disorderly Nazi and two hoodlums who attempted to interfere with the demonstration. Police found little to do other than succor crippled, feeble, or fainting marchers. And Negroes and whites sang:

> Black and white together,
> We'll march hand in hand.

Something went wrong. Something went grievously wrong in the four years that followed.

TWENTY

The Report of the National Advisory Commission on Civil Disorders 1968

The National Advisory Commission on Civil Disorders produced its final report* four months before the date called for by the President. In view of "the gravity of the problem and the pressing need for action," it had worked "with a spirit of the greatest urgency." A summary, which filled two and a half pages in major newspapers, was released on February 29, 1968. The full report, of 250,000 words, was issued on March 2. It gave a deeply disturbing picture of the situation and urged drastic and costly remedies.

The commission saw the nation "moving toward two separate societies, one black, one white—separate and unequal." Continuation of present policies would risk "a seriously greater problem of major disorders." Large-scale violence, if it came, would lead to "white retaliation. This spiral," the commisison said, "could quite conceivably lead to a kind of urban apartheid with semi-martial law in many cities, enforced residence of Negroes in segregated areas, and a drastic reduction in personal freedom for all Americans, particularly Negroes."

* "Some studies still under way" would be issued later as supplemental reports.

The commission's compilation showed 164 disorders reported in 128 cities during the first nine months of 1967. Eight of these—taking place in Buffalo, Cincinnati, Detroit, Milwaukee, Minneapolis, Newark, Tampa, and Plainfield, New Jersey—were classified as "major"; 33 were classified as "serious," and 123 as "minor."

The conspiracy theory, after exhaustive investigation, was firmly rejected. The report said:

> On the basis of all the information collected the Commission concludes: The urban disorders of the summer of 1967 were not caused by nor were they the consequence of any organized plan or conspiracy.

It was noted, however, that "militant organizations, local and national, and individual agitators, who repeatedly forecast and called for violence, . . . helped to create an atmosphere that contributed to the outbreak of disorder."

The commission threw the blame for the situation essentially upon the white majority. It said:

> White racism is essentially responsible for the explosive mixture which has been accumulating in our cities since the end of World War II. . . .
>
> Pervasive discrimination and segregation in employment, education and housing have resulted in the continuing exclusion of great numbers of Negroes from the benefits of economic progress.

The resulting poverty in black ghettos had led to "crime, drug addiction, dependency on welfare, and bitterness against society in general and white society in particular." At the same time, through television and other media, affluence outside the ghetto had been "endlessly flaunted before the eyes of the Negro poor and the jobless ghetto youth."

White Americans were directly implicated in the development of the ghetto: "White institutions created it, white institutions maintain it, and white society condones it."

The alternative to "the continuing polarization of the American community and, ultimately, the destruction of basic democratic values," the commission said, would "require a commitment to national action—compassionate, massive and sustained, backed by the resources of the most powerful and the richest nation on this earth. From every American it will require new attitudes, new understanding, and, above all, new will. . . . The vital needs of the nation must be met; hard choices must be made, and, if necessary new taxes must be enacted."

The twelve "deepest grievances" were listed, ranked in three levels of relative intensity, as follows:

First Level of Intensity
1. Police practices
2. Unemployment and underemployment
3. Inadequate housing

Second Level of Intensity
4. Inadequate education
5. Poor recreation facilities and programs
6. Ineffectiveness of the political structure and grievance mechanisms

Third Level of Intensity
7. Disrespectful white attitudes
8. Discriminatory administration of justice
9. Inadequacy of federal programs
10. Inadequacy of municipal services
11. Discriminatory consumer and credit practices
12. Inadequate welfare programs

The report contained a broad sweep of recommendations for dealing with these grievances. Several would be difficult, as the attitude of Congress had already shown, but not a significant burden upon federal finances. The commission recommended that Congress "enact a comprehensive and enforceable federal open housing law to cover the sale or rental of all housing, including single family homes." It also urged "new and vigorous action to remove artificial barriers to employment and promotion," and maximum efforts to break down de facto public school segregation.

Some other recommended action, as the commission said with understatement, "would involve substantially greater federal expenditures than anything now contemplated." This included:

• Creation of two million new jobs—a million each by the public and private sectors—with federal subsidies for training of the unskilled.

• Bringing "within the reach of low and moderate income families within the next five years, six million new and existing units of decent housing, beginning with 600,000 units in the next year."

• Expansion of the public housing, urban renewal, and Model Cities programs.

• Greater federal funding of education programs for the disadvantaged.

• Establishment of a national standard of welfare assistance at least higher than the social security administration's "poverty level," and federal assumption of 90 per cent of welfare payments.

• Development of "a national system of income supplementation to provide a basic floor of economic and social security for all Americans"—an approach to the guaranteed annual income plan.

Estimates of cost were not given, but it was evident that the full implementation of the recommendations would involve outlays comparable to the cost of prosecuting the war in Vietnam. The commission said nonetheless that the nation's financial resources were "enough to make an important start on reducing our critical 'social deficit' in spite of a war and in spite of current requirements."

In its survey of 24 disorders in 23 cities, the commission found that "disorder did not erupt as a result of a single . . . incident," but "was generated out of an increasingly disturbed social atmosphere. . . ." However, it gave the following description of how an average riot gets under way:

The final incident before the outbreak of disorder and the initial violence itself, generally took place in the evening or at night at a place in which it was normal for many people to be on the streets.

Violence usually occurred immediately following the occurrence of the final precipitating incident, and then escalated rapidly. With but few exceptions, violence subsided during the day, and flared rapidly again at night. The night-day cycles continued through the early period of the major disorders.

Disorder generally began with rock and bottle throwing and window breaking. Once store windows were broken, looting usually followed.

Rumors aggravated tensions in 65 per cent of the disorders. Routine arrests triggered wild accounts of Negroes being beaten or murdered by police. In Tampa and New Haven false rumors led directly to the outbreaks. On the other hand, the commission found many instances of "excessive and indiscriminate shooting" by law enforcement officers. Hysteria fed the flames on both sides.

To maintain control of incidents that could lead to disorders the commission recommended that officials

● Develop plans which will quickly muster maximum police manpower and highly qualified senior commanders at the outbreak of disorders.

● Provide special training in the prevention of disorders and prepare police for riot control and for operation in units, with adequate command and control and field communication for proper discipline and effectiveness.

● Develop guidelines governing the use of control equipment and provide alternatives to the use of lethal weapons. . . .

● Create special rumor details to collect, evaluate, and dispel rumors that may lead to a civil disorder.

The commission also urged the recruitment of more Negro policemen and the establishment of community relations programs. Police should cultivate friendly, nonadversary contacts and draw closer to citizens in neighborhood service activities.

Here in brief are some pithy nuggets from the commission's findings:

● The typical rioter was . . . a lifelong resident of the city in which he rioted, a high school dropout, . . . usually underemployed or employed in a menial job.

● Nearly 53 per cent of those arrested were between 15 and 24 years of age. . . .

● Most reported sniping incidents were demonstrated to be gunfire by either police or National Guardsmen.

● The overwhelming majority of the persons killed or injured in all the disorders were Negro civilians.

● Numerous Negro counter-rioters walked the streets urging rioters to "cool it."

● A Detroit survey revealed that only approximately 11 per cent of the residents of the two riot areas participated in the rioting.

● While the civil disorders of 1967 were racial in character, they were not interracial. . . . They involved Negroes acting against local symbols of white society—authority and property—rather than against white persons.

● The Black Power advocates . . . have retreated from a direct confrontation with American society on the issue of integration and, by preaching separation, unconsciously function as an accommodation to white racism.

● Little basic change in the conditions underlying the outbreak of disorder has taken place. Actions to ameliorate Negro grievances have been limited and sporadic; with but few exceptions, they have not significantly reduced tensions.

● Race prejudice has shaped our history decisively; it now threatens to affect our future.

Veteran Negro leaders thought the report said what ought to be said—but what they had said many times before. Martin Luther King commented unenthusiastically that the recommendations "have been made before almost to the last detail—and have been ignored before almost to the last detail." Whitney Young said: "The answer to whether we have riots this summer depends on whether the nation adopts the cures recommended by the commission, cures which the National Urban League called for four years ago." Even the belligerent Floyd McKissick said: "We're on our way to reaching the moment of truth." From a New Orleans jail Rap Brown commented that the commission was "saying essentially what I've been saying." (The NAACP's Roy Wilkins was a member of the commission.)

The mayors of six major cities that had been hit by riots in recent years, appearing on NBC's "Meet the Press" on March 3, agreed substantially with the commission's report. They were Cavanagh of Detroit, Addonizio of Newark, Stokes of Cleveland, Yorty of Los Angeles, Allen of Atlanta, and Maier of Milwaukee. Exception was taken only by Mayor Yorty, who disagreed with the commission's finding that the riots were not started by outside agitators.

Most of the striking things in the report had indeed been said before in some quarter, but now they were said with reasoned judgment in the voice of the—preponderantly white—establishment. They were said by the governor of Illinois, the mayor of New York, two senators and two representatives—evenly divided between the two national political parties—and five other distinguished Americans—assigned to this study by the President of the United States. These had been aided by over 100 staff members and assistants at various levels. Several hundred officials, businessmen, labor leaders, civil-rights activists, scholars, and others had been consulted. In its seven-months inquiry the commission had visited eight riot-torn cities, and had held 44 days of hearings, 24 full days of executive sessions, and additional night sessions. Its staff had made field surveys in 23 riot cities and carried out formidable research.

What had come out of all this was a work on the condition and temper of Negroes in the United States reminiscent in its thoroughness and insight of the classic study of Gunnar Myrdal published at an earlier and quieter stage in *An American Dilemma*. Appropriately in the contemporary context the report included a considerable development of what might be called "riotology." It provided an invaluable resource alike for student and statesman.

In the opinion of the *New York Times* the report of the Commission on Civil Disorders "is sure to mark a turning point in the history of this nation." Whether its advice is heeded soon or disastrously late, it gave to the cause of racial justice and racial peace in the United States an arsenal of truth and wisdom which must ultimately triumph.

Five weeks after the publication of the report of the Commission on Civil Disorders, Negroes rioted in Washington, D.C., and in many other cities across the land. It was not a trivial incident that set off this upheaval. It was a tragedy of immeasurable proportions: the greatest Negro leader, and one of the greatest Americans of our time—the apostle of nonviolence—had been murdered.

In Memphis on April 4, 1968, the career of Martin Luther King, Jr., was ended by an assassin's bullet.

Dr. King's passion for the Negro cause never turned into hatred of the white man, and he cherished to the end a faith that the day of interracial justice and brotherhood would yet dawn in the United States. In a seeming valedictory he told a Negro audience the night before his death:

> I just want to do God's will. And He has allowed me to go up to the mountain, and I've looked over. And I've seen the promised land. I may not get there with you, but I want you to know tonight that we as a people will go to the promised land.

Statement of Principles, Goals, and Commitments

Emergency Convocation: The Urban Coalition

Washington, August 1967

We are experiencing our third summer of widespread civil disorder. In 1965, it was Harlem, and the disaster of Watts. In 1966, it was the Hough area of Cleveland, Omaha, Atlanta, Dayton, San Francisco and 24 other cities. This summer, Newark and Detroit were only the most tragic of 80 explosions of violence in the streets.

Confronted by these catastrophic events, we, as representatives of business, labor, religion, civil rights, and local government have joined in this convocation to create a sense of national urgency on the need for positive action for all the people of our cities.

We are united in the following convictions:

We believe the tangible effects of the urban riots in terms of death, injury, and property damage, horrifying though they are, are less to be feared than the intangible damage to men's minds.

We believe it is the government's duty to maintain law and order.

We believe that our thoughts and actions should be directed to the deep-rooted and historic problems of the cities.

We believe that we, as a nation, must clearly and positively demonstrate our belief that justice, social progress, and equality of opportunity are rights of every citizen.

We believe the American people and the Congress must reorder national priorities, with a commitment of resources equal to the magnitude of the problems we face. The crisis requires a new dimension of effort in both the public and private sectors, working together to provide jobs, housing, education, and the other needs of our cities.

We believe the Congress must move without delay on urban programs. The country can wait no longer for measures that have too long been denied the people of the cities and the nation as a whole—additional civil rights legislation, adequately funded model cities, anti-poverty, housing, education, and job-training programs, and a host of others.

We believe the private sector of America must directly and vigorously involve itself in the crisis of the cities by a commitment to investment, job-training, and hiring, and all that is necessary to the full enjoyment of the free enterprise system—and also to its survival.

We believe the sickness of the cities, including civic disorder within them, is the responsibility of the whole of America. There-fore, it is the responsibility of every American to join in the crea-tion of a new political, social, economic, and moral climate that will make possible the breaking of the vicious cycle of the ghetto. Efforts must be made to insure the broadest possible opportunity for all citizens and groups, including those in the ghetto, to partici-pate fully in shaping and directing the society of which they are a part.

This convocation calls upon the nation to end once and for all the shame of poverty amid general affluence. Government and business must accept responsibility to provide all Americans with opportunity to earn an adequate income. Private industry must greatly accelerate its efforts to recruit, train, and hire the hard-core unemployed. When the private sector is unable to provide employ-ment to those who are both able and willing to work, then in a free society the government must of necessity assume the responsibility and act as the employer of last resort or must assure adequate in-come levels for those who are unable to work.

This convocation calls upon the federal government to develop an emergency work program to provide jobs and new training opportunities for the unemployed and underemployed consistent with the following principles:

—The federal government must enlist the cooperation of government at all levels and of private industry to assure that meaningful, productive work is available to everyone willing and able to work.

—To create socially useful jobs, the emergency work program should concentrate on the huge backlog of employment needs in parks, streets, slums, countryside, schools, colleges, libraries, and hospitals. To this end an emergency work program should be initiated and should have as its first goal putting at least one million of the presently unemployed into productive work at the earliest possible moment.

—The program must provide meaningful jobs—not dead-end, make work projects—so that the employment experience gained adds to the capabilities and broadens the opportunities of the employees to become productive members of the permanent work force of our nation.

—Basic education, training, and counseling must be an integral part of the program to assure extended opportunities for upward job mobility and to improve employee productivity. Funds for training, education, and counseling should be made available to private industry as well as to public and private nonprofit agencies.

—Funds for employment should be made available to local and state governments, nonprofit institutions, and federal agencies able to demonstrate their ability to use labor productively without reducing existing levels of employment or undercutting existing labor standards or wages which prevail for comparable work or services in the area but are not less than the federal minimum wage.

—Such a program should seek to qualify new employees to become part of the regular work force and that normal performance standards are met.

—The operation of the program should be keyed to specific, localized unemployment problems and focused initially on those areas where the need is most apparent.

All representatives of the private sector in this Urban Coalition decisively commit themselves to assist the deprived among us to achieve full participation in the economy as self-supporting citizens. We pledge full-scale private endeavor through creative job-training and employment, managerial assistance, and basic investment in all phases of urban development.

The alternatives to a massive and concerted drive by the private sector are clear. They include the burden of wasted human and physical potential, the deterioration of the healthy environment basic to the successful operation of any business, and the dangers of permanent alienation from our society of millions of citizens.

We propose to initiate an all-out attack on the unemployment problem through the following steps:

—In cooperation with government, to move systematically and directly into the ghettos and barrios to seek out the unemployed and underemployed and enlist them in basic and positive private training and employment programs. We will re-evaluate our current testing procedures and employment standards so as to modify or eliminate those practices and requirements that unnecessarily bar many persons from gainful employment by business or access to union membership.

—To create a closer relationship between private employers and public training and emergency employment programs to widen career opportunities for our disadvantaged citizens. To this end, we will proceed immediately to promote "Earn and Learn Centers" in depressed urban areas that might well be the joint venture of business, labor and local government.

—To develop new training and related programs to facilitate the early entry of under-qualified persons into industrial and commercial employment.

—To develop large-scale programs to motivate the young to continue their education. Working closely with educators, we will redouble our efforts to provide part-time employment, training, and other incentives for young men and women. We also pledge our active support to making quality education readily accessible to deprived as well as advantaged young people.

—To expand on-the-job training programs to enhance the career advancement prospects of all employees, with particular emphasis on those who now must work at the lowest level of job classifications because of educational and skill deficiencies.

We pledge to mobilize the managerial resources and experience of the private sector in every way possible. We will expand part-time and full-time assistance to small business development. We will strive to help residents of these areas both to raise their level of managerial know-how and to obtain private and public investment funds for development. We will work more closely with public agencies to assist in the management of public projects. We will encourage more leaders in the private sector to get directly and personally involved in urban problems so that they may gain a deeper understanding of these problems and be of greater assistance.

We pledge our best efforts to develop means by which major private investment may be attracted to the renovation of deteriorating neighborhoods in our cities. We will explore and encourage governmental incentives to expedite private investment. We will develop new methods of combining investment and managerial assistance so that the residents may achieve a leadership position in the development of their areas.

This convocation calls upon the nation to take bold and immediate action to fulfill the national need to provide "a decent home and a suitable living environment for every American family" with guarantees of equal access to all housing, new and existing. The Urban Coalition shall, as its next order of business, address itself to the development of a broad program of urban reconstruction and advocacy of appropriate public and private action to move toward these objectives, including the goal of rehabilitation and construction of at least a million housing units for lower-income families annually.

This convocation calls upon the nation to create educational programs that will equip all young Americans for full and productive participation in our society to the full potential of their abilities. This will require concentrated compensatory programs to equalize opportunities for achievement. Early childhood education must be made universal. Work and study programs must be greatly expanded to enlist those young people who now drop out of school. Financial barriers that now deny to youngsters from low-income families the opportunity for higher education must be eliminated. Current programs must be increased sufficiently to wipe out adult illiteracy within five years.

This convocation calls upon local government, business, labor, religious, and civil rights groups to create counterpart local coalitions where they do not exist to support and supplement this declaration of principles.

This convocation calls upon all Americans to apply the same

determination to these programs that they have to past emergencies. We are confident that, given this commitment, our society has the ingenuity to allocate its resources and devise the techniques necessary to rebuild cities and still meet our other national obligations without impairing our financial integrity. Out of past emergencies, we have drawn strength and progress. Out of the present urban crisis we can build cities that are places, not of disorder and despair, but of hope and opportunity. The task we set for ourselves will not be easy, but the needs are massive and urgent, and the hour is late. We pledge ourselves to this goal for as long as it takes to accomplish it. We ask the help of the Congress and the Nation.

Index